MW01093168

LEGAL PHANTOMS

Legal Phantoms

*Executive Action and the Haunting
Failures of Immigration Law*

JENNIFER M. CHACÓN,
SUSAN BIBLER COUTIN,
AND STEPHEN LEE

STANFORD UNIVERSITY PRESS
Stanford, California

Stanford University Press
Stanford, California

© 2024 by the Board of Trustees of the Leland Stanford Jr. University. All rights reserved.

No part of this book may be reproduced or transmitted in any form or by any means, electronic or mechanical, including photocopying and recording, or in any information storage or retrieval system, without the prior written permission of Stanford University Press.

Printed in the United States of America on acid-free, archival-quality paper

Library of Congress Cataloging-in-Publication Data

Names: Chacón, Jennifer, 1972– author. | Coutin, Susan Bibler, author. |
   Lee, Stephen, 1975– author.
Title: Legal phantoms : executive action and the haunting failures of
   immigration law / Jennifer M. Chacón, Susan Bibler Coutin,
   and Stephen Lee.
Description: Stanford, California : Stanford University Press, 2024. |
   Includes bibliographical references and index.
Identifiers: LCCN 2023029771 (print) | LCCN 2023029772 (ebook) |
   ISBN 9781503611719 (cloth) | ISBN 9781503637573 (paperback) |
   ISBN 9781503637580 (ebook)
Subjects: LCSH: Emigration and immigration law—United States. | Deferred
   Action for Childhood Arrivals (U.S.) | Children of noncitizens—Legal
   status, laws, etc.—United States. | Noncitizens—United States. |
   Illegal immigration—United States.
Classification: LCC KF4819 .C43 2024 (print) | LCC KF4819 (ebook) |
   DDC 342.7308/2—dc23/eng/20230907
LC record available at https://lccn.loc.gov/2023029771
LC ebook record available at https://lccn.loc.gov/2023029772

Cover design: Gabriele Wilson
Cover painting: Jose Ramirez, *The Magic Tree* (2014)
Typeset by Newgen in Arno Pro Regular 11/15

CONTENTS

ACKNOWLEDGMENTS

Our deepest debt of gratitude goes to the countless people and organizations who supported this project by participating in interviews, allowing us to observe their events, sharing deeply personal (and painful) aspects of their lives, and recounting their dreams and future goals. To preserve confidentiality, we name neither individuals nor organizations, but please know that we are deeply appreciative. We hope that this book does justice to your experiences.

We are also grateful to our funders. Our research was supported by the National Science Foundation (grant number SES-1535501), the UC Irvine School of Law, and the UC Irvine School of Social Ecology. The UCLA School of Law and Stanford Law School also funded the work of research assistants who contributed to this project. The Russell Sage Foundation (grant number 88–14–06) provided funding for a preliminary study that paved the way for this research. Any opinions, findings, and conclusions or recommendations expressed in this material are those of the authors and do not necessarily reflect the views of the National Science Foundation or other funders.

Earlier drafts of ideas and material that informed our writing were presented at the American Anthropological Association annual meetings, the American Association of Geographers annual meeting, California State University, Northridge; the Center for the Study of Law and Society (CSLS) at UC Berkeley, Humboldt University of Berlin, the XXXVI

International Congress of the Latin American Studies Association in Barcelona, Law and Society Association annual meetings, UC Berkeley School of Law, UC Davis King Hall School of Law, UC Law, San Francisco (formerly UC Hastings) School of Law, UCLA School of Law, the UCLA Critical Race Studies Program, UC Irvine School of Law, UC Santa Cruz, the University of Chicago Law School, the University of Connecticut, the University of Florida Levin College of Law, Fordham University School of Law, the University of Georgia School of Law, the University of Hawaii William S. Richardson School of Law, the University of Iowa College of Law, the University of North Carolina School of Law, the University of Pittsburgh, USC, the USC Gould School of Law, the University of Texas School of Law, the University of Wisconsin Law School, Stanford Law School, the Tulane University Law School, and Yale Law School. We are grateful to session, workshop, and conference organizers for the opportunities to share our work in progress. We also benefited from feedback provided by discussants and audience members.

The following individuals offered insightful comments on particular chapters or on papers that we drew on to write the book: Kathryn Abrams, Mario Barnes, Rabia Belt, Richard Boswell, Devon Carbado, Angélica Cházaro, Erwin Chemerinsky, Ming Hsu Chen, Michael Churgin, Pooja Dadhania, Seth Davis, Ingrid Eagly, Mary Fan, Catherine Fisk, Trevor Gardner, Denise Gilman, Laura Gomez, Tanya Hernández, Barbara Hines, Cheryl Harris, Laila Hlass, Aziz Huq, Anil Kalhan, Emma Kaufman, Joseph Landau, Eunice Lee, Michelle Lipinski, Hiroshi Motomura, Carrie Rosenbaum, Daria Roithmayr, Joel Sati, Shirin Sinnar, and Jayashri Srikantiah. This book has been in the making for many years, and benefitted from many thoughtful comments. We apologize to those whose names we have failed to include. We also appreciate the comments provided by the anonymous reviewers. The book is much improved as a result of their critical feedback.

We have been privileged to work with numerous research assistants, including Gray Abarca, Edelina Burciaga, Alma Garza, Yasmin Moreno, Jason Palmer, Lovlean Purewal, Elizabeth Hanna Rubio, and Jose Torres. They carried out interviews, wrote fieldnotes, tracked down citations, helped organize our data, did legal research, coded data, and commented on drafts in progress. This project also benefited from the help of dedicated support staff at our various institutions, including Naomi Aguilar and Ana Duong. We are fortunate to have been able to work with them during key moments in their own academic journeys.

This book consists of original material, but some chapters draw on ideas or material that we previously published elsewhere. Our introduction draws on Coutin, Susan Bibler, Sameer Ashar, Jennifer Chacón, and Stephen Lee, 2017, "Deferred Action and the Discretionary State: Migration, Precarity and Resistance," *Citizenship Studies* 21(8): 951–968. There is some overlap between Chapter 1 and Chacón, Jennifer, and Susan Coutin, 2018, "Racialization through Immigration Enforcement," in *Race, Criminal Justice, and Migration Control*, ed. Mary Bosworth, Alpa Parmar, and Yolanda Vázquez (Oxford University Press). Chapter 2 draws from Ashar, Sameer, and Stephen Lee, 2019, "DACA, Government Lawyers, and the Public Interest," *Fordham Law Review* 87: 1879–1912. Chapter 5 overlaps with and draws upon the text of Chacón, Jennifer, 2019, "Immigration Federalism in the Weeds," *UCLA Law Review* 67: 1630–1694. Chapter 6 draws on material published in Coutin, Susan Bibler, Sameer Ashar, Jennifer Chacón, Stephen Lee, and Jason Palmer, 2022, "Shapeshifting Displacement: Notions of Membership and Deservingness Forged by Illegalized Residents," *Humanity: An International Journal of Human Rights, Humanitarianism, and Development* 12(3): 339–353. Aspects of Chapter 6 are also discussed in Chacón, Jennifer, Susan Bibler Coutin, Stephen Lee, Sameer Ashar, Edelina Burciaga, and Alma Garza, 2018, "Citizenship Matters: Conceptualizing Belonging in an Era of Fragile Inclusions," *UC Davis Law Review* 52(1): 1–80.

Our institutions supported our work in multiple ways. At UC Irvine, colleagues in the School of Law and the Department of Criminology, Law and Society were a source of support and encouragement as we pursued this project. Susan Coutin also thanks colleagues at USC, where she spent a sabbatical in 2017, for conversations relevant to the project. Colleagues at the UC Irvine School of Law also provided valuable intellectual support, and Deans Erwin Chemerinsky and L. Song Richardson also ensured needed material support. Colleagues at the UCLA School of Law and UC Berkeley School of Law were also instrumental in bringing this project to completion.

We thank Stanford University Press for supporting our project, Michele Lipinski for seeing its potential when we were still at the book proposal stage, and Marcela Maxfield and Sarah Rodriguez for shepherding the manuscript through the publication process.

We are grateful to each other. We especially would like to acknowledge Sameer Ashar, who launched our collaboration by reaching out to Susan Coutin to suggest that we apply for a small grant to develop an immigration scholarship-advocacy network. That effort led to involving Jennifer Chacón and Stephen Lee in offering a workshop, coteaching a course in the UC Irvine School of Law, and developing a grant proposal for Russell Sage, and then for the National Science Foundation. Sameer's insights, acumen, and sensitivity have been key throughout the project, and while he decided to pull back when we were at the book-writing stage, we acknowledge his contributions through coauthorship of the introduction and Chapter 4. Over the years that we worked on this project, we have appreciated the ways that each of us contributed ideas, time, energy, resources, and sometimes delicious meals to our collaboration. We leave this project with deeper friendships and a renewed commitment to doing the work that matters to us.

Lastly, we are grateful to our families, who were part of this journey in more ways than one. They were in the background—or the back seat—during Zoom calls, and they put up with absences when we were out doing interviews for the project, or when we were at our computers trying (and often failing) to meet writing deadlines. We appreciate our parents, siblings, partners, children, and the many members of our chosen families: your support means more than we can say.

LEGAL PHANTOMS

FIGURE 1.1. Obama's image at a downtown Los Angeles rally to listen to the announcement of executive relief. Photo by Susan Coutin.

Introduction

Sameer M. Ashar is a co-author of this chapter.

ON NOVEMBER 20, 2014, President Obama went on national television to announce Deferred Action for Parents of Americans and Lawful Permanent Residents (DAPA) and an expansion of the 2012 Deferred Action for Childhood Arrivals (DACA) program (DACA+). In the streets outside of an immigrant detention facility in downtown Los Angeles, community members gathered to watch the announcement. A huge screen was inflated so that the speech could be projected. The mood was festive. A band played and a crowd of people circulated, holding signs advocating for immigrants' rights. As night fell and the time for the speech began, viewers sat on the street pavement, which had been closed to traffic, to watch the telecast.

President Obama appeared on the screen, and as the audience listened, he described the importance of immigration for the United States and the ways that the immigration system was broken. The President emphasized his enforcement accomplishments, characterizing the increased arrivals of unaccompanied migrant children at the US southern border in the summer of 2014 as a "brief spike." After outlining his administration's frustrated efforts to encourage Congress to pass comprehensive immigration reform legislation, he described the actions that he could legally take as president. As many in the audience feared, he began with increased enforcement

efforts: "First, we'll build on our progress at the border with additional resources for our law enforcement personnel so that they can stem the flow
of illegal crossings and speed the return of those who do cross over." This
announcement led to a cascade of boos from the crowd that sat on the pavement watching the screen.

Next, he turned to the matter of greatest interest to those present:
"Steps to deal responsibly with the millions of undocumented immigrants
who live in this country." Taking these steps, he said, would enable enforcement activities to focus on "felons, not families. Criminals, not children.
Gang members, not a mom who's working hard to provide for her kids." In
essence, the president offered longtime undocumented immigrants what he
described as a "deal":

> If you've been in America for more than five years; if you have children
> who are American citizens or legal residents; if you register, pass a crimi-
> nal background check, and you're willing to pay your fair share of taxes—
> you'll be able to apply to stay in this country temporarily without fear of
> deportation. You can come out of the shadows and get right with the law.
> That's what this deal is.

The offer of this "deal," like the distinction between "families" and "felons,"
created artificial categories of deserving and undeserving immigrants at
odds with the lived experience of many members of the assembled crowd.
The proposed "deal" did not draw cheers from those assembled on the
streets of Los Angeles. Instead, there seemed to be a stunned silence among
onlookers as the president finished his speech. In fact, as the president
signed off, there were more boos. While the details of this "deal" were still
unclear, the inclusion of only parents of US citizens and lawful permanent
residents and the exclusion of parents of DACA recipients appeared to
many onlookers to be a major injustice. Moreover, the facile dichotomies—
between children and "criminals," mothers and "gang members"—belied
the complexity of the lives of people living in places where police labeled
mothers as gang members haphazardly, and where intrusive policing practices ensured that many children would also bear criminal records.

The negative response of the audience that night was a striking contrast
to the ways that the officials who designed deferred action programs imagined that the announcement would be received. It was widely understood

that the president announced the original DACA program in 2012 with the hope that Republicans, who controlled the House of Representatives at the time, would pass a law creating a more lasting legal status for intended DACA recipients and many other longtime immigrant residents. When the Republican-controlled House refused to even consider a 2013 Senate bill that did precisely that, officials within the Obama administration imagined that immigrants would welcome the news of the 2014 "deal," which expanded on the basic framework of DACA, with not only relief, but enthusiasm. One official we interviewed for this book said that he "really did picture tears of joy just streaming down the faces of people in millions of immigrants' households around the country." Some people undoubtedly felt some degree of relief, or at least hope of relief. But many were disappointed by the details of the announcement.

Ultimately, DAPA and DACA+ ended before they began. On February 16, 2015, just days before the programs were set to go into effect, a federal district court in Texas issued a nationwide preliminary injunction preventing them from being implemented while litigation on the merits of the programs proceeded. As the litigation wore on, the programs remained frozen in the courts. In 2017, Donald J. Trump assumed the presidency after running on a racist, anti-immigrant platform. Unsurprisingly, his administration rescinded DAPA and DACA+ altogether. President Obama's "deal" never came to pass, but it has left traces everywhere—a phantom program that continues to haunt.

At the same time, the original DACA program, created in 2012, is still in place as we put the finishing touches on this book in mid-2023. Lawyers and government officials who worked in the Obama administration continue to view the program as a significant success, and it has had an important, ameliorative effect on the lives of DACA recipients. During President Trump's administration, acting Department of Homeland Security (DHS) secretary Elaine Duke announced the rescission of the DACA program, but those efforts were stopped by the US Supreme Court, which concluded in a 5–4 decision that the administration's attempted rescission of the program failed to comply with the requirements of the Administrative Procedures Act. When Joseph R. Biden—President Obama's former vice president—entered the White House in 2021, DACA's legacy appeared more secure.

Still, the program remains endangered by ongoing litigation, with a federal court injunction barring the grant of new applications, and with a built-in degree of obsolescence ensured by the requirement that recipients have been in the US since June 15, 2007. A new legal challenge is headed to the nation's highest court, and the Supreme Court appears to be ready to declare DACA illegal. Nevertheless, for those recipients who obtained and maintained eligibility, DACA has provided work authorization and reprieve from the threat of banishment for over a decade. And some recipients have been able to use DACA as a bridge to more permanent forms of status.

Given the unceremonious thwarting of the DAPA and DACA+ programs, and the survival of the original DACA program across administrations, it is easy to overlook the period from 2014 through early 2017, when the promise of DAPA and DACA+ hung in the balance. Those interested in understanding how the law shapes and is shaped by immigrants, advocates, and government officials often focus on the events leading up to June 2012, when the Obama administration announced DACA, or on the early days of President Trump's administration, with its flurry of entry bans, enforcement pronouncements, and the attempted rescission of DACA.

This is a book about the interstitial space connecting these landmark political and legal moments over a ten-year period, from 2012 to 2022. Our 135 interviews and focus group sessions with immigrants, community organizers and leaders, lawyers, and government officials document these years of political and legal uncertainty. We tell a story of government action gone awry, the continued immiseration of immigrants in limbo in the United States, and advocates and organizers navigating a shifting and complex terrain. We document the ways that people continue to be haunted by the failed promise of phantom DAPA and DACA+ programs, and the broader failures of immigration policy. Ultimately, we tell a story about the limits of political imagination, sharply restricted by the central logic of US immigration law and policy as it has developed in the past century—a logic rooted in racism and manifested in discretionary, racialized enforcement. Even when government officials imagined themselves to be bold actors developing unprecedented programs of relief for undocumented immigrants, they were in fact operating within a narrow field circumscribed by the legal and political terms of the governing discourse of the day. In fact, officials' most imaginative political thinking was directed not toward immigration relief, which in the end was limited to a relatively small set of beneficiaries, but rather toward enforcement measures that devastated communities within the US and markedly increased the militarization of the external border. The United States' governing discourse allowed for the exercise of nearly unfettered enforcement authority, while it kept discussions about relief contained within narrowly established parameters.

Despite these developments, those directly affected by legal uncertainty—immigrants, immigrant justice advocates, and organizers—withstood the violence of state action (and inaction), drawing on deep reserves of material, spiritual, and intellectual resources. Advocates and organizers showed how policy discourse could be made elastic to accommodate new terms. They resisted legal violence and they argued strenuously for new political horizons of possibility for immigrants in the US. Not only did they argue *for* the DREAM Act, various deferred action programs, and other, more comprehensive legalization measures, they also argued *against* immigration and criminal law enforcement programs and practices that imperiled large swaths of society regardless of immigration status. Their transformative vision, rooted in an expansive political imagination, still has the potential to transform immigration law and policy in the wake of the devastation wrought by the Trump era and by decades of violent immigration enforcement. Over the course of this book, we recount these hopes and aspirations, and the context in which they were forged, as we tell the story of the phantom DAPA and DACA+ programs.

A Brief History of Deferred Action and Enforcement

To understand the immigration policy developments over a ten-year arc from 2012 when DACA was initiated, through 2022, the midpoint of the Biden administration, it is important to have a clear sense of what came before. In the simplest terms, during the three decades that preceded the 2012 announcement of DACA and the 2014 announcement of DAPA and DACA+, policymakers wove the methods and ever-expanding excesses of what scholars have come to refer to as "the carceral state"[1] throughout the fabric of immigration enforcement efforts.

Immigration enforcement has always been connected with police spending, incarceration, and other forms of punitive control in the United States. Criminal law has been used throughout US history to structure and backstop immigration policies, and vice versa. Even before there was a federal immigration control system in place, many states attempted to exclude individuals convicted of crimes.[2] Criminal convictions or individuals' alleged propensity to commit crimes also became the basis for some of the earliest federal immigration exclusions.[3] In the first half of the twentieth century, federal criminal law—and particularly the newly enacted and racially motivated criminal penalties on entry without inspection and felony unauthorized reentry—was deployed against Mexican workers as a means of controlling the migrant labor force.[4] Immigrants deemed "undesirable" or "radical" were contained and deported through a mix of criminal and immigration law tools, with immigration officials relying on criminal records created and maintained by state and local law enforcement to target certain immigrants.[5] And state and local law enforcement agents collaborated with federal immigration officials in sweeps and roundups of Mexican immigrants (and US citizens of Mexican descent) on a massive scale in the 1930s and 1950s.[6]

By the 1970s, these converging forces resulted in a large, permanent, unauthorized population—usually racialized as "Mexican" and increasingly cast as criminal or "illegal." As historians have noted, the end of the Bracero Program in 1964, the imposition of per-country caps on legal immigration from the Western Hemisphere in 1976 and the growth of a border patrol focused on controlling Mexican migration ensured that efforts to control "illegal immigration" in the second half of the twentieth century generally targeted populations racialized as "Mexican," even though in reality, the immigrant population—including the undocumented population—is much more diverse.[7] Even efforts to liberalize immigration laws reinforced these patterns. The 1986 Immigration Reform and Control Act (IRCA), for example, is widely remembered (and derided by some) for the mechanisms it created to allow about three million undocumented residents to regularize their immigration status and ultimately apply for citizenship. While IRCA regularized the status of millions of residents, millions of others were excluded from that law's protections and became the target of increasingly aggressive enforcement efforts. In other words, the cost of creating legal stability in the lives of millions of immigrants was the normalization of a legal culture that targeted and punished the remaining and future migrants.

Systemic bonds between immigration and criminal law were cemented and elevated in importance by the late twentieth-century expansion and federalization of the criminal enforcement system[8] and Congress's significant expansion in the 1990s of criminal offenses that qualified as the basis for deportation and exclusion.[9] In the mid-1990s, Congress enacted a series of laws that concretized the discursive and legal linkage between immigration, crime control, and national security.[10] While the immigration and criminal law systems have deep historic connections, and while criminal justice actors at all levels of government have cooperated with federal immigration enforcement agencies for as long as they have existed, recent policy innovations have rendered this integration more systematic and ubiquitous than ever before.

Many immigrant communities were subject to racialized over-policing as the carceral state expanded in connection with the ongoing national "wars" on crime and drugs.[11] The September 11, 2001 attacks on the United States also prompted Congress to increase federal spending on national security, which included enforcing these criminalizing provisions and expanding state and local involvement in immigration control efforts.[12] But the most consequential systemic integration of the criminal and immigration enforcement systems occurred, ironically, not under the presidency of Republican George W. Bush, but during the presidency of Barack Obama, a Democrat who campaigned on a promise of immigration reform.

In the lead-up to the 2008 election, Obama promised that if he were elected, he would work to sign a comprehensive immigration reform bill during his first year in office. Democrats controlled both chambers of Congress during his first two years in office, but no immigration reform bill was passed. Instead, the Obama administration rolled out an enforcement program that had been initiated in seedling form in the final year of President George W. Bush's second term. Inaptly named "Secure Communities" ("S-Comm"), the program was designed to allow DHS to harvest the fingerprints of every person arrested by state or local law enforcement. Under S-Comm, fingerprints collected by any law enforcement official at the time of arrest automatically cycled through DHS databases. This information sharing purportedly allowed DHS to determine whether the person was present in violation of immigration law, though in fact, the databases were riddled with errors. Based on this fingerprint screen, DHS would determine whether the agency wished to pursue removal of the arrested individual. In tens of thousands of cases, DHS opted to do so, sending out detainers, requesting that the state or local agency hold individuals until they could be transferred to DHS custody.

Some members of the Obama administration apparently envisioned that the nationwide use of DHS screening would restore the federal government's control over discretionary decisions about immigration enforcement. By that time, hundreds of localities like Farmer's Branch, Texas, and Hazleton, Pennsylvania, and states like Arizona and Alabama had enacted subfederal migration control laws that inserted their own law enforcement agents (and private actors) into immigration enforcement. The Obama administration fought against subfederal migration controls in federal courts across the country[13] even as it rolled out S-Comm. Official announcements suggest that the administration thought S-Comm would answer subfederal political demands for more aggressive immigration enforcement while allowing the federal government to make the ultimate determination on whether immigration enforcement was warranted against any particular individual.

Instead, automated arrestee screening simply meant that local policing choices and biases were amplified—elevating to the notice of federal immigration agents every arrest, whether that arrest was justified or not. The program magnified the consequences of existing racial disproportionality in arrests, which flowed not just from express racial profiling but also from a host of institutionalized arrest practices. At the same time, S-Comm decreased the costs of improper racial profiling for state and local actors. Racial profiling is explicitly allowed in immigration enforcement efforts, and illegally obtained evidence is generally admissible in immigration proceedings, even if it would be excluded in criminal proceedings.[14] Once S-Comm was operative within their jurisdictions, any law enforcement agents who were engaged in racially discrepant policing or using illegal policing tactics had a new form of cover for doing so.[15]

Affected communities mobilized and organized in opposition to what they experienced as unjustly exclusionary laws and racially discriminatory enforcement. The number of organizations dedicated to immigrant rights advocacy grew, but those organizations were not uniformly distributed, and access to services remained uneven. The federal enforcement budget continued to balloon, even as federal authorities lacked the resources and political will to remove all unauthorized or deportable residents, placing the choice of how to prioritize enforcement goals in the hands of the executive branch.[16]

In place of comprehensive immigration reform, a patchwork of discretionary enforcement decisions allowed temporary reprieve for some immigrants. Responding to intense pressure from immigrants and their allies, and in the face of congressional gridlock on legalization programs, DHS secretary Janet Napolitano announced in 2012 that "childhood arrivals"—individuals who had entered the United States before age 16—who also met specific age, presence, and educational requirements, and who passed a criminal records check would be eligible for deferred action. Deferred action meant a two-year stay of removal and legal work authorization. One indication of how important the program was to the administration is that President Obama announced the creation of this program in a televised speech from the White House Rose Garden. Eventually, around 800,000 individuals qualified for relief through what came to be known as the DACA program.[17]

After the 2013 Senate bill that would have created a pathway to citizenship for these childhood arrivals (and many other people) failed to become law, President Obama once again turned to discretionary enforcement tools to provide temporary relief to immigrants. In 2014, the Obama administration attempted to extend deferred action to a broad swath of longtime residents without legal status. This was the "deal" referenced at the top of this chapter, which would have covered the undocumented parents of US citizen and lawful resident children, as well as a broader range of childhood arrivals than those covered by DACA (programs colloquially identified as DAPA and DACA+).[18] Some studies suggested that more than a third of the undocumented population not already covered by DACA would have potentially been eligible for one of these two programs, though our own work leads us to believe that is probably an optimistic estimate.[19] Regardless of the precise scope of the program, DAPA and DACA+ would have significantly altered the immigration enforcement landscape of the United States.

Before DAPA could be implemented, however, Texas and twenty-five other states sued the federal government, and the expansion of deferred action was enjoined, meaning that it was at least temporarily stopped from going into effect.[20] After the Fifth Circuit Court of Appeals upheld the injunction, litigation reached the US Supreme Court, which deadlocked on the issue, allowing the lower court's injunction to stand throughout the remainder of the Obama presidency, pending ongoing litigation relating to the constitutional and statutory challenges to the program.[21]

Republican President Donald J. Trump, who ran on an anti-immigrant platform that included calls to build a wall along the US-Mexico border, took office in January 2017. In June 2017, his administration rescinded both DAPA and DACA+.[22] Consequently, the litigation surrounding DAPA and DACA+ never ended with a conclusive ruling on the legal merits of those programs by the courts. Technically, a future presidential administration could try to reinstate these programs. But the Biden Administration has not attempted to do so, perhaps anticipating the disapproval of federal courts.

As for the original DACA program, several months into the Trump presidency, the administration announced the rescission of the program, to go into effect after a six-month wind-down.[23] DACA recipients and their allies sued in several courts across the country to prevent this, and in June of 2018, the US Supreme Court invalidated the Trump administration's attempt to rescind DACA, leaving the program intact, but in a form that allowed for no new applicants to gain protection under the law. DACA remains vulnerable to possible rescission and legal challenges.

This complex legal history gave rise to renewed activism on the part of immigrants and their allies. It also exacerbated deep uncertainty over the future of longtime residents of this country who lack legal immigration status. This uncertainty gave way to heightened anxiety with the election of Donald Trump. While the Obama administration had aggressively enforced immigration laws, particularly during President Obama's first term, the Trump administration combined tough, if scattershot, interior immigration enforcement efforts with harsh new restrictions at the border and explicitly racist and anti-immigrant rhetoric. The federal government adopted a more restrictive approach to immigration policy toward a broad range of immigrants. The Trump administration reduced the availability and scope of legal protections for asylum seekers and refugees, trafficking victims, crime victims, those with Special Immigrant Juvenile status, Temporary Protected Status (TPS) recipients, individuals with cases warranting administrative closure, and individuals who might be viewed as low enforcement priorities.[24]

President Joseph R. Biden assumed office in early 2021 after a successful campaign that included promises to reverse Trump-era immigration policies. In its first two years, his administration implemented substantial changes to the immigration system, including 296 executive actions on immigration in Biden's first year in office.[25] In the face of significant resistance from Republican-led states, the Biden administration issued a number of orders and policies that substantially restructured interior immigration enforcement after the Trump era: introducing a more nuanced approach to enforcement priorities, putting an end to massive workplace raids, and ending family detention practices.[26] At the same time, however, many of Trump's restrictive border policies, including a ban on the entry of most asylum seekers, remained in place two years after Biden assumed office, due to a combination of litigation challenges from Republican-dominated states and the administration's own concerns about the potential political fallout of loosening immigration restrictions. Moreover, President Biden's efforts to persuade Congress to enact comprehensive immigration reform have failed. Individuals with DACA still have no legislative path to citizenship. Individuals who would have been eligible for DAPA or DACA+ still lack work authorization and can only hope for acts of official discretion to avoid removal.

This book explores the consequences of these developments for immigrants, for the organizations that serve them, and for the broader local, state, national, and transnational communities of which these immigrants are a part.

A Critical Approach to Deferred Action

Our analysis of the announcement, injunction, and withdrawal of DAPA and DACA+ contributes to critical immigration scholarship by exploring the impact of phantom programs on immigrant communities and immigration policy. We refer to DAPA and DACA+ as "phantoms" because they were spectral: after they disappeared, the programs continued to structure the political and legal landscape, to influence advocacy, and to haunt potential beneficiaries with the memory of what might have been. In 1990, Hiroshi Motomura developed the notion of "phantom norms" in the context of immigration law.[27] Motomura observed that when courts construed immigration statutes, they often brought to bear "phantom constitutional norms" that were "not indigenous to immigration law but come from mainstream public law instead."[28] These norms pushed statutory interpretation in immigration cases in a more rights-protective direction than the formal case law seemed to support. We focus not on interpretive norms, but administrative programs—specifically, two programs that were jointly announced, challenged, withdrawn, and largely forgotten, but that continue to exert a gravitational pull on law and policy, and on the lives of the people and organizations who would have helped to implement them and those who might have benefited from them. Phantom programs exert their influence in the development of case law, but they do their most important work in the social sphere: influencing how people think about and plan for the future, how organizations devise advocacy strategies, and how activists attempt (and fail) to mobilize responses from policymakers.

Ana Muñiz employed the eighteenth-century concept of *phantasmagoria* to explain how racialized gang allegations haunt people. Such allegations, like the phantoms in the analogy, are illusory, monstrous, and fear-inducing.[29] Many of the individuals in our study have similar, haunting presences in their own lives in the form of criminal allegations, criminal records, and records of prior exclusions and removals in the immigration system. But they are also haunted by programs that never were. Our interviews reveal how, long after lawyers and policy makers have declared a legal policy innovation dead, and long after it has been frozen by the courts, that program continues to shape lives.

The phantom DAPA and DACA+ programs were products of prolonged political struggles on the part of immigrant communities and their allies. President Obama's announcement of these programs was a partial policy success for immigrant rights advocates. The programs would have had concrete benefits for successful applicants. At the same time, even if these programs had gone forward, the benefits would have been limited. Many people would have been excluded from the DAPA program because they lacked a qualifying relative, specifically, a US citizen or lawful permanent resident son or daughter. Many more would have been disqualified from both DAPA and DACA+ because of their prior encounters with the criminal legal system or the immigration enforcement system. For those who did qualify, deferred action would not render the bearer eligible to adjust their status, vote, petition for family members, exit and reenter the country at will, or maintain their status for an indefinite period. Deferred action is, in essence, an enforcement measure, a form of prosecutorial discretion exercised when the costs of enforcing laws outweigh the benefits, or when humanitarian considerations come into play.[30] Its boundaries are shaped by political considerations—recall the stunned silence when Los Angeles viewers learned that DAPA would not be extended to parents of DACA recipients. Deferred action is therefore part and parcel of criminalization. It is the kind of relief that can be created when enforcement is the water that noncitizens swim in: it provides relief from the worst elements of a life governed by criminalization but cannot guarantee anything close to the certainty and security that the law is often imagined to provide through administrative benefits. Studying this form of relief therefore exposes the punitive underbelly of what might otherwise appear to be a humanitarian gesture.

Phantom programs such as DAPA and DACA+ both reveal and perpetuate criminalization and racialized exclusion in immigration policy. Our conversations with immigrants in Southern California revealed very clearly how the criminalization of noncitizens and other marginalized groups has ensured that immigration policy reforms will likely remain illusory for many immigrants, no matter how long they have been here and how hard they work. Their criminal records and contacts with the criminal and immigration enforcement system would have rendered ineligible for relief many of the people with whom we spoke. At the same time, the creation and announcement of these phantom programs were used to justify enforcement initiatives that grew ever bolder and more invasive. Even as the relief programs failed to go into effect, parallel enforcement efforts carried on and multiplied. Phantom programs thus continue to haunt us in many ways, including the ways that they have justified severity without delivering their promised lenity.

Our exploration of phantom programs thus contributes to critical immigration scholarship by helping to excavate some of the legal and social mechanisms that produce immigrant illegalization and that naturalize racialized exclusions. Over the past two decades, critical immigration scholarship has highlighted the global inequalities that underlie immigration policy-making. Scholars working in this field have sought to denaturalize categories and practices that earlier scholarship took for granted.[31] Traditional immigration scholarship has defined *immigrants* as people who engage in a type of behavior, specifically, moving from one country to another. This definition suggests that immigrants are a type of person, that movement entails crossing borders, that borders are located at the edges of national territories, and that movement is a key and defining step in the life of immigrants.[32] Central questions in traditional immigration scholarship are: how do immigrants move, why, and with what effects? To describe impacts on individuals, scholars have examined incorporation, assimilation, and social mobility.[33] Scholars have also studied how receiving countries are impacted by new arrivals, the "brain drain" experienced by sending countries,[34] the ways that an immigration "escape valve" works to limit political dissent on the part of marginalized groups,[35] and the nature of global labor markets.[36] Within such accounts, immigration law is defined as a system that regulates movement, reinforcing national sovereignty, bounding citizenries, and structuring opportunity.

In contrast, critical immigration scholarship interrogates many of these notions. Critical scholars have insisted that, instead of being an intrinsic characteristic of personhood, being an "immigrant" involves being constituted as such through state processes like illegalization.[37] Law is therefore a mechanism that produces illegality.[38] Borders are located not only at territorial limits but also within countries' interiors and outside of their formal territory,[39] and are created in the process of excluding noncitizens[40] and in sorting members of the political community. Illegalization impacts not only immigrants themselves but also their family members, limiting life opportunities.[41] In addition to documenting such harms, critical scholars have also studied exclusionary systems and processes. Exclusionary laws and practices often produce ambiguous or liminal social positions, in which noncitizens are in some ways part of the societies where they live but are also partially excluded.⁴² Concepts such as labor extraction and deportability highlight the ways that immigration law structures and is produced through global inequalities and hierarchical relationships within nation states—for example, between capital and workers.⁴³ Instead of merely playing a regulatory role, critical scholars assert, immigration law is part of a system of power, one that can sometimes be mobilized to confer rights but that often is punitive and exclusionary in nature.

Our analysis of interviews with government officials, immigrant rights advocates, and members of immigrant communities builds on critical immigration studies by putting forward three theoretical insights. First, we argue that criminalization is a central element of the processes that produce illegalization, which has been the term favored by critical scholars. While a focus on "illegalization" has the advantage of highlighting the ways that individuals are constituted as undocumented or unauthorized, in the US context, it also can overemphasize the importance of federal law and immigration status at the expense of a focus on other legal regimes and actors, most notably, pervasive criminal regulation. Our interviews with members of immigrant communities reveal that individuals were subject to low-level policing by a wide variety of actors—police officers, hospital staff, school officials, and employers—and that interviewees felt that they were often targeted due to their race. Low-level police stops for things like a traffic violation could lead to confiscated vehicles, expensive tickets, or arrests, which in turn could bring individuals to the attention of immigration officials. Over-policing in low-income communities and communities of color therefore was key to defining individuals as noncitizen subjects. A variety of nonstate and state actors, not only federal ones, were involved in these processes. Ironically, the ever-elusive promises of immigration relief in the form of phantom programs and failed immigration reform were wielded by policy makers at all levels of government as justification for turning the harsh tools of criminal and immigration law enforcement on immigrant communities. Attending to criminalization counters both citizen/noncitizen and deserving/undeserving binaries by explicating the processes to which multiple marginalized communities are subjected.

Second, our exploration of phantom programs brought us face-to-face with the liminality and precarity experienced by low-income workers, members of racialized communities, and others across a range of immigration and citizenship statuses. Undocumented residents excluded from DACA, and denied the benefits of DACA+ and DAPA, were exceptionally vulnerable as a legal matter. But many people who gained the protections of immigration and citizenship law, up to and including US citizens, nevertheless experienced various forms of legal precarity and exclusion. In this book, we attend to the various precarious social conditions that result from criminalization, whether this takes the form of incarceration, detention, removal, being unhoused, or confinement to particular social positions or geographic locations. These forms of precarity are interconnected. Being unhoused can lead to incarceration and incarceration can lead to detention and precarious employment, which can inhibit social mobility. For interviewees who were members of immigrant communities, deportation was one of many concerns related to this broader concept of banishment. Social exclusion, therefore, not only derives from borders, but from various sometimes-interrelated forms of precarity.

Third, our exploration of phantom programs allows us to build on previous insights into race, power, and immigration restrictions that have been generated by critical race theory[44] and Third World Approaches to International Law (TWAIL).[45] Our focus on phantom programs allowed us to document, in real time, how communities struggled to come to terms with the promise of programs that would not meet their needs under the best of circumstances and that exacerbate their vulnerabilities when even the limited promises go unfulfilled. We bear witness in this book to the ways that empty promises of legal relief exact slow violence on marginalized communities.[46] In charting these struggles, we observe how abstract concepts of sovereignty and state power are used to justify exclusions and how these exclusions operate in furtherance of projects of racialization and the construction of racial hierarchy.

Looking "to the bottom," as critical race theory urges,[47] also gives us insight into how people resist the exclusionary effects of law and build communities that are more broadly protective than any program ever promised. While elected officials can rescind programs at their discretion (though not without political and legal battles), those who have been the subjects of immigration law also have devised means of transcending its limits. These strategies include strategically deploying personal narratives to build political power, applying for status as opportunities present themselves (or strategically declining to do so), forming alliances across borders and issues, mobilizing support through organizing, and remaining in the United States in the face of mounting enforcement initiatives. Examining these resistance strategies in detail reveals the complex ways that people both engage in and critique respectability politics. Resisting criminalization primarily by prioritizing status regularization benefits some people, but also leaves others vulnerable to enforcement practices. Recognizing this vulnerability, immigrant communities and their allies have been creative in developing politically imaginative approaches that challenge traditional notions of deservingness, sometimes pursuing social justice for a broad swath of citizens and noncitizens in ways that extend well beyond deferred action.

Our deep dive into the phantom programs that shaped the last decade of immigration policy reveal how enforcement practices undercut the very distinctions on which exercises of discretion are based. Deferred action is grounded in categorical thinking that seeks to differentiate the "deserving" from the "undeserving"—families, not felons, as President Obama put it. Yet, the overreach of enforcement initiatives marks many individuals' records in ways that counterintuitively yet categorically define them as undeserving. In a climate of heightened enforcement, otherwise innocent actions or evidence—a discrepancy in someone's record, a period of time that cannot be accounted for, a trip outside of the United States—have come to be treated as suspect. Overt racial profiling and pervasive, intrinsically racialized enforcement practices concentrate this suspicion on certain groups, regardless of their citizenship. The sort of betrayal experienced by noncitizens who had hoped to apply for deferred action is therefore also faced by other precarious groups, including workers who lack a living wage and those racially profiled by the police. As a result, securing legal status is not enough to guarantee full social inclusion, an observation that is not lost on the immigrant-serving organizations with which we worked.

Our conversations with people haunted by phantom programs thus returned again and again to our three theoretical themes: the role of criminalization in illegalization processes; the interdependence of legal and social sources of liminality and precarity; and the centrality of racialized systems of power in the operation of contemporary US immigration policy. Charged with navigating the terrain shaped by these forces, organizations and individuals often sought instead to change the map. Organizations providing legal services pushed to change immigration law and policy, but they also drew connections between immigration and other issues like housing, employment, and criminal legal system reform, and made immigration law less threatening by building out protections in those other areas of law and policy. They also sought to change the underlying narrative of immigration reform. A student activist and DACA recipient who came to the US from Hong Kong by way of Canada told us that granting relief to a small subset of immigrants could never be enough. "What I would like to see is," she said, "[a] move away from the DREAM Act narrative [about idealized, high-achieving, young, predominantly Latinx, students]. And instead talk a lot more about undocumented workers, undocumented parents, LGBTQ immigrants, undocumented Black immigrants." She, and others, were trying to construct a world in which nobody had to be perfect, and in which there would be a place for everyone.

Studying a Phantom Program

Before going any further, we must offer a confession: this book is the product of a thwarted research plan. When we first conceptualized this project in 2013, the Obama administration was still hoping to sign into law some form of comprehensive immigration reform, or CIR, as it came to be known in policy circles. In fact, S. 744, the Border Security, Economic Opportunity, and Immigration Modernization Act of 2013, received bipartisan support in the Senate but was not considered by the House of Representatives, and therefore never reached President Obama's desk. Had it become law, this legislation would have created a new temporary "Registered Provisional Immigrant" (RPI) status. Successful applicants would have had to meet numerous requirements to maintain RPI status and would have had to do so for ten years before being eligible for lawful permanent residency. Our original plan was to study this process in order to understand who would be able to qualify, the barriers that would-be applicants encountered, and the role of immigrant-serving organizations in helping applicants overcome these barriers. When the CIR bill failed to pass into law, activists pressured the Obama administration to develop more expansive forms of executive relief, modeled on DACA, and our research strategy changed. We decided to study the role of immigrant-serving organizations as brokers who would likely serve as intermediaries between the federal government and potential applicants, sharing information about this new program, interpreting its provisions, preparing applications, and advocating on behalf of community members.

We launched a preliminary study in the summer of 2014, when planned announcements of immigration relief were being postponed due to a so-called "surge" in arrivals of unaccompanied minors from Central America at the southern border. The widespread use of the term "surge" to describe what was happening mischaracterized the arrival of these migrants—mainly children—as uncontrollable and unforeseen, when in fact, it was a predictable effect of emerging developments in Central America and of US policy. Decrying a "surge" purposefully invokes an image of invading masses, allowing government officials to dodge the institutional failures indicated by the lack of capacity to deal with regular migration flows. The notion of "surge" is invoked to justify an "emergency" response that suspends the normal construction of productive responses to migration. And it does so again and again. Rhetoric about a "surge" certainly did so in the summer of 2014.

Although the Obama administration delayed the announcement of DAPA and DACA+, we began interviewing community-based lawyers and activists in Southern California in the summer of 2014 to better understand their work and their goals with respect to the proposed programs. We also applied for, and received, funding from the National Science Foundation with the hope that we would be able to study the DAPA and DACA+ programs when they were announced and implemented.

When organizations began holding forums on DAPA and DACA+ and on California's 2014 legislation permitting undocumented residents to acquire a driver's license, we were permitted to announce our project and to recruit interviewees who hoped to apply for deferred action. We continued our study after DAPA and DACA+ were enjoined, reinterviewing lawyers, organizers, activists, and would-be applicants while continuing to recruit new participants. We also interviewed government officials who were involved in creating these programs. Over the next three years, we carried out participant observation when possible, attending informational forums, trainings, document review workshops, meetings, conferences, and protests, and shadowing service providers during their workdays. We also collected documents relating to the legal challenges to DACA and DAPA+, including the *United States v. Texas* case that reached the Supreme Court in the October 2015 term. We gathered administrative guidance documents, the text of local immigration-related ordinances, news articles, and materials produced by the organizations that participated in our study. We focused not only on deferred action but also on the broader system of laws and regulations affecting long-term residents who lacked legal immigration status.

Our collaborative research crosses the boundaries between law and social sciences. Between 2014 and 2017, our research team interviewed more than 135 individuals, including immigrants who were potentially eligible for executive relief, immigrants excluded from proposed relief, the family members of these immigrants (including some who received relief through DACA), activists and attorneys at immigrant rights organizations, and government officials who crafted executive relief programs. Approximately one-third of this sample was interviewed multiple times, allowing us to trace changes in individual lives and organizational histories. Together, these interview transcripts, field notes, and documents comprise an unprecedented dataset that provides insight into the dilemmas experienced by government officials, the strategies of immigrant rights advocates, and the experiences of immigrants themselves as these played out during a time of great legal turmoil and uncertainty.

Our study is grounded in Los Angeles County and Orange County, California, sites that have large immigrant populations and that also present striking contrasts. Both counties have long histories of settler colonial displacement of Native peoples, beginning in Spanish colonial times and continuing as the national flag flying over the region changed from that of Spain to Mexico to the United States. Both counties were also sites of racist policies perpetrated by white settlers, policies that were virulent and overt through much of the nineteenth and twentieth centuries. Anti-Black racism was pervasive, and a host of exclusionary laws and practices took aim at both immigrants and citizens of Latin American, Asian, and African origin.

But the histories of Los Angeles and Orange Counties diverged, particularly as the twentieth century gave way to the twenty-first. Los Angeles, with its abundance of long-standing immigrant-serving organizations, adopted more welcoming official policies toward immigrants. Orange County, with fewer immigrant-serving groups, largely retained its more exclusionary policies (though there are exceptions, such as the city of Santa Ana). Our research strategy has allowed us to engage a broad range of interviewees in these contrasting geographic spaces, including multiple language groups (Spanish, Korean, and English), generations, and political ideologies. Likewise, our research team has a broad range of expertise, including administrative law, immigration law, criminal law, clinical training, and social science methodology. This breadth of expertise allows us to train a rich analytical lens on our research data, resulting in a text that engages policy questions from a perspective grounded in human experience, social theory, and legal knowledge.

Our research approach was collaborative in multiple senses. The four co-authors of this introduction worked together throughout the project. We all conducted interviews and participant observation, often separately though sometimes jointly, focusing on different organizations and constituencies depending on our connections, geographic locations, and language skills. Through frequent research team meetings, we shared ideas and initial analyses. We also collaborated with research assistants including Edelina Burciaga, Alma Garza, Jason Palmer, Elizabeth Hanna Rubio, Jessica Santiago, and Jose Torres. Research assistants played multiple roles in the project, conducting interviews, writing fieldnotes, and coding data. In addition to doing all of those things, Jason Palmer helped to create a website so that the documents we collected for our study could be publicly available.[48] Additionally, we collaborated with the organizations that participated in our study. Our analyses reflect issues that they were interested in and wanted us to ask about, and we shared findings with them early in our research. We also collaborated with interviewees in that we attempted to pursue interview topics that they cared about. Interviews were semi-structured. We had an interview guide, but we also tailored interviews to the expertise and interests of each interviewee. Interviewees also contributed to the study by referring us to others, thus we employed snowball sampling methods in addition to reaching out to those we met during participant observation. The data were double and triple coded according to salient themes. This iterative coding process ensured that our analysis reflects the expertise of all members of our study team. When the time came to write the book, one member of our research team, Sameer Ashar, had to step back due to other commitments and life events. We recognize Sameer's many contributions through coauthorship on the introduction and Chapter 4, the two chapters that he helped write.

One challenge we faced during the writing process is the inadequacy of terminology for the people and phenomena that are the subject of this book. Like many scholars, we reject the term "illegal alien" as stigmatizing and dehumanizing. "Undocumented" is preferable and is often used by members of immigrant communities, but this term can be inaccurate, as those who lack legal status in the United States are often hyperdocumented,[49] since they collect check stubs, receipts, and other evidence of their stay in the US. Moreover, some people who are removable under immigration law maintain their legal status unless and until they receive a court order, so they are fully and legally "documented." "Unauthorized" is in some ways more accurate in that it references the role of state authorities in producing conditions of illegality, yet this term is dichotomous, implying that there are two neatly divided groups: the authorized and the unauthorized. In reality, there are gradations that include people with temporary authorization, such as deferred action.[50] Moreover, even lawful permanent residents can lose their "authorization" very quickly given their vulnerability to immigration enforcement, particularly if convicted of certain crimes. The term "noncitizens" highlights the shared vulnerabilities experienced across gradations of legality, yet this term distinguishes citizens from all others which is problematic because in reality, forms of precarity transcend the citizen/noncitizen binary. For instance, both citizens and noncitizens confront discriminatory policing practices and spatial exclusion. Even the term "immigrant" can be stigmatizing in the current political context.[51] Elites who move to the United States do not necessarily call themselves immigrants and are often excluded from public discourse concerning immigrants.

Because of these terminological dilemmas, we use varied terms for the individuals who are the subject of this book, and when the issue is salient, we stress their specific legal status (e.g., "DACA recipient") or another aspect of their identity, such as their profession or area of residence. Through such terminology, we hope to communicate the complexity of our interlocutors' experiences and social positions, and to avoid reductionist labels.

We also grapple with the limits of language when writing about race, gender, national origin, and nationality—concepts that intersect in complex and shifting ways. We cannot talk about immigration without talking about race. Immigration laws and racial categories are mutually constitutive. But race itself is a fluid concept. We recognize that our attempt to use broad racial categories to sort individual experiences is fraught, but we also cannot avoid this peril without masking realities of law and law enforcement.

Throughout the book, we generally use the term "Latinx" to refer to individuals who trace their origin (at least in part) to Mexico, Central and South America, and portions of the Caribbean, and we use the term "API" (Asian and Pacific Islander) to refer to those who trace their origins (also at least in part) to Asian and Pacific Island nations. These terms apply to individuals regardless of their nationality and citizenship status. Given the geographic context of the study, we prefer the term "Latinx" to the census term "Hispanic" and "API" to "Asian" or "Asian American."[52] We chose to use the relatively new and less common term "Latinx" rather than the more common "Latino" because of the term's potential for inclusivity.[53] We appreciate the fact that these terms are the same, regardless of US citizenship status. We recognize, however, that our choices still obscure important intra-group differences, sweeping together people from many different countries and lumping together individuals who identify as Black, those who identify as members of nations preexisting European colonialism, those who identify as mixed race, and those who identify as white descendants of European colonizers. Where it is more appropriate, we describe a person with reference to their country of origin.

Sensitivity to terminology, diversity, and individuals' forms of self-identification are even more important as we move past the Trump era, a time when use of anti-Black and anti-immigrant terminology abounded. President Trump denounced Mexican immigrants as rapists,[54] referred to Haiti, El Salvador, and African nations as "shithole countries,"[55] and conflated all Central American immigrants with gang members.[56] President Biden has eschewed the use of such overtly racist terminology, but the continued use of racist epithets and stereotypes by those charged with enforcing criminal and immigration laws persists, as does the use of racial epithets by important politicians and political commentators.[57] We deliberately strive to counter such racist depictions, presenting a more complete and humanizing portrayal as social movements focused on immigrant rights continue to fight and move forward under President Biden's administration.

A Story in Two Parts

We tell this story in two parts—the first explores the complex and pervasive consequences of deferred action against a backdrop of cresting immigration enforcement, and the second delves into the various responses to these developments. In the first half of the book, we focus on the legal context for, and provide descriptive clarity on, the various deferred action programs created and challenged between 2012 and 2022. Beginning with a discussion of the background conditions that set the stage for DACA and later executive relief proposals, including the phantom DAPA and DACA+, we show in Chapter 1 that these programs are impossible to disentangle from a broader set of criminalization processes. Federal immigration enforcement infrastructure bears considerable responsibility for the uncertainties and fear experienced by migrant communities, and Chapter 1 documents some of the many ways that local law enforcement could both exacerbate or alleviate these uncertainties and fears. Ultimately, criminal conduct—past, ongoing, or presumed—largely sets the terms of inclusion for immigrant residents. This chapter concretely illustrates the centrality of criminalization in the illegalization process.

Centering the criminal law principles and processes at the heart of the Obama administration's approach to immigration policy allows for a more accurate understanding of the significance and limitations of temporary relief programs like DACA and DAPA, which define only certain, exceptional immigrants as "deserving" of relief. In Chapter 2, we reveal how the government officials who created and implemented programs like DACA underestimated the degree to which the benefits were curtailed by many of the criminalization processes and immigration enforcement pathologies that existed before the program was launched and that continued throughout. As the Obama administration–era officials we interviewed tell the story, DACA was conceptualized as a stepping stone toward broader reform. But broader reform never materialized, forcing undocumented individuals to develop and employ survival strategies during the Obama administration's second term, a period characterized by continued, if modulated, enforcement efforts. The phantom DAPA and DACA+ programs might have provided further measures of modulation, but they similarly failed to grapple with the pervasive criminalization of long time, undocumented residents. And, in any event, they never came into being.

In Chapter 3, we explore how immigrants and their allies actively charted paths for themselves in this period of shifting enforcement strategies. They expended significant energy preparing for programs that never materialized. Many engaged in "hyperdocumentation" to create, collect, and curate a record establishing a life lived but unseen in the United States. Migrant-serving organizations and other community groups who figured into the process by which deferred action programs were negotiated helped mediate and explain to migrants, as best they could, the risks and benefits of the various deferred action programs. At the same time, even as the political class offered a narrow view of who deserved immigration relief, immigrant communities showed their willingness to set their own terms of belonging, merit, and deservingness.

After mapping out the contours of the phantom programs of the past decade—and their very real footprint in immigrant communities—we explore how individuals, organizations, governmental actors, and communities tried to create new realities in spaces haunted by phantom programs. Chapters 4, 5, and 6 explain how individuals, organizations, and some government officials tried to mitigate the punitive elements of immigration law and respond productively to the enforcement climate they confronted. While Chapter 3 centers on individuals' efforts to navigate lives against a hostile and uncertain legal terrain, Chapter 4 turns to the question of how organizations sought not only to navigate, but also to transform that domain. While Chapter 2 focuses on federal officials that helped to change the federal enforcement landscape, Chapter 5 applies a local lens to those issues, exploring how states and localities developed their own responses to the shifting federal landscape. The deferred action experiment has prompted a broad reimagining of the role that subfederal immigration governance strategies play in shaping the conditions of daily life for residents regardless of immigration status. The pervasive local differences in immigration policy prompted individuals and organizations to reconfigure their advocacy efforts between and among levels of government as they sought sites responsive to their claims. Finally, while Chapter 1 lays out the enforcement climate and the effects it had on individuals' daily lives, Chapter 6 pivots to exploring how individuals worked to conceptualize their own belonging in the face of shifting policies at all levels of government. We present the various ways that immigrants "perform citizenship" or engage in citizenship "passing," and we also unearth more transformative strategies and attitudes. The long history of racism in the US, represented and compounded by overly punitive enforcement of criminal and immigration law, has diminished the social meaning of citizenship for at least some of the people with whom we spoke. They had embarked on new ways of imagining belonging.

We conclude our book by describing the ways that the legal shapeshifting of the immigrant residents, and their allied organizers and activists, have created possibilities for a more inclusive future. Their work revealed the ways that individuals, organizations, and government officials could work toward a world in which deferred action would not be necessary because no one would be at risk of deportation. For the past three decades, scholars and politicians have centered on a mass legalization program as the solution to the pathologies of the immigration system. Current political realities suggest that any such legalization program will be forged within a difficult political compromise and will entail significant tradeoffs in terms of further criminalization and increased enforcement against those left out of the compromise. Among the people with whom we spoke, there were some who had great enthusiasm for this kind of reform. But others insisted that we need to think about immigration reform in a much more capacious way. Instead of criminalization, many individuals, organizers, and advocates yearned for political engagement marked by free movement, equality, freedom from over-policing, and opportunities to thrive at school, in the workplace, and in longer-term life projects. Liminal legal status suppresses these aspirations, but also creates openings through which communities have created opportunities to break through.

As we envision what more breakthroughs might look like, we must also recognize the many ways that people are haunted—not just by the failure of DAPA and DACA+—but by all of the unfulfilled promises of immigration law reform. We witnessed, and bear witness to, the human costs of decades of criminalization, unrealized political aspirations, and the slow violence of exclusionary immigration policies. Scholars are still developing a vocabulary to describe the secondary and long-term effects of living within a constant state of uncertainty and liminality. In writing this book and working our way toward that vocabulary, we have tried to be respectful of people's experiences and to present them not in soundbites, but in all their complexity. Ultimately, we strive to convey how a wide variety of people cope with the legal phantoms of DAPA and DACA+ in a context of fast-moving social and legal changes.

ONE

Enforcement

ERASMO ARRIVED IN THE United States from Durango, Mexico, when he was twenty-one years old—fourteen years before we first interviewed him in Los Angeles. He remembered being in the US when the Twin Towers fell on September 11, 2001. Crossing into the US before that event was quite easy for him, but even then, getting a job without documents was not.

As a young man struggling to find employment and his footing in a new country, he ran into trouble with the law. As he put it, "I started misbehaving due to lack of experience." He was pulled over for drinking and driving, and his cousin's gun was in the trunk of his car. He did not remember many details of the legal proceedings or the specific charges that followed, but he recalled that he pled guilty and spent several months in jail.

When he was released, Erasmo related, "They made me sign my deportation order." As he explained in a December 2014 interview, he took the word of the government officials that signing the order was the best way to ensure his speedy release. He says that he was not informed of, nor did he understand, the immigration consequences of this decision:

> I didn't want to sign my deportation but being there, it's the first thing the police tells you, sign your deportation. This way you'll leave faster. And that's what you do thinking that's the best thing. But if I would've known in that time, I wouldn't have signed the deportation. I didn't consult with an attorney, because the people who were inside said that I would be released fast, that I didn't have too many problems, so I thought, well then why

consult with an attorney? And that's the problem I had, because there were some people that could help me post bond, but I didn't want to, because I didn't want to thin out those resources since I was going to be released fast. So I went to court, got released, and thought I'd stay in LA.

Erasmo said that he would not have signed the order if he had understood its legal consequences. Because he was undocumented, he was not released, but was instead sent to an immigration detention facility in Arizona. He spent two months in immigration detention and was removed to Nogales, Mexico. From there, he moved to Tijuana, where he worked for several months before reentering the United States. In so doing, he not only violated civil law requiring authorization to enter, but also violated the terms of his removal order, which, as he understood it, included a ten-year bar to reentry. Erasmo's record is now likely marked in two ways that will impede his future efforts to regularize his status: he has a criminal record, and he has reentered the country in violation of a formal removal order.

Crossing the border was harder for him in 2004 than it had been the first time. Erasmo recalled that he was detained at the border and returned to Mexico two or three times. But after a month of failed attempts, he did make it back. He has lived in Los Angeles since his return in 2004, and he had a child who is a US citizen. Yet, despite his more than two decades in the country and his family ties to US citizens, the paths to legal status for Erasmo seemed to be blocked by his prior criminal and immigration records. He told us of his desire to "clear" his record, though he does not know the exact nature of that record. Under existing law, it is very difficult to eliminate the immigration consequences of many criminal convictions.[1]

Erasmo's migration story cannot be described as "typical." Among the Southern California residents we interviewed, migration trajectories and experiences with law enforcement varied. But some of the themes that surfaced in Erasmo's story were common: the increased difficulty of crossing the border in a post-9/11 world, the frequent police encounters of low-income immigrants in heavily policed spaces, and the lack of counsel readily able to provide knowledgeable legal advice about the immigration consequences of any resulting contacts with the criminal legal system. These and other elements of Erasmo's story highlight the increasingly intertwined nature of criminal and immigration law enforcement in the US.

Erasmo's account is very different from those of Benjamin and Samuel, yet similar themes run through their experiences as well. When we spoke to Benjamin, he was eighteen years old and living in Los Angeles. He had entered the US from Mexico around the time he was nine years old, crossing the border from Tijuana without inspection. In 2014, he had received deferred action through the DACA program, but he had not applied to renew when his deferred action designation expired in 2016. By that time, he was confused about the legal status of the program, erroneously thinking that the Supreme Court's April 2016 split ruling, which kept in place a lower court injunction of the DAPA program, applied to DACA. He was also concerned about the impact that a new traffic ticket would have on his renewal application.

Samuel, an Orange County resident who came from Mexico more than two decades earlier as a young boy, participated in the immigrant justice movement that generated momentum toward creating DACA. In an ironic twist, however, he was unable to apply for DACA himself, because he was over 31 years of age when the program was announced. Although he had a college degree and wanted to become an accountant, he found that his legal status had complicated his ability to get a professional license. In some ways, Benjamin and Samuel were quite different from each other and from Erasmo. And yet, there were many common elements to their accounts, in addition to their lack of legal status. Most notably, as we will see, they both experienced low-level interactions with police that made their hold on life in the US feel increasingly tenuous.

Nor were the elements of these stories limited to the men that we interviewed. Although men are significantly overrepresented among people deported from the US—leading one scholar to label deportation in the US a system of "racialized and gendered mass deportation"[2]—many of the women with whom we spoke also had experienced what they perceived as racially discriminatory law enforcement practices. They also confronted the same realities of a hardening border over the past twenty years, as ever-expanding enforcement efforts made it more difficult to enter the country and work in the formal economy. As we discuss in greater detail in this and other chapters, regardless of their gender, people shared stories of workplace exploitation and discrimination that resulted from their lack of work authorization.

This chapter explores the historical forces that produced the landscape in which Erasmo, Benjamin, Samuel, and many others negotiated their daily lives in Southern California over the past decade. By the time we began interviewing immigrant residents in 2014, many of them were confronting daily the realities of an enforcement landscape that had fundamentally changed over the past two decades. Changes in immigration laws in the 1990s that widely expanded grounds for deportation and exclusion were followed by bureaucratic reorganizations and immigration enforcement funding infusions after September 11, 2001. As a result, beginning in 2001, the US government spent unprecedented sums to militarize the southern border and heighten surveillance and tracking at every port of entry; digitized workplace enforcement; integrated state and local law enforcement into the process of immigration enforcement through 287(g) agreements, joint task forces, and the Secure Communities program; increased capacity for immigration detention; and substantially increased the size of federal immigration enforcement agencies charged with enforcing immigration law in the interior.[3] Numerically, the Latinx community in the US bore the brunt of these border and interior enforcement measures,[4] but Black,[5] API, and Muslim immigrants from around the world experienced significant and specific enforcement-related harms as well.[6]

The effects of these changing immigration enforcement practices in the US were manifest in the lives of people we interviewed. At the border, repeat crossings and multiple encounters with border patrol agents were common experiences for immigrants who had entered and resided in the US without authorization. As a result, many had complex immigration histories, sometimes including one or more removal orders. Away from the border, immigration enforcement efforts were shaped primarily not by federal immigration agents but by local law enforcement—here broadly defined to include state, county, and local law enforcement officials. For everyone, daily life became more complicated, and conditions of normalcy more remote.

In the period from 2012 to 2022, interior immigration enforcement efforts came to rely much more heavily on transfers from local law enforcement than on field arrests or comparable efforts by Immigration and Customs Enforcement (ICE).[7] At the same time, the question of whether to prioritize an individual for removal was often answered based on criminal records largely shaped by local officials. Interactions with local law enforcement officials therefore became the most frequent entry point into the deportation pipeline, and the substantive outcomes of those interactions were critical determinants of whether immigrants were removable, and whether they were entitled to any possible relief.[8]

This shift in federal enforcement gave additional importance to local policing choices, including racially discrepant policing practices. This is significant, because many of the immigrant residents we interviewed felt that they were policed differently and more aggressively than white residents of their cities. They argued that police relied on markers of race and class as proxies for immigration status, and that they profiled residents accordingly, imposing fines and fees on residents for legal vulnerabilities tied to immigration status, such as a lack of a driver's license.[9]

Collectively, interviewees' experiences suggest that the federal turn toward cooperative interior immigration enforcement had normalized and further institutionalized longstanding policing practices that illegalize immigrant residents by identifying and exploiting their legal status vulnerabilities. Latinx residents repeatedly reported to us that police routinely profiled them on the basis of race and class markers precisely because law enforcement viewed certain characteristics as markers of undocumented immigration status.

When he ran for president in 2008, Barack Obama campaigned on a pledge to support a broad immigration reform bill—one that included generous legalization provisions—in his first year in office.[10] That legislation never materialized. Blame for this legislative failure does not rest solely with President Obama; he lacked willing partners in Congress. But it is also clear that Obama deprioritized immigration legislation during his first years in office. And during this same period, when Obama administration officials had an opportunity to rethink the tightening linkages between federal immigration enforcement and local law enforcement, they instead opted to formalize, systematize, and strengthen those ties, rather than disrupt them. Instead of questioning the logics of the nascent Secure Communities program, which fatefully linked local policing with immigration enforcement, President Obama oversaw its nationwide implementation—beginning in jurisdictions with the highest percentages of Latinx residents.[11] The administration developed enforcement priorities that focused on individuals with criminal records, with insufficient regard for individuals' equities, the needs of communities, or the realities of inequitable policing practices. Federal officials thus linked a criminal law enforcement system known to be racially biased with an immigration enforcement system that has relied since its inception on racial profiling.[12]

These immigration enforcement choices, made in the early days of President Obama's first term, continue to have lasting, deleterious effects on undocumented residents in the US. Individuals who might otherwise be good candidates for DACA, cancellation of removal, or other forms of immigration relief have instead been labeled "high priority" for removal based on low-level interactions with law enforcement. These interactions, in turn, have occurred against a backdrop of federal policy choices that have effectively encouraged over-policing in the immigrant neighborhoods that were home to most of the people we interviewed. Although the Obama administration came to accept some of the more pointed critiques of the Secure Communities program and sought to restore greater discretion and local input into the enforcement processes in 2014, the architecture of the Secure Communities program remained in place and was deployed to facilitate aggressive enforcement tactics when President Trump took office in 2017. Jurisdictions that favored tighter restrictions on immigration were readily able to use their criminal legal systems to funnel immigrant residents into the federal immigration enforcement system.[13] Notable differences emerged between jurisdictions interested in expanding federal immigration enforcement efforts and those wishing for more constrained approaches.[14] And although the Biden administration has downplayed the linkages between state and local criminal law enforcement and immigration enforcement, ceasing to operate the Secure Communities program, the federal government continues to check the fingerprints of state and local arrestees against a DHS database and file immigration detainers—and continues to criticize jurisdictions that seek to limit these connections—under the auspices of the Criminal Apprehension Program.[15]

Programs like the 2012 DACA program and the proposed DAPA and DACA+ programs of 2014 have to be understood in this context. As our discussions with Southern California residents reveal, these programs purport to protect "good" immigrants while allowing for prioritizing the deportation of the "worst of the worst." But this system, which permits profiling and intrusive policing of economically marginalized immigrants, draws a line between those who are "good" and those who are "the worst" that is thin and often arbitrary, while offering no guarantees to today's DACA recipient who might—through encounters with law enforcement that are overdetermined based on race and place—become tomorrow's enforcement priority.

Immigration Enforcement Infrastructure

Over the past three decades, the resources expended on immigration enforcement in the United States have grown exponentially. In 1990, the federal government spent about $263 million on border policing. By 2021, that figure was $4.9 billion.[16] In 1990, the budget for the entire Immigration and Naturalization Service (INS)—which handle both immigration enforcement *and* immigration services functions—was about $1 billion.[17] By 2021, the funding for enforcement functions alone was $26 billion.[18]

The exponential growth in immigration policing is more significant than these numbers suggest, because during this same period, the immigration enforcement system formally yoked itself to a criminal enforcement system that is excessively punitive and deeply unequal. Criminal law enforcement officials throughout the country have long cooperated with federal immigration enforcement officials,[19] but the bureaucratic linkages between these systems is of a more recent vintage. In 1996, Congress outlined a process whereby state and local governments could contract with the federal government to gain immigration enforcement authority.[20] Known as 287(g) agreements, named after the section of the Immigration and Nationality Act that outlines the legal authority for these agreements, memoranda of understanding enacted pursuant to this provision allow state and local law enforcement agents to perform immigration enforcement functions with the same authority as federal immigration agents, provided that local agents are trained and supervised by the federal government.[21] Although there was clearly some congressional enthusiasm for such collaborations, the executive branch did not enter into its first 287(g) agreement until 2002.[22]

But governmental reluctance to embrace the program changed markedly after the terrorist attacks on the United States on September 11, 2001. Spurred in part by a push from states and localities and in part by increased federal interest in and capacity for immigration enforcement, the largely dormant 287(g) program took off. By 2011, there were 72 such agreements, the vast majority of which formed after 2006.[23]

Beginning in 2008, administration officials also designed and began to implement a broader integration effort—the Secure Communities program—which Congress first funded in 2008.[24] Initially, Secure Communities functioned as a sort of automated expansion of ICE's Criminal Alien Program (CAP), whereby incarcerated individuals convicted of crimes were screened for potential removability. But the program quickly grew to include fingerprint screening not just individuals incarcerated for criminal convictions, but rather, of all individuals at the time of their arrest by any government official. By 2013, the Department of Homeland Security automatically screened all state and local arrest data to determine whether arrestees had any immigration offenses. This screening occurred whether or not the state or locality wanted to engage in such a joint effort and whether or not the arrest that led to the screening ultimately resulted in charges, much less convictions.[25] Police officers' decisions to arrest thus became the critical determinant of whether an immigrant would be screened by DHS.

Many immigrants and their allies had hoped that when he took office in January 2009, President Obama would reverse the trends that had increasingly criminalized their communities and encouraged the overpolicing of immigrant neighborhoods. After all, he had campaigned on the promise of such reforms. But that reversal did not happen. Throughout his first term and part of his second term, President Obama continued the immigration policies and practices of the Bush administration: mass prosecutions continued on the border, long time lawful permanent residents continued to be removed for relatively minor offenses, government lawyers continued to push for expansive judicial interpretations of crime-related removal grounds, and the Obama administration continued to expand its reliance on immigration detention.[26] Most critically, as previously noted, the Secure Communities program expanded from a handful of jurisdictions doing jail screenings to nationwide fingerprinting of all arrestees.[27] Ironically, President Obama—who went further than any other president in calling out the racial injustices of the criminal enforcement system[28]—oversaw the nationwide implementation of an immigration enforcement program that was tethered directly to that same racially unjust criminal enforcement system. The completion of this Secure Communities rollout occurred around the same period that the administration was announcing DACA, marking the ways that the Obama administration sought to carve out an elite and select group of immigrants from interior enforcement efforts that were otherwise reaching unprecedented levels.

The announcement of DAPA in late 2014 coincided with the Obama administration's first baby step to scale back Secure Communities. Attempting to rebrand Secure Communities as the "Priority Enforcement Program" (PEP), administration officials pledged to work with localities to find ways to target enforcement resources on individuals who were priorities for removal. The number of removals from the interior, particularly removals of people without criminal convictions, did decrease after the rollout of PEP. But the continued fingerprint screening of arrestees, overbreadth of priority categories, and hyperpunitiveness of the criminal legal system ensured that tens of thousands of long-term residents with strong equitable claims to stay were deported under PEP.

The criminal enforcement system was also linked to the immigration enforcement system in another important way during this period. As the federal "war on crime" heated up, Congress had enacted legislation in 1994[29] and again in 1996[30] that tied immigration control objectives to crime control objectives. The result is an immigration system that is extraordinarily harsh for a wide array of noncitizens who have contact with the criminal legal system. Congress legislated severe immigration consequences for almost all drug offenses, no matter how minor. Congress also significantly expanded the list of drug crimes and other criminal offenses that qualify as "aggravated felonies." An aggravated felony triggers mandatory detention during proceedings, mandatory removal, and a lifetime bar on return. This expanded definition of "aggravated felonies" applies retroactively, meaning that pre-1996 offenses are recharacterized as aggravated felonies in post-1996 removal proceedings.[31]

The confluence of massive enforcement budget increases, the systematization of bureaucratic linkages between immigration enforcement and local policing, and the expansion of criminal grounds of removability in the midst of a misguided and racially discriminatory "war on crime" led to an explosion in immigration detentions and deportations. In fiscal year 2000, the total number of noncitizens removed from the US was 188,467; by 2011, that number was 391,953,[32] and in 2013, it was 435,000.[33] In fiscal year 2000, only about 17 percent of federal criminal prosecutions were for immigration crimes.[34] By 2010, immigration prosecutions made up more than 50 percent of federal prosecutions,[35] and the numbers of removals and criminal prosecutions for immigration crimes did not peak until 2013.[36] The divide between immigrants treated as "good" or "bad," with those categories generally defined in terms of contact with the criminal justice system, became a centerpiece for both enforcement and relief initiatives. And even as reform conversations evolved in the criminal justice space, officials seemed to have few qualms about using systems widely viewed as racially biased and overly punitive as a reliable indicator of immigrant worthiness.

Through conversations with Orange County and Los Angeles County residents in the years immediately following these early Obama-era policy changes, we gained a better understanding of how these residents experienced enforcement trends on the ground. There are, of course, differences between and among the many jurisdictions encompassed in this region, both between and within the two counties that we focus upon. In Chapter 5, we home in on these jurisdictional differences to better examine how local policies impact immigrants' experiences. Here, it suffices to note an overall pattern suggesting that public officials in Los Angeles have been, on balance, less committed to cooperating with federal immigration enforcement officials in the decade of our study than officials in Orange County, though there are agencies and localities in both jurisdictions that serve as exceptions to this general rule. There are sufficient commonalities in the experiences of Los Angeles and Orange Counties during the period, however, that it is instructive to draw out some repeating themes that surfaced in our interviews with residents.

First, we find that many of the people we interviewed, and particularly, low-income Latinx residents, experienced frequent low-level contacts with criminal enforcement actors (including police officers, sheriff's deputies, and municipal court judges). In their experience, the legal vulnerabilities associated with immigration status—which include difficulty in accessing driver's licenses and being limited to low-wage work, often outside of the formal economy[37]—incentivized law enforcement to target immigrant communities.

Second, the residents with whom we spoke experienced policing as racially discriminatory. In particular, interviewees of all races and nationalities suggested that the police disproportionately targeted Latinx residents (regardless of immigration status) for immigration-driven street policing. Latinx respondents experienced this profiling at the hands of officers of all races and ethnicities. This profiling compounded the disproportionate policing of Black and Latinx communities more generally.[38]

Third, picking up once again on the stories of Erasmo, Benjamin, and Samuel, we trace the consequences of over-policing in immigrant communities combined with a contemporary enforcement system that focuses indiscriminately on criminal records as a marker of unworthiness. Contact with the criminal enforcement system (whether in the remote past or more recently) often stands as a permanent impediment to immigration relief and generates ongoing stress for impacted residents.

The Criminal Law Enforcement Landscape

Since his return to the US in 2004, Erasmo had avoided serious run-ins with law enforcement. But our interviews with him revealed the fact that he still frequently encountered the police. In 2014, he reported that his lack of a driver's license created recurring problems for him:

> We've been struggling due to the documents—that we don't have a license and all of that. We're running around—like my job, I work in construction, but we always wonder, what if the police pulls us over. All of that and the risks we run. I've had cars taken away from me. They leave my toolbox thrown on the ground. But here we are, surviving. [The police have] taken—what is it?—about three cars. I've paid about, what is it to retrieve my cars, like four or five thousand dollars. From there we've also paid tickets ranging from three hundred to six hundred dollars. . . . The tickets I've easily paid four to five thousand dollars.

Erasmo identified an issue that many of the people we interviewed had encountered—the recurrent cycle of automobile seizures, fees, and fines that occurred in communities where significant numbers of drivers lacked a driver's license.[39]

At the time we spoke with Erasmo, the California legislature had just passed a law, A.B. 60, which was signed by Governor Jerry Brown and would restore the ability of undocumented residents to access driver's licenses. By April 2018, more than one million California residents had accessed driver's licenses under the program.[40] But in the early days of our research, most residents who were out of status and not DACA eligible had no way of obtaining a license. And even after A.B. 60, many residents still lacked a license because they assumed they were ineligible and did not apply, because they were unable to pass the driving test, or because they felt it was not worth the risk of sharing their information with state law enforcement. Racialized barriers to access, including lack of information due to language barriers, also likely impeded the efforts of some of the API respondents to access driver's licenses.[41] In Erasmo's case, worry about past traffic stops kept him from moving forward, meaning that two years after the passage of A.B. 60—and notwithstanding the many problems that his lack of a license had caused him—he was still without a driver's license.

Consistent with findings in studies carried out in other geographic locales,[42] fear of deportation was not the central concern of immigrant residents during many of these police encounters. Erasmo, for example, did not express concern that his encounters with police would result in deportation. Although police had pulled him over and impounded his vehicles "four or five times," no immigration enforcement actions had followed. As he understood it, "if the police officers don't run your fingerprints, the police officer doesn't have access to your [immigration] record." In Los Angeles, Special Order 40—which limits communications between the Los Angeles Police Department (LAPD) and federal immigration enforcement officials—has been in effect since 1979. Perhaps because of his past experience, deportation was not a pressing daily concern for Erasmo and other Los Angeles immigrants when they encountered the police—at least, not one that they articulated. Nevertheless, the revolving-door nature of the auto seizures and the payments of fines and fees was a frequent and costly fact of life for Erasmo.

These interactions were not just expensive; they could also be violent and frightening. Erasmo described one particularly memorable encounter:

> [My partner and I] had a small, old car, not too new. We had just acquired it. We had only one week with it. We left the car across [the] street from where we were visiting. When we were heading back to the car, and we saw two police officers in a bike. . . . They waited until we got into the car to return. They pulled out their handguns and told us to [show] our hands and to turn off the car. The car wasn't even on. They forced us to get out of the car at gunpoint and the first [thing] they asked for was a driver's license. I told them I didn't have any. The car had about a month before the plates expired and they said the plates were expired. The reality is that the plates were not expired. So we argued back and forth with them because they had no reason to take the car away from us and they left us on foot, without a car. It was frustrating because they had us at gunpoint. What were we doing? We weren't doing anything, only getting our car and trying to drive. We left upset but what could we gain? And that's one of the toughest experiences we've had. I've been pulled over on other occasions but none like that episode.

Other Southern Californians shared similar stories of police encounters. As in Erasmo's case, for others, driving without a license frequently became the basis for a citation and other legal consequences in the course of police encounters. Fátima, Erasmo's wife and a small business owner in her forties who is originally from Mexico, explained:

> [N]o matter what, wherever you go, the unfortunate thing is that there are police that are going to ask you for documents. It doesn't matter where you are. You are never safe from the police, because the police are everywhere. . . . The streets I have taken, where there isn't very much traffic, there can still be an officer on a motorcycle, a patrol car, . . . they have impounded my car four times. I remember that once they took a car from me—they took it from me one day, my husband got it out for $1,300, and I had been driving it for two days and it was taken from me again by the same officer. So it isn't safe anywhere. What is the reason they stop you? Because your light isn't working, or because you look suspicious . . . or for whatever. Or it can be because they are like, "Well, I haven't done anything today, and here you are, so I'll impound your car."

Nor did the people we spoke with see these practices as random. As Mario, a Mexican national and long-term Los Angeles resident in his seventies at the time of our interview, explained, "The police sometimes set up squads. . . . They are checking people and if you don't have a license they are going to take your car away and they are going to throw you in the slammer. . . . They put them in certain places where there are more Latinos. All that area between Alvarado [Street] and MacArthur Park [in mid-city Los Angeles], they put up squads every week, they would take cars away exclusively from Latinos." Other individuals whom we interviewed talked about their efforts to avoid driver's license checkpoints when going about their daily business.

The tickets immigrants received for driving without a license, the fines and fees that accumulated as a result of these tickets, and the costs of the auto impoundment that sometimes follows are reminiscent of the racially disproportionate criminalization through fines and fees that have been documented in Black neighborhoods in places like Ferguson, Missouri.[43] These informal criminal law enforcement practices create what some critics call the "new debtor's prison,"[44] a system motivated by fiscal prerogatives rather than by rule of law principles like fairness or proportionality. As residents move through this informal system, which metes out seemingly arbitrary outcomes, the vulnerability created by immigration status only exacerbates the system's broader pathologies. Put differently, even when police formally separate themselves from federal immigration enforcement, policing practices appear designed to capitalize on legal vulnerabilities created by immigration status, and race frequently serves as a proxy for immigration status.

The resulting humiliating and frightening encounters leave people feeling not only marginalized and vulnerable, but also angry and ripped off. For example, Samuel, the Orange County resident who wants to become an accountant, discussed what happened to him after he was stopped and then cited for driving without a license. He said that the initial fine was $150, but because he did not have the money and missed a payment, an additional $250 penalty was added to that amount. He recalled:

> I went to see the judge and he made a big deal like in TV: that "you didn't pay the bill," that "you are robbing the state," and blah-blah, but it was a big deal. It made me feel really bad. . . . It's easy for them to send you to jail. So

I was like, "here you go." He was like, "It's fine," and I just thought, "It's all about the money." . . . Every day they have, like, in every session, they have like maybe fifty or seventy people without driver's licenses at that time and paying $750 each. So you think they have these sessions of how much money they make out of us. It's a lot of money.

Of course, for some people who lack US citizenship, and particularly those lacking lawful immigration status, there is an additional component to the cycle of fines, fees and incarceration that plague many poor communities of color. Given programs like Secure Communities, fear of deportation lurked under the surface for some immigrant residents. While it was not always the biggest concern, it was an additional source of stress. This was particularly true among those who lived in jurisdictions more inclined to cooperate with the federal government in immigration enforcement. Raul, a young activist and DACA recipient working in Orange County, noted that at a forum held in Santa Ana, shortly after the 2016 election, attendees were frightened. Raul said, "I don't know if folks are going to feel safe to be in Santa Ana. You know, you get picked up by the police for a traffic violation . . . and . . . you get taken into an ICE detention cell." (In fact, as we document in Chapters 4 and 5, these kind of post-election concerns spurred successful local activism, driven by young immigrant residents of Orange County, to pass a sanctuary ordinance in Santa Ana to interrupt this tight bond between local police and federal immigration enforcement agents.)

For the hundreds of thousands of people whose right to remain depends upon temporary, discretionary forms of relief like DACA and TPS, even low-stakes encounters can have dramatic immigration consequences. Benjamin, the Los Angeles County resident whose DACA-related work authorization had recently expired at the time we spoke to him, was ticketed for driving without a license and had his car impounded. Because he was uncertain of the legal effect this ticket would have on his deferred action status, he decided not to apply for DACA renewal. As he described it to us, Benjamin's encounter with law enforcement had the hallmarks of racial profiling. He and his other teenage friends were parked in a parking lot at Seal Beach late at night. He recounted:

So the cop, the highway patrol, he just told me, "You guys look suspect." I was like, "Why?" He was like, "You guys are the only ones here." But there was more cars, you know? But just because we were like, a lot of people, we were outside. They just said we looked suspect. They were like, "Do you have a driver's license?" I was like, "No, I don't. I have a permit though." He was like, "Unless you are with someone that's over twenty-one, your permit doesn't work." So I was like, "Okay, that's fine." He's like, "Can I see your registration and everything?" So I gave it to him. And he was like, "Okay." So he just told me, "Hold on a second." He went inside to check everything. The tow truck had already come. So he came. He was like, "Your car's gonna get towed away, you know, for this and this and for no license."

The officer left him at Seal Beach in the middle of the night with no transportation. Nor was this incident Benjamin's only encounter with law enforcement that seemed to him to lack a valid predicate for the stop and interaction. In Los Angeles some time earlier, he had been pulled over and asked for his license and registration. The alleged reason the officer gave to him was that he was driving with a minor. Yet, the woman he was with was not a minor. She was 19 years old and had identification to that effect. But since Benjamin did not have a driver's license during the stop, he was cited for *that* offense—which was unknown to the officer at the time of the stop.

Benjamin's understanding of his own interactions with law enforcement was also influenced by the experiences of other people he knows. When asked if he felt like his experiences were unique or reflected common attitudes among law enforcement, he was quick to choose the latter explanation, noting in passing, "I'm pretty sure, yeah. 'Cause for my brother, they have taken like four or five cars, different cars."

Benjamin's encounters with law enforcement also had consequences that extended beyond humiliation, degradation, cost, and serious inconvenience. For Benjamin, these encounters also impeded his willingness to file for DACA renewal—something that left him vulnerable to removal and unable to retain the job he worked when he had DACA. Benjamin was uncertain whether the citations he had received were barriers to DACA renewal, and he did not want to risk drawing attention to himself by filing a renewal application that might be rejected. He told us that he could not apply for renewal because of his "ticket for no license. So first, I have to fix that." When asked if he was certain that his ticket would bar renewal, he answered that, based on the information he had received at the DACA workshop he attended prior to his initial application, he understood that "you can't have nothing unless you fix everything." Whether or not Benjamin was correct that his tickets were barriers to DACA renewal, it was clear that he (and other DACA recipients and potential recipients) felt anxious or unable to file for DACA renewals after contacts with law enforcement.

In 2016, the Supreme Court deadlocked on the DAPA program in *United States v. Texas*, and even though that holding did not affect DACA as a strictly legal matter, this discouraging outcome only enhanced the anxiety of Benjamin and others contemplating whether and how to seek a DACA renewal. Benjamin was not alone in thinking that the ruling put a hold on DACA renewals, although the injunction by its own terms applied to DAPA and DACA+, and therefore had no effect on people who already had DACA. Even those who understood the legal distinctions between the programs felt that the DAPA litigation signaled looming challenges to the continued legal viability of DACA.

They were not wrong. On September 5, 2017, President Trump's acting secretary of Homeland Security, Elaine Duke, announced the rescission of the DACA program. Deferred action renewals could be filed only through March 2018, and all existing deferred action grants and work authorization would expire at the end of an individual's authorized two-year deferred action period.[45] Several federal district courts enjoined the rescission of the program, finding violations of the Administrative Procedures Act and the equal protection guarantee of the Fifth Amendment's due process clause, and ordering US Citizenship and Immigration Services (USCIS) to continue processing renewal applications.[46] The Trump administration appealed these decisions. Although the US Supreme Court ultimately affirmed the lower courts' invalidation of the DHS's attempt to rescind the DACA program, in an important way, the rescission effort seemed to accomplish the broader goals of the Trump administration, namely undermining confidence in legal institutions in the context of immigration policy. Even if the DHS failed to secure a legal victory before the Supreme Court, the agency and the broader administration still alienated noncitizens like Benjamin who might have a valid claim for relief but who hesitate to move forward for fear of what awaits around the corner. Moreover, the DACA program only survived in truncated form, because the Supreme Court kept in place the lower court's prohibition on the government's ability to extend DACA to those who did not already have it. People who, like Benjamin, had failed to renew their status, are now locked out.

Undocumented immigrants were at risk for targeted law enforcement actions not only as drivers, but also as employees in the informal economy. Selling food from food trucks or otherwise conducting commerce in informal marketplaces could bring on law enforcement actions.[47] As Marc, a young advocate working at an immigrants' rights advocacy organization in Los Angeles, explained, the arrests, criminal processing, and removal of immigrants who engaged in these sorts of commercial activities actually fueled a narrative of migrant criminality: "They frame it as, like, the only people we capture are, like, criminals, when really . . . this person was selling stuff on the streets and you guys started doing a raid, and what do you mean, 'He's a criminal?' He's selling, like, food for his family to survive. What do you mean he's a criminal?"

Participation in the labor market created other perils for individuals who lacked legal work authorization. Some enter the formal labor market using social security numbers that do not belong to them.[48] Knowing use of a means of identification belonging to another person can serve as the basis of aggravated felony identity theft charges,[49] as well as similar state offenses.[50] These convictions, in turn, can serve as grounds for removal.[51] Though women are statistically less likely to be arrested in public encounters with police, these kinds of violations create another path by which they might nevertheless find themselves caught up in the criminalized immigration system.

This was true for Julieta, a Mexican national and longtime Los Angeles resident, whose story is told in greater detail in Chapter 3. In the 1990s, Julieta applied for a driver's license using a social security number that did not belong to her. "I would like to know," she said, if the number "that I used years back is a nonexistent number, or if it belongs to someone." Twenty years ago, she felt that her immediate need to work outweighed the possible long-term consequences of using a social security number that was not hers. Several years later, "when the time to renew the driver's license came, I just got a letter from the DMV [Department of Motor Vehicles], saying the social security number that you provided doesn't match our records. That's all. . . . So now that the [California] Governor Jerry Brown passed the law [the previously mentioned A.B. 60, allowing undocumented immigrants to apply for driver's licenses], I could apply, but I could get into serious trouble. . . . I feel bad for using that number, to be quite honest. I feel guilty for doing so. But, unfortunately, there's not much I can do." Julieta relied on Los Angeles's public transportation system because she was not comfortable driving without a license and did not see a clear way to apply for one.

Students living in low-income communities with large immigrant populations often experience enforcement practices that increase the likelihood of contact with the criminal and immigration enforcement systems. César, a Mexican American immigrant rights advocate based in Santa Ana in Orange County, spoke of the system as an "incarceration-to-deportation pipeline," noting that "at every single step where a kid would be processed [in Orange County], they would get the maximum highest sentence. So, sentence number one, you got in a fight, you got expelled. Sentence number two, they would press charges. And sentence number three, once the DA [district attorney] would have you, if you would happen to be undocumented, they have the discretion to either contact ICE or not. At every step you'd get completely the maximum, okay. So Orange County deported more young men than any other county in the state of California, okay? So we've had a pipeline for years."

Racialized and Gendered Enforcement

Erasmo, whose story opened this chapter, did not necessarily fear that his numerous low-level encounters with the LAPD would put him on a path to deportation. But he was still leery of coming into contact with LAPD officers because, in his view, they targeted "Latinos" for license checks. These encounters were potentially costly as well as humiliating. Other people with whom we spoke expressed more direct concerns about deportation. An important question is how these individuals came to be stopped by the police. The people we spoke with suggested these law enforcement encounters were the result of departmental policy decisions that focused street policing efforts on low-income neighborhoods with large Black and Latinx populations—particularly, but not exclusively, men. Many participants in our study expressed the belief that, within this already racialized context, officers targeted individuals on the basis of race.

For example, when asked about the basis upon which the police decided to stop him and others, Erasmo indicated that he believed it was race. He stated that officers stopped individuals whose outward appearance matched that of a stereotypical "Latino," and in some cases would issue a citation when the lack of a license then provided a rationale, after the fact. As previously noted, these stops generate fines and fees that are expensive for immigrants and that provide a source of revenue for the county. Erasmo said that he thought he was pulled over because the police "see [him] as Latino." He continued by explaining that when police initially decide to make a stop:

> They don't know your status yet, whether you're an immigrant or not. I've seen people who are Latino, who have their license. They're not immigrants and they've been pulled over. The first thing [the police] ask for is the license. When they see that you have a license, they just give you a pretext or a random fee. They'll say, "I pulled you over because you don't make a complete stop, because you didn't turn correctly. Try to do it right," and that's it. They don't even fine you after that. When [you are] Latino, they'll pull you over just to investigate whether [you are] licensed or not. Sometimes even though you don't do anything, they'll pull you over.

Many of the Southern Californians that we interviewed shared Erasmo's sense that police-initiated traffic stops were often based on physical appearance associated with Latinx racial identity. When asked to explain what motivated police stops in his neighborhood, Tomás, a middle-aged Mexican national who lives in the San Fernando Valley replied, "[t]he police profile you on the basis of your color. If they see that you are *güerro*, a *gabacho* [white person],[52] they leave you alone. All of the enforcement of the laws they use against Latinos. And they don't help people who don't have documents." In the view of many people we spoke with, race motivates the initial stop. A lack of immigration status worsens the consequences.

Citizenship status operates as a protection from deportation and from legal consequences associated with undocumented immigration status but does not stop the profiling on the front end. César, the Mexican American community organizer introduced earlier, discussed how the police stopped him when he was riding his bike through the park at dusk, citing an ordinance that prohibits being in the park at night: "[I]f you're wearing a Raiders jersey and you're young, younger than 40, and you're walking down the street, the chances are you are going to get stopped. And unfortunately, that's across the nation, not just here, you know. And, of course, that's not the type of community I would like—I don't have kids, but to raise my kids in. But as a person of color, my biggest fear in America is some man with a badge."[53]

Moreover, those whose appearance did not match widespread stereotypes[54] of "undocumented immigrants" reported feeling that they were less likely to be stopped and questioned than their relatives whose physical appearance, language ability, and accent aligned more closely with those stereotypes. Mireya, a college student and DACA recipient born in Mexico who is fair-skinned and fair-haired, mentioned her concern that her father would be profiled by the police when he drove with her from her home in Los Angeles County to her university in Orange County. She said, "I fear profiling, especially when [my dad] goes to Santa Ana . . . I fear it for myself, too. But I think it's less, mainly because I can prove that I have a license . . . and I can speak English . . . . and I'm white so it's not like they are going to profile me all that much." Mireya used "white" to describe her physical appearance, not her racial identity, and noted the contrast to her father's appearance. In this way, she implicitly debunks the notion, embraced by the Supreme Court, that reliance on "Mexican appearance" is a useful way to police immigration status, while at the same time revealing how race and gender can increase (or decrease) an individual's likelihood of being stopped by police.

In short, while immigration status created unique risks and anxieties for many Southern California residents, these residents almost universally expressed the view that certain racial (and, in some contexts, gender) markers rendered them more susceptible to being racially profiled by law enforcement officials. They felt that law enforcement officials interested in either using their law enforcement powers to enforce immigration laws or to target certain criminalized conduct associated with immigration status (like driving without a license) used racial profiling to achieve this objective.

An estimated 1.8 million people currently present without authorization are from Asia. On balance, the experiences of our API respondents with local police differed from those of Latinx respondents. While a number of API respondents reported being concerned that driving without a license would increase the risk of deportation for themselves or for a family member if they were discovered during the course of an otherwise valid stop, few of them were concerned that they would be stopped arbitrarily by the police on account of their race. Stephanie, a college student and Korean national, suggested that her race, along with other factors, might have escalated a police stop. "I remember in Arcadia," she said, "I was driving with my taillight out and they thought I had drugs . . . cuz, I guess, I'm an Asian and I have a somewhat nicer car." But generally (and even in Stephanie's case), people did not worry that the police would stop them on the sole basis of their race, even if they did believe that racial stereotypes could reconfigure those encounters as they unfolded. At the same time, some of the API immigrants with whom we spoke were convinced of the reality of racial profiling, identifying it as something that was a more significant problem for "Mexicans" or Black residents.

Organizers and advocates similarly expressed divergent perceptions and experiences with the police. Marilyn, an organizer and activist living in Los Angeles, indicated that neither she nor her API clients generally feared that they would be the target of excessive use of police force or of any other targeting based on their immigration status. She said, "We have May Day. We have marches. We call up the local you know, the sheriff, and say we're gonna have a rally. We'll be peaceful. And they're usually like, 'Okay.' They're not too bad." In contrast, Samuel in Orange County and Yupanqui, a Latinx organizer and activist in Los Angeles, spoke of Latinx demonstrators experiencing violence at the hands of police during political actions in Anaheim and Los Angeles, respectively.

These generalizations do not signify a universal lack of hardship or negative experiences with the police among API residents. As we discuss in great detail in Chapter 3, Joonseo, a South Korean national who lacked lawful immigration status, experienced police profiling and mistreatment. More broadly, data from Orange County collected during the time of our study revealed that Vietnamese residents were overrepresented among those transferred to ICE custody by the Orange County Sheriff's Department relative to their presence in the population detained in the county,[55] perhaps because police in Orange County frequently targeted young Vietnamese residents for policing based on purported gang ties.

Moreover, the API residents we interviewed frequently reported the experience of being treated as "other"—and experiencing dual exclusions. Law enforcement agents and other government officials frequently did not treat them as "American," but programming for unauthorized residents also frequently overlooked them. In short, our discussions with the respondents in our study reaffirm the findings of other scholars that illegalization has taken on a particular racialized forms in the US.[56] Individuals with characteristics associated with Latinx identity were likely to be policed as unauthorized immigrants. At the same time, many nonwhite immigrants experienced treatment that made them feel excluded and under suspicion.

Although we do not have enough interview data to speak definitively about the experience of Black residents, existing data demonstrate that Black communities were subject to pervasive racial profiling, including in Los Angeles and Orange Counties, during the time of our study.[57] Immigrant organizations that focus on the needs of Black migrants have explained that this racial profiling means that even if immigrant communities are not singled out for immigration policing, Black residents who lack US citizenship disproportionately wind up in the immigration enforcement system.[58] The widespread and prevalent problem of police profiling and the disproportionate targeting of Black communities also has been compounded in immigrant communities by the excessive federal surveillance of Black Muslims under the guise of national security policing.

The Consequences of Over-policing

Individuals who experience high levels of police contact in their neighborhoods can accumulate an official record of low-level offenses. As uncertainty around immigration reform continues, for the many people who lack a permanent legal right to remain in the US, these records haunt them. They can carry long-term and retroactive implications that may well limit the bearer's ability to take advantage of any immigration relief that might be designed for long-term residents. This generates its own form of stress and exacerbates legal precarity.

First, not only do police contacts threaten to obstruct future paths toward regularizing immigration status, but as Benjamin's case illustrates, they also push people out of liminal forms of protection that they may have. Benjamin's decision not to renew his DACA status after his low-level contact with police was not unique. Several of the Southern California lawyers with whom we spoke highlighted the ways that high levels of police contact posed a serious problem for people with liminal legal status. In the period from 2012 to 2022, the number of DACA recipients fell from over 830,000 students to fewer than 610,000 in 2022. Some of this attrition is good news. Marilyn, a lawyer in Los Angeles at a community-based organization, noted that some DACA recipients had been able to gain access to more permanent relief through marriage.[59] But she also pointed out that others had lost their deferred action status "because they get DUIs or have other, like, criminal things happening in their lives." Furthermore, since July 2021, the federal government has been under an injunction issued by a federal district court in Texas that prevents USCIS from extending DACA to new applicants.[60] Though individuals who had received DACA prior to the injunction can currently apply for renewals, other people who meet the criteria cannot apply. That case is still on appeal, and the Supreme Court could still strike down the DACA program in its entirety.

Second, as explained by Gerarda, a Latinx lawyer who works at a Los Angeles–based organization, the repercussions of law enforcement contact often extend beyond one person, affecting whole families. Much of her work focused on assisting people who were applying for T visas, which are available for individuals who are "victims of severe forms of trafficking in persons," and the more common U visa, available for individuals who are victims of certain serious crimes and are willing to assist law enforcement in furthering legal investigation. There are long backlogs for U visas because Congress capped the number of visas at 10,000 a year. As of 2022, U visas were becoming available to individuals whose visas had been approved in 2016, and wait times are increasing. Individuals whose visa petitions have been approved but for whom a visa is not yet available remain out of status. They are allowed to live and work in the US only through acts of discretion on the part of federal officials. Encounters with law enforcement are devastating for such applicants, and Gerarda estimated that about 10 percent of her clients fell into this situation. If those individuals were removed and their U visa eligibility terminated, that also ended the eligibility of all dependent immediate family members who otherwise could obtain a U visa derivatively based on their relationship to the principal applicant.

Gerarda had also been involved in several cases where a client had a law enforcement encounter after receiving their U visa but before naturalization. Here again, the law enforcement encounter could end the process of legalization. In one particularly stressful case, the mother of a U visa recipient, who had received her visa derivatively through her daughter, had completed her naturalization, but her daughter had not. The woman's daughter was then placed in removal proceedings after a run-in with the law arising out of her substance abuse issues. This placed significant strain on the family relationship. Gerarda noted that measures like A.B. 60, which legalized driving for many of her clients, had made an important difference in their lives. Nevertheless, she said that her clients remained fearful of law enforcement encounters and the possible immigration consequences they engendered. The long wait times for U visas simply lengthen the anxious period during which police encounters can complicate or end a path to citizenship.

Police contact can also impede efforts to regularize immigration status, now and in the future. Arrests can limit an arrestee's future access to housing, employment, and immigration relief, regardless of whether that arrest ever results in a criminal conviction.[61] Michaela's story illustrates the point. Michaela, a Mexican national, entered the country with a visa and overstayed its expiration date. In 1993, she was involved in an altercation at work. Because she was working with scissors and wearing work boots, she recalls being initially arrested on grounds of felony assault with a deadly weapon. After spending a couple of days in jail, she was bailed out by her sister. It appears that charges were eventually dropped because she served no additional time and was only admonished by the judge at her hearing to do better in the future. But Michaela remained uncertain as to what was recorded on her criminal record. Her application for low-income housing was once rejected, purportedly on the basis of her criminal record, though an advocate at a Los Angeles–based immigrant rights organization investigated and found her record to be clean. So while she was proactive in investigating the possibility of DACA for her twenty-two-year-old son, she was reluctant to take any steps to change her own status. Haunted by the uncertainty of her record and the ambiguous information she received about it, she told us, "Now I don't know what to do."

Not only did concerns about records of prior police contact impede some people from pursuing immigration relief, but their fear that information might be shared with immigration officials also prevented some from applying for state-run governmental programs like driver's licenses. Erasmo expressed no concern that LAPD officers would share his data with federal immigration enforcement officials, but that confidence did not necessarily extend to the Department of Motor Vehicles (DMV). As previously noted, when the state implemented A.B. 60 to allow undocumented residents to apply for and receive state driver's licenses, Erasmo was fearful about applying. He attended an informational forum with an LA-based organization, where he was informed that he could apply without fear that his data would be shared with the federal government, but he was still concerned that his past deportation order would resurface in this process and cause trouble for him. He knew that "supposedly our information is secret." But when pressed on whether he was convinced of this fact, he admitted, "It's confusing for me because if I sign or I go to apply for a driver's license and they hand over my information, then it's difficult. [It's] frustrating because we don't know if it's really true. . . . There are no guarantees. That's what we're doubting slightly."

Erasmo's concern is reasonable. In other jurisdictions, ICE has accessed state DMV data.[62] As Erasmo saw it, there was risk either way. Without a license, he knew that he was susceptible to fines and fees when stopped by police. But he saw a bigger risk in handing over his data to a faceless state agency than to taking his chances with police officers on the street.

Twenty-five Years of Heightened Border Policing

The precarity generated by interior policing practices in the context of everyday policing is compounded by immigration enforcement along the US-Mexico border. For the last three decades, spending on such enforcement has been on the rise. There are two distinct and interrelated consequences of this trend. First, it dramatically increased the number of formal removal orders that the government has issued (with a concomitant decline in informal returns, which do not show up as part of an individual's immigration history). Second, along the US-Mexico border, criminal prosecutions for crimes of migration (especially misdemeanor illegal entry and felony reentry) have risen dramatically. The consequences of both developments are evident in the lives of many of the Southern California residents whom we interviewed. Again, Erasmo's story is instructive. Not only would a very old criminal conviction complicate his efforts to regularize his status, but his situation was further complicated by the fact that he was detained while attempting to reenter the country in violation of his prior removal order. Beginning in the 2010s, such an event could well result in a criminal prosecution for felony reentry. At the time, however, he was simply returned. But he worries (without really knowing) that his 2004 contact with a border patrol agent is a part of his record.[63]

Such complex immigration histories were a reality for many residents who appeared to be the ideal beneficiaries of perennial immigration reform proposals—individuals who resided in the United States for decades, were working, had US citizen children, and had no recent contact with law enforcement. Our conversations frequently revealed that such seemingly ideal candidates had old records that would impede legalization under any recently proposed version of comprehensive immigration reform. For example, Karina, a Mexican national and DACA recipient, told us of her father who had resided in the US since before 2001, but who had returned home for his brother's funeral around 2002 or 2003. Her father sought to reenter the country using someone else's identification card, was caught, and was charged with a felony. When DAPA was announced, Karina explained, her father decided that he wanted to try to clean up his record so that he might be eligible for that program, or for eventual legalization. She said:

> He was like, "I'm going to start seeing if there's something I can do because if I can fix it, I want you guys to be able to get your situation fixed." He went to two different lawyers, and he was just like, "Ugh. This is ridiculous." One of the lawyers told him, "Oh, no. You're not going to be able to ever fix [your papers]. Your entire family, two kids, are never going to be able to fix [your papers]." He was like, "Okay, that I don't really believe." Then he

went to a different lawyer and that other lawyer was just straight out with him. He's like, "I'm not going to take your money. I'm not even going to try to help you because there's nothing I can do for you right now."

But Karina's father still hung on to life in the US. She explains, "Even with all that, he's still hopeful. He's like, 'I don't care if I'm in my grave, you guys are going to change my status.' . . . It's heartbreaking."

Alfaro, a business owner in his thirties who is originally from Mexico, told a similar story. At one time, he had a visa that allowed him to visit the US, but federal officials confiscated the visa, which he was using to reside in the country. To reenter and return to his home in the United States, he used someone else's visa and was caught by border officers. When he finally did make it back to the US after that, he never tried to cross again. But he explained to us that this encounter had frustrated his ability to regularize his status because, as he understood it, he would not be eligible for a waiver of the ten-year bar on his presence in the US, even if he did have a path to legalization. "[I]n my case there is no pardon here on the inside, so I have to leave the country, stay out for ten years, even if I have married an American wife and I have citizen children, that doesn't matter."

Some people did not even realize that their immigration records presented bars to regularization. In some cases, this is the result of faulty notice in immigration proceedings.[64] Many people are unaware that they have missed hearings, and they often do not know when immigration courts have issued removal orders against them. It can also be difficult for people to access their own records in immigration proceedings.[65] In addition, in recent years, immigration judges have issued tens of thousands of removal orders against individuals who failed to appear at their hearings. Often, this failure to appear was not by choice, but rather the result of the government's failure to properly notify them of their hearings.[66] (The Supreme Court imposed new limits on this practice in 2021[67] but notice problems persist.[68]) Consequently, when some people try to regularize their status after becoming eligible for a family-based visa or other form of relief, they are instead removed without hearings based on prior—often procedurally flawed—outstanding removal orders. Marc, who worked at an API-serving community organization, explained to us that one of his clients went to a visa interview with USCIS officials and wound up being detained because there was an outstanding removal order against him of which he was unaware. Not only was it devastating for the client, but it was also difficult from a community relations perspective for the organization, making it more challenging to encourage people to attempt to regularize their status. The idea that old and unknown records pose a threat to their ability to access immigration relief haunts both individuals seeking relief and the organizations that try to help them.

There is also a connection between these old immigration records and the over-policing patterns discussed earlier. Individuals who, unbeknownst to them, have outstanding removal orders are at particular risk in an era when police share their arrest data with DHS. That agency can flag arrestees on the basis of existing in absentia removal orders. And, as we discuss further in Chapter 5, even jurisdictions with noncooperation agreements were, during the period of our study, routinely sharing information with federal immigration agents in the cases of noncitizens with a wide range of criminal convictions.

Prosecutorial Discretion and the Enforcement State

The discussion above illustrates how immigration and criminal law enforcement work together to create a condition of hypercriminalization in low-income Latinx communities. This hypercriminalization forms the backdrop for the relief programs developed by members of the Obama administration. It is within this legal landscape that DACA and DAPA emerged. They were offered as an immigration benefit for a certain subset of long-term immigrant residents, but they were designed in such a way that the criminal enforcement system served as a key sorting mechanism to determine eligibility. The Obama administration's framing of DACA, which defines applicants' worthiness in large part based on the presence or absence of criminal convictions, ignored the injustices of the criminal enforcement system itself.

In the years following the DAPA announcement, federal enforcement expanded further, particularly under President Trump. At the same time, not only DAPA but also DACA and other forms of prosecutorial discretion have become increasingly embattled, as Republican state attorneys general have repeatedly challenged in federal courts any effort on the part of any administration to enact lenity through enforcement discretion. Texas's challenge to the DACA program (in the one of the many litigation challenges recently captioned *Texas v. United States*) is still winding its way through the courts in the middle of 2023, even as Congress yet again failed at the end of 2022 to enact any legislative protection for DACA recipients. Texas and several other Republican attorneys general also challenged the Biden administration's enforcement priority memo in a case (also captioned *United States v. Texas*). And although the Supreme Court recently concluded that these states lack standing to challenge the administration's enforcement priorities, Justice Kavanaugh's opinion expressly noted that the reasoning of the opinion does not apply to administrative programs that not only set enforcement priorities but that also provide benefits—a clear allusion to DACA.[69]

The stories of DACA recipients like Benjamin illustrate how problematic this is for young adults who, by virtue of race and class, are more likely to be the targets of heightened police scrutiny and excessive police contact. It was striking that even in our relatively small sample of young adult residents, his story was not unique. Nicolas, a twenty-three-year-old Mexican national living and working in Orange County, had similar experiences. Nicolas initially believed himself to be eligible for DACA but was charged with a misdemeanor in the middle of his application process. Uncertain whether his conviction would be disqualifying and concerned about sharing his information with the federal government, he stopped the application process midstream.

Nicolas noted the perverse relationship between the federal government's intensification of removal for individuals with criminal records alongside programs like DACA that provided immigration relief for individuals without such records. He stated:

> What does worry me is when the president announced the new, the extension of DACA and the new DAPA program, he also announced the PEP program, the Priorities Enforcement Program. . . . So what happened before this announcement was that the misdemeanor that I had was something that disqualified me from the DACA program, but with this new announcement, it makes me a *priority* for deportation, right? Yeah. And so

that's kind of like, that sucks. And so yeah, and I mean, there's been cases of people who've done stuff in the past, and twenty, fifteen years later, and like through the recent Operation Cross Check[70] that they had, there were various cases of people who were deported through this program because of that. So that really worries me. And it kind of like makes me feel like my chances of being able to remain here are coming down.

With no legislative solutions on the horizon for longtime residents lacking legal status and increasing judicial constraints on executive enforcement discretion, Nicolas's worries have only increased with each passing year.

TWO

Discretion

IN A FORMER LIFE, Edgar was an attorney in private practice and far removed from the byzantine and often cruel world of immigration law. But
the election of Barack Obama became an inflection point in Edgar's life. He
found his way into the leadership of the Department of Homeland Security
(DHS) and over the course of the Obama administration, Edgar developed
expertise in immigration law, experience that he still uses at the time of this
writing in the private sector working for a firm that assists organizations with
a range of immigration-related problems. In the broadest sense, his work for
the DHS consisted of fixing the United States' dysfunctional system of immigration regulation and enforcement. For many immigrant residents and
immigrant rights advocates, the problem was that during President Obama's
first term, "fixing" often meant removing as many "undesirable" noncitizens
as possible. Between the years 2008 and 2012, removals climbed to record
numbers and they remained high in Obama's second term. With no legislative relief for immigrants on the horizon, for some immigrant rights activists,
the temporary relief provided by DACA was not enough to erase the deportation machine unleashed during the early years of the Obama administration.
Against this backdrop, National Council of La Raza president, Janet Mur-
guía, called President Obama the "deporter-in-chief" in March of 2014.[1]

Edgar, like many immigration officials at the time, felt that these removals were not only defensible, but laudable. Immigration and Customs
Enforcement (ICE), the agency responsible for initiating removals against

migrants, had limited bandwidth, so President Obama gave orders to prioritize migrants presumed to pose a threat to public safety, like "criminal aliens," or those less likely to have meaningful ties to this country, like recent entrants. In fact, this approach actually prioritized the removal of tens of thousands of people who were deeply integrated in their communities through family and work—hardly the kind of people who threatened public safety.

To function properly even on its own imperfect terms, President Obama's priority enforcement system would have required applying broad screening tools on the front end to everyone. In theory, ICE could just screen out those individuals deemed lower enforcement priorities, such as young immigrants who had spent the majority of their lives in the United States. In reality, neither the officers nor the lawyers in ICE had the interest or the capacity to provide such childhood arrivals—or anyone else—with meaningful relief. Against this backdrop, the DHS unfurled the DACA program in 2012, giving a particular subset of childhood arrivals temporary and renewable reprieves from removal.

DACA has become a key part of the Obama administration's broader legacy on immigration policy, a mishmash of uplift and terror. The same administration that formally removed more noncitizens than any prior administration also created DACA, arguably the most significant administrative program in a generation. This program not only paused immigration enforcement but also created opportunities for noncitizens to obtain immigration benefits, like employment authorization. When viewed next to the high removal numbers of most of Obama's first term, at first glance the 2012 DACA program might look like an abrupt change in policy—a change of heart. Indeed, in a candid moment, describing the decision to create DACA, Edgar bluntly stated: "To be honest with you, . . . I think a lot of our internal reflection was, boy, everything we've done has been half-measures—everything's been compromises, you know with [Immigration and Customs Enforcement]. Well, maybe we should just say fuck the compromises, you know, and just get something done."

But the reality was more complicated. Edgar's words offer a striking contrast to the views of many on the ground, the immigrants and advocates who viewed DACA itself as a half-measure, one that unfolded against, and was impossible to separate from, the backdrop of an unprecedented immigration enforcement effort. Chapter 1 sketched out those contemporaneous efforts, most notably the Secure Communities program, which converted all state and local law enforcement contacts into potential immigration apprehension moments. Those policies expanded the number of immigrant residents brought to the attention of federal immigration enforcement agents. This expansion, in turn, ensured that more people were flagged for potential removal than federal agencies had the budget and capacity to remove.

This chapter explores how high-ranking immigration officials worked to structure decisions about the exercise of removal power. These officials sought to inject immigration enforcement policies with greater pragmatism and humanitarianism, but they coupled these efforts with aggressive expansions of enforcement. Government officials involved with immigration policy during the Obama administration were drawn to the logic of a legal landscape organized around principles of discretion. DACA was part of this story, and it is the part that has come to define President Obama's second-term approach to immigration policy. But it is only part of the story. Immigration enforcement choices made during Obama's first term established the benefits and boundaries of the DACA program even as they limited the practical effects of enforcement discretion.

Long before DACA was announced, and throughout the early part of Obama's presidency, the DHS's strategy was to train government attorneys to approach immigrant removal cases the way a prosecutor might assess a criminal case file. An exclusive focus on DACA would obfuscate the much earlier internal push made by senior officials to encourage, foster, and coax immigration lawyers to embrace their discretionary authority along the lines of criminal prosecutors. The administration's pivot to DACA suggests that its earlier approach—the prosecutor-centric approach—failed at the task of protecting the immigrant residents that administration officials had hoped to spare from removal.

By highlighting these earlier attempts to professionalize a subgroup of government lawyers, this chapter also provides important context for DACA. Far from representing a radical policy reversal, DACA reflected a logical evolution of administrative policies that valued discretionary authority as a means of governance. During the Obama administration, senior officials encouraged subordinates to exercise this authority as a way of partially counterbalancing expanding enforcement capabilities. More than a decade after the program's announcement—a decade of nearly continuous legal challenges—immigration officials continued to insist that DACA did not change the fundamental nature of the immigration enforcement enterprise, which still focuses on principles of discretion and exercises of authority largely unreviewable by courts.[2] Rooting DACA within principles of enforcement discretion rather than within a suite of affirmative rights reflects an attempt to reconcile competing political forces: an immigrant rights movement growing stronger in its demands for inclusion, on the one hand, and, on the other, a Republican-led Congress unwilling to create a legislative solution for long-term residents lacking legal immigration status.

DACA unquestionably changed lives for the better. And the related deferred action programs, DAPA and DACA+, would have undoubtedly done likewise had they been implemented. But it is also true that these deferred action programs affirmed and legitimized an immigration enforcement system that racialized, criminalized, and illegalized migrants like those featured in Chapter 1. The frustration, fear, and anger expressed by Erasmo and others are the predictable consequence of a legal system that enables immigration officials to reach deep into the lives of migrants and then provide relief defined in terms of holding back these punitive elements of law. By occupying the negative space created by expanding enforcement policies, programs like DACA enabled immigration officials to offer and dispense relief at their discretion and on their terms. This allows, and indeed requires, officials to frame their efforts as responses to requests for administrative grace rather than as a recognition of the rights of long-term residents.

Priorities and Nonpriorities

Policy debates often fixate on numbers, and debates involving immigration are no different. One important number is eleven million, which is the approximate number of unauthorized immigrants living in the United States without a meaningfully available way to regularize their status.

Restrictionists—those who favor reducing or eliminating immigration to the United States—often point to this number as proof of the enormity of our country's "immigration problem."[3] Because of this number, they argue, the United States must do something—anything—to stop the alleged problem from getting even worse. For restrictionists, immigration enforcement is akin to being in a sinking ship armed with a bucket—stop bailing water and the whole ship goes under. But to us the figure of eleven million suggests something else entirely. The number has been largely static, notwithstanding the vagaries of domestic enforcement practices, because US immigration policy is only one factor in how people make decisions about whether to stay or whether to move. Even with a continuous push to remove as many noncitizens as possible, the size of the pool of potentially removable immigrants has not meaningfully changed. In other words, the US has pursued an aggressive set of enforcement policies that have created a great deal of human suffering while doing relatively little to decrease the overall numbers of unauthorized migrants.

During interviews, high-level federal officials—those who are appointed and who therefore come and go with changing administrations—tended to emphasize another number: four hundred thousand. This is the number of noncitizens ICE can actually remove in a given year with the resources appropriated by Congress. And this number is important, they often say, because it shows that ICE cannot remove more than 4 percent of the total unauthorized population a year. It also shows that Congress neither intends nor funds full enforcement. So the relevant question for them is: *which* 4 percent should frontline ICE officers remove?

This question was of intense interest to the political leadership during the Obama administration. Shortly after Barack Obama assumed the presidency, Congress confirmed Janet Napolitano as secretary of Homeland Security. Working closely with senior leadership in the three major immigration agencies—ICE, US Citizenship and Immigration Services (USCIS), and Customs and Border Protection (CBP)—Secretary Napolitano and the DHS senior leadership sought to prioritize the expenditure of their (expanding) enforcement resources. The DHS was created as a part of a massive governmental reorganization effort and encompasses a diverse array of agencies meant to prevent future attacks on the US. This includes but is

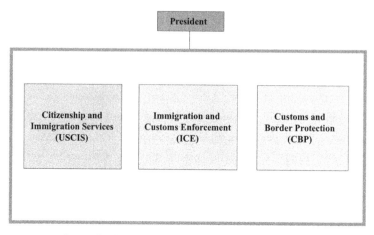

Core Immigration Agencies of the Department of Homeland Security

FIGURE 2.1. Core Immigration Agencies in the Department of Homeland Security.

not limited to the core immigration agencies. During the early years of the Obama administration, ICE's primary immigration enforcement strategy was priority-setting—that is, identifying the specific groups that officials should target for removal.[4] John Morton, then director of ICE, played a critical role in setting these policies. He issued a series of memoranda articulating the types of people ICE officials should target as priorities for enforcement, establishing policies on prosecutorial discretion and instituting interagency collaborations to ensure that immigrants who were otherwise removable, but who had nonfrivolous claims for relief, had the chance to pursue that relief on an expedited basis.[5]

The purpose of the memos was to provide guidance to immigration officials within ICE. In the broadest of terms, the Morton memos divided noncitizens in the United States who were potentially removable under the immigration statute into enforcement "priorities" and "nonpriorities." On August 20, 2010, Morton instructed field agents in ICE to identify noncitizens in the removal pipeline who had pending family-based petitions for relief. Individuals with pending applications for these types of immigrant visas could be deprioritized for enforcement. In deciding whether to proceed with the removal of apprehended migrants, John Morton instructed agency personnel to focus on whether the migrant had a pending application with USCIS that might serve as the basis for relief against removal.[6] This directive both focused ICE's attention on the presence of these factors in the removal process, and instructed USCIS to engage in an expedited review of the underlying applications for relief.[7] But again, the most that immigration officials could offer noncitizens in this scenario was relief in the form of administrative closure; any genuine change in status depended on the outcome of other processes. Administrative closure was a docket management tool that enabled immigration judges to remove cases from their active docket.[8] In this regard, administrative closure closely resembles deferred action. It provides relief, but only by offering indefinite forbearance from the consequence of removal.

Morton further instructed ICE agents to prioritize those noncitizens who posed a danger to national security or the public generally, those who had entered the United States relatively recently, and those for whom removal orders had already been issued.[9] More specifically, a memo issued on March 2, 2011, directed all ICE employees to consider potentially removable migrants within the context of three categories of noncitizens: (1) those who threatened "national security" or "public safety"; (2) those who had "recently violated immigration controls" most notably at the border or at ports of entry; and (3) those deemed to be fugitives or absconders.[10] A few months later, on June 17, 2011, Morton again issued another memo providing technical details on the suite of legal tools available to immigration officials in exercising prosecutorial discretion. Moreover, this memo articulated several factors illustrating the kinds of scenarios meriting a favorable exercise of prosecutorial discretion including the presence of familial ties to the United States and the absence of a criminal history.[11] These "Morton memos" trickled out steadily over a span of two years beginning in the summer of 2010.[12] They represent some of the clearest examples of the Obama administration's approach to immigration law, namely the attempt to redirect the punitive elements of immigration and criminal law enforcement policies in ways that are more systematic and less random.

This enterprise was doomed. ICE is a large agency with varied and often conflicting mandates. Where ICE officials and agents stand on a particular policy question often depends on where they sit within the agency.[13] Popular representations of ICE often focus on the agency's officers and the agents

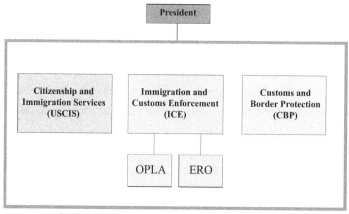

Core Immigration Agencies of the Department of Homeland Security

FIGURE 2.2. Core Immigration Agencies in the Department of Homeland Security.

in the field wearing parkas emblazoned with the letters "ICE" or "POLICE ICE" on their backs investigating, pursuing, harassing, and sometimes detaining people. Most of these agents work within the Enforcement and Removal Operations (ERO) unit. But ICE attorneys also perform the task of seeking removal orders against individuals after an arrest or sometimes without any preliminary arrest. These lawyers work within a subdivision of ICE called the Office of the Principal Legal Advisor (OPLA) and are tasked with representing the DHS in removal proceedings before immigration judges.[14] Put in the terms of the criminal enforcement system, ERO agents function as the rough equivalent of the police, while OPLA attorneys act as prosecutors within the realm of immigration enforcement.

The government officials we spoke with all spent time working within immigration agencies during the Obama administration and indicated that, in the pre-DACA era, immigration officials often measured success in terms of the number of both apprehensions and removals. Senior officials describe the Morton memos as a signal to immigration officials—both lawyers and frontline agents—that the *types* of apprehensions and removals also mattered. One such interviewee was David, whose long career in federal law enforcement included spending many years managing and overseeing prisoners in the Federal Bureau of Prisons. Throughout the interview, David emphasized that he sympathized with and understood "both sides" of the immigration debate, that is, both those who wanted greater enforcement and those who opposed existing enforcement practices. David served as part of senior leadership in ICE during the first several years of the Obama administration. After leaving government, David spent quite a bit of time lecturing and talking to students and the public more generally about immigration enforcement. In David's estimation, a system that focused on criminal noncitizens made for sensible policy. In his view, such a system posed little threat to the vast majority of noncitizens in the United States without authorization: "Let's say the majority of the eleven or twelve million people who are here in undocumented status . . . you know, they have virtually no chance of being arrested these days. ICE is not out there looking for undocumented aliens who have not committed crimes, who don't pose a threat to the community. They're just not. So you don't want to put yourself in the situation in the future where you might become a priority."

Another senior official, Frank, who also worked within ICE during the Obama administration concurred in this assessment. After graduating from law school, Frank spent several years working for the federal government in an international context before joining the ranks of DHS senior leadership. When asked about the fear generated by expansive immigration enforcement policies, Frank opined confidently: "If they're not committing a crime, we're not gonna get them out anyway, and that should not be our priority." In theory, ICE was setting priorities for the purposes of targeting people who posed a danger to their communities, those whose ties to the United States were minimal (at least as measured in time spent within the United States), and those whose removability had already been adjudicated. But the experiences of Erasmo, Samuel, and many others illustrate how imperfect and malleable categories of deservingness can be. In the exercise of their largely unfettered discretion, local police can easily transform an unauthorized immigrant from a potential DACA recipient into a "high-risk" priority through their handling of encounters on the street or in the workplace. Moreover, Frank's comment reaffirms the pervasive quality of criminal law thinking within immigration enforcement and reflects the distance separating his reality from Erasmo's. For Erasmo and others who had to navigate the world without authorization, everyday encounters, especially with the police, appeared as the moment when immigration officials might apprehend them.

"The Beauty of Prosecutorial Discretion"

ICE bears the primary responsibility for initiating immigration proceedings against noncitizens. And while immigration law is treated by courts as a civil matter, ICE's culture is heavily organized around criminal law principles. During President Obama's first term, for example, ICE organized much of its enforcement efforts around newly forged linkages with criminal law enforcement agencies around the country. In other words, ICE pursued its civil enforcement priorities within a broader network of legal actors and agencies expressly empowered to police, punish, and imprison. The nationwide implementation of the Secure Communities program institutionalized and federalized an approach to immigration enforcement that relied on state and local law enforcement as front-end screeners. But ICE's familiarity with and embrace of criminal law norms played out in different ways. Some of the senior officials we spoke with described ICE as an agency in which the identities of frontline officers explicitly embraced labels like "police" or "prosecutors," identities that are primarily associated with criminal legal proceedings. Some of the officials expressly described frontline ICE officers as a kind of federalized police force.

Prior to working in the Obama administration as a high-ranking DHS official, Gail spent several years as a federal prosecutor and had a career in politics. Gail expressed sympathy for unauthorized immigrant residents, especially those residents whose parents brought them to the US when they were children, but her view of policy was politically pragmatic and fundamentally unquestioning of the core rationality of dedicating billions of dollars and extensive efforts to removing longtime residents. For her, prosecutorial discretion was a necessary legal doctrine that could inject some proportionality into enforcement policy. As she explained: "the sanction in immigration enforcement, deportation . . . ha[s] significant consequences on a person's life. And although it's civil or administrative, it's kind of quasi-criminal. And even in administrative law there's the concept of prosecutorial discretion." When a member of our research team asked whether any specific ICE field offices resisted the prioritization efforts by the Obama administration, Gail had this to say: "Basically all of them. I mean, these are immigration cops. That's what they do—that's what they're trained to do. And they tend to attract a fairly conservative group of officers. . . . And when you get into middle management or even in some of the nonappointed people in ICE, there was a lot of reluctance [to the Morton memos] because, you know, to them, if someone is deportable, they're deportable and that's kind of the beginning and end of the analysis."

Janelle, a senior advisor within USCIS, expressed similar sentiments. Before working in the Obama administration, Janelle had a very successful career advocating for immigrants as a lawyer. From her vantage point, "The people in ICE, the long knives were always drawn. They were a police agency—not a very good one, but that's how they see themselves." Initially, it seemed as if Janelle was referring to the frontline officers in ICE, the bureaucrats who worked across administrations. But as she continued with her observations about the culture at ICE, it was clear that she was referring to the political appointees as well, people like Edgar and Frank. As she recounted her experiences, a stream of frustrating memories spilled out. Janelle grew more agitated, speaking at a faster clip as she continued:

> That's the routine in Washington; I'm certainly not telling you anything you don't know, but it was not routine for me and it's not the way I operate. Remember, I've already retired from a very successful career. The last thing I'm going to do is sit down and let a bunch of teenagers—guys who, by the way, have only one major word in their vocabulary: fuck. I've never heard guys use a word so much in my life. It was unbelievable. You felt like you were in a [pro-President] Trump locker room. And so, for me, they were just irrelevant. I wasn't going to spend any time courting them or anything. And I knew, literally . . . in the first six months I was on the job that this was going to be a short-lived experience, so I decided, quite analytically, that I would go down in flames for something I cared about.

During the Trump administration, journalistic accounts reported that field agents, especially in ERO, understood themselves as possessing nearly unfettered discretion to identify targets for removal.[15] Gail's and Janelle's observations suggest that this identity can be traced back at least to the Obama administration. Their accounts paint a picture of ICE officers bristling at the idea that political appointees like John Morton would set an enforcement agenda that did not permit them to make these types of choices. In their view, they, the civil servants who worked across administrations and political parties, not Obama loyalists, were in the best position to make these choices.

In the face of this bureaucratic recalcitrance, senior officials within the Obama administration did not back away from the criminal law paradigm but instead firmly embraced it. Rather than de-escalate and disentangle immigration policy from criminal law's punitive traditions, senior officials attempted to empower and encourage ICE lawyers to curb the blunt enforcement tactics of frontline ICE officers, the so-called "immigration cops." High-level political appointees asked OPLA attorneys to screen out those people they thought were deserving of relief. Effectively, they asked government lawyers to lean into an identity as prosecutors, the key lawyers guiding and shaping criminal punishments. In their messaging, political officials indicated that low-level government lawyers should think of themselves as prosecutors who had broad discretion to decide which people should ultimately be removed from the United States. While ICE agents could arrest and detain noncitizens, the decision to actually initiate removal proceedings belonged to the OPLA attorneys. Senior leaders acknowledged that distrust characterized the relationship between senior DHS leadership and career ICE officials. Horace worked in the DHS General Counsel's office during the Obama administration. He described the relationship between OPLA attorneys and ICE field agents this way: "And so, you know, if you don't have the trust and the buy-in, something of this nature is not going to succeed, right? 'Cause ultimately it has to rise or fall in the field. And as we've seen, there are pockets of pretty mass resistance." The theory behind this approach was to empower OPLA attorneys to act as gatekeepers in the removal pipeline. If OPLA attorneys declined to issue Notices to Appear (NTAs)—the legal document that officially initiated removal proceedings—against noncitizens apprehended by ERO who didn't fit ICE's enforcement priorities, then eventually, ERO officers would alter their behavior to make better use of their time and resources.

According to some officials, the Morton memos failed to overcome the agency's bureaucratic inertia, born of distrust. After graduating from law school, Georgia began working in the White House as a special advisor. Unlike many of the appointees within DHS—like David, Frank, or Edgar—Georgia was a young woman of color who was at the start of her career. She notes that White House officials frequently experienced pushback from ICE officials who disapproved of Obama-era policies. Georgia stated:

> The policies we were setting weren't fully taking hold. . . . [A] part of that is just, you know, it was a real shift in how an agency . . . did business, right? They were used to just saying, "Whoever we run into we're gonna pick up. If . . . we think they're undocumented or bad actors, it doesn't matter what their kind of equities are, right?" So it was a shift in kind of saying, "No, we don't want you to just pick up everyone, we want you to think about do these people really pose a threat to our communities?" And you know that really took time to take hold.

Central to this turn in policy is the view that lawyers played a crucial role in creating and implementing the program. Janet Napolitano's 2014 speech provides helpful insights:

> DHS was a new entity—a vast department that brought together many distinct agencies in the aftermath of 9–11. Our earlier call for a review of the backlogged cases in removal proceedings through the lens of our stated priorities helped a bit. But in the end, it did not have the desired impact. The Dreamers[16] remained in limbo, ensnared within the sputtering debate over immigration reform. And so it came to pass that in the spring of 2012 I assembled a small team of advisors, including our brightest lawyers, and I asked them this: What can we do about the Dreamers? What can we do short of a blanket amnesty? What can we do within the parameters of the law?"

From his vantage point within the DHS, Frank confirmed that early efforts to make immigration enforcement less harsh and more equitable focused on empowering government lawyers, as opposed to field agents, to guide the removal process. He saw the push toward a prosecutorial mentality as tantamount to professionalizing the business of removing immigrants—an undertaking that career OPLA attorneys heavily resisted and that the administration never really achieved.

> It's not a vote issue, it's not a Latino issue, it's not an Asian issue, it's an issue of justice, and seeing oneself as the prosecutor in the system. And having

that authority and that power to decide which cases to move through the system and which cases to stop. And you know, I tried . . . to create a more, umm, for lack of a more diplomatic term . . . a more professional rank of OPLA attorneys that weren't just, ya know, nonthinking, take an NTA, treat every case alike, spend two hours when it's an asylum case or ya know, female genital mutilation case on the one hand versus when it's a visa over-stay. You'd be shocked at the resistance to treating those cases differently, which is just mind-boggling to me. But it's gonna take a generation now or longer because now you've really politicized the process . . .

But some officials who worked within the agencies themselves suggested that the notion of agency pushback was overblown. Steve, who served in the DHS during Obama's second term—that is, well after the Morton memos era had passed—deflected criticisms against ICE as a rogue agency:

[Y]ou know, there may have been people at ICE that were initially hesi-tant. But you know, ICE followed orders. You didn't see a lot of dissent, you didn't see a lot of leaking of information the way you do now. . . . [W]ere they happy about everything? No. But also know they weren't out there . . . when people are really offended or running roughshod they go out there and leak . . . that wasn't happening either.

David noted that the agency was heterogeneous and comprised of agents with a variety of views on the wisdom of whatever mandate senior lead-ership doled out. Still, he did not believe such disagreement ultimately mattered:

[A]ny law enforcement officer—federal, state, or local—has their personal opinions, but they work in at least quasi-paramilitary organizations. And when they are directed to do something, they do it. And their . . . personal opinions don't really matter. Ya know, I'm sure if you talked to certain police officers in Colorado and said, "Hey what's your personal opinion about legalizing marijuana," some of them probably weren't all that happy about it. But they do what they have to do.

Whether or not the characterization of ICE at that time as a "rogue agency" is valid,[17] what is clear is that the DHS leadership set about con-ducting trainings around the country to close the gap separating senior leadership from career officers. Senior leadership conducted these train-ings by visiting the various field offices to expand on the mechanics of the prosecutorial-discretion system and to address concerns. Central to this endeavor was the reconceptualization of lawyers in the field in the model of federal prosecutors. The message political appointees circulated was clear: the power immigration lawyers in the agency exercised was akin to the criminal law enforcement powers of their Department of Justice counterparts. These political appointees targeted their message toward the career civil servants most likely to buy into this approach, namely the OPLA lawyers (as opposed to the ICE enforcement agents) charged with overseeing the removal process.

Georgia noted that "there was a series of trainings that happened after all the different [Morton] policy memos that were put out." She referred to these as "town halls," where Secretary Napolitano and ICE director John Morton "would talk about various issues impacting the agencies, particularly ICE. . . . And, you know, really make a pitch that this is smart law enforcement . . . this is the way to kind of do your job effectively."

Senior officials plainly referenced the criminal law enforcement model in explaining the pre-DACA years. When speaking with David about the challenges of implementing the Morton memos' priorities, he argued that immigration officials, like other law enforcement agents, could appropriately exercise discretion:

> You can look at other examples where a . . . district attorney, umm, because of workload, may make the decision that . . . we will no longer arrest people for . . . possession of small amounts of marijuana. We're gonna issue a summons, something similar to a traffic citation. And local jurisdictions and states . . . and even the federal government does that sort of thing all the time. And you know, the officers charged with implementing those decisions, they do. It doesn't [necessarily] mean they like it or support it . . .

Horace, from his vantage point within the DHS General Counsel's office, described ICE infrastructure this way:

> ICE's infrastructure is more what you would imagine from a law enforcement case management structure. You know, where . . . they have things where they're tracking . . . aspects of cases and individuals from . . . a case perspective but that's a lot different from . . . a benefits agency, right, where there's a lot more paper, or . . . whatever material, to justify a thing.

Another senior ICE official confirmed this account. Frank, as previously mentioned, spent many years working overseas on behalf of the federal government before joining the leadership team in ICE. One of his duties was trying to translate the Morton memo directives into meaningful change in the field offices. As he described his role:

> I pleaded with the administration, as did others, to try to change the hearts and minds of many of those thousand attorneys, to take a different role than they have previously had in some cases literally for decades, in that they should not treat all cases alike, and that they should focus their efforts, their talents, and their energy on truly high-priority cases, like terrorists and human rights violators and murderers and rapists and immigration frauds, and to not spend as much time and perhaps in some cases, not spend any time on visa overstays of individuals who had come into the country as young people or people that had frankly come into the country later in life but had been good civil citizens in a sense, quotation marks around "citizens," and had not committed crimes, and had contributed to their communities, and had paid their taxes.

Members of our research team were unable to secure interviews with the front-line officers and field agents who carried out these policies because they work as civil servants within bureaucracies governed by strict protocols regarding data collection by outsider researchers. Our interviews therefore focused on the views of political appointees, rather than career civil service agents. At the same time, other data tend to confirm the account provided by the high-level officials we interviewed. Most notably, through a 2011 Freedom of Information Act (FOIA) request, journalists from the *Houston Chronicle* obtained documents from ICE's Houston field office.[18] These documents include a variety of forms of communications and cover a period of approximately six months, from June 2010 to January 2011, which was squarely in the middle of President Obama's first term and during the period of prosecutorial training referenced and discussed by the government officials we interviewed.[19] This period captures the months leading up to the issuance of the March 2, 2011, Morton memo articulating the different enforcement priorities and the June 17, 2011, Morton memo providing immigration officers with guidance on the exercise of prosecutorial discretion.[20]

The Houston field office documents tend to confirm that ICE lawyers viewed the Morton memos in terms of increasing efficiency in the office rather than in terms of realizing equity-oriented outcomes. Agenda items for meetings included titles such as "Improving the Efficiency of the Removal Process: Prosecutorial Discretion" with a focused examination of administrative devices such as joint motions to reopen, appeals, and remands.[21] Leadership in the Houston office seemed to commit to the task of changing office culture through the development of local implementation policies and regularly held team meetings.[22] In a memo to the attorneys in his office, Chief Counsel Gary Goldman explained that the "universe of opportunities to exercise prosecutorial discretion is large."[23] Goldman then continued to impress upon the legal staff a particular vision of lawyering, one that reflects traditional notions of prosecutorial power long used with criminal cases:

> We have been empowered with independent authority to exercise prosecutorial discretion. We work not in a world of black and white but one of many shades of grey. That is the beauty of prosecutorial discretion. . . . ICE Senior Leadership does not want their attorneys to merely fill a seat in immigration court and blindly prosecute every case handed to them. The current administration wants attorneys of greater sophistication, independence, and complexity in decision making.[24]

Set Up to Fail

The effort to transform OPLA attorneys into a cadre of quasi-prosecutors ultimately failed. This was true for many reasons. First, the deals the government was willing to offer to immigrants in removal proceedings did not provide a robust form of immigration relief. In formal terms, the legal relief that ICE government lawyers offered during President Obama's first term was usually administrative closure, which was a government decision not to initiate removal proceedings against the person who had been apprehended.[25] This provided relief to migrants in only the barest sense. Administrative closure did not create a pathway to regularizing immigration status.[26] Nor did it offer immigrants the chance to secure the employment authorization documents necessary to open up access to the formal labor market. Edgar—the government official featured at the top of this chapter—explained administrative closure this way: "[i]t wasn't a good enough deal. They'd rather take their chances on a cancellation claim or their asylum claim . . . than they would accept administrative closure." These were the types of half-measures Edgar wanted the DHS to push beyond in creating the DACA program. Once the Morton memos were issued in 2011, it became clear to the public that to the extent they offered any kind of relief, such relief was defined in the negative—that is, migrants who were *not* enforcement priorities could take some comfort in knowing that they faced a statistically low chance of being expelled from the country. During this pre-DACA period, the only type of administrative action that might be characterized as "relief" was the decision to not initiate removal proceedings against those who had pending applications that might eventually result in status if the individuals in question were not removed first.

A second reason that the administration's attempt to transform immigration enforcement through merciful or equitable exercises of prosecutorial discretion on a case-by-case basis fell short was that relief during the Morton memo era was hard to predict. The groups categorized as nonpriorities for removal remained fairly ad hoc and ill-defined. To implement the Morton memos, ICE often would mash together different traits to create a generic range of equitable qualities that might merit relief for vague "humanitarian" reasons. These traits included illness, absence of criminal record, or being the parent of citizens.[27] Senior officials also fielded complaints from the immigrant-advocacy community. A common complaint was that many immigrants with no or minor criminal records were being swept up into the removal pipeline.[28] In this sense, some of the officials found the memos to be insufficiently helpful in identifying appropriate priorities for enforcement. Although the putative focus of the Morton memos was on those who posed a national security threat or a danger to their communities, the memos also prioritized immigration violators, such as those with a prior deportation and reentry, even though many of these individuals were long-time members of their communities who would be ideal beneficiaries of discretionary relief, not the dangerous "criminal aliens" of popular discourse.[29] As Edgar explained: "Much later I realized what a problematic area that was in the priorities. It was only after I got to ICE and had access to a lot better data that I was, you know, able to dig into their data pretty deep [and] realized that a substantial portion of the 11.5 million [undocumented migrants in the United States] fell into that bucket."

Recall Frank's earlier comments that he and other political appointees pleaded with frontline OPLA attorneys to focus their efforts on "truly high-priority cases" like "terrorists and human rights violators" rather than on those who "had not committed crimes." Edgar's comments suggest that such a task was arguably pointless, at least if the goal was to identify and remove from the United States people who pose a threat to the broader population. Indeed, the distinctions that Frank draws assume a great deal about how the law identifies and labels people as dangerous. After all, terrorists and human rights violators are not the only types of people who commit crimes. People like Erasmo from Chapter 1 have criminal records, and yet their stories do not fit either the profile of dangerous residents or relative newcomers. The mismatch between their individual stories and the rhetoric around who was prioritized undercut the credibility of the administration's message. According to Edgar, this helps explain why immigrants and their advocates were not "feeling the change quick enough." As Edgar noted, drawing attention to the flaws in efforts to shape enforcement priorities: "Everyone's searching for an answer as to why . . . no one's following the policies when—without realizing they are following the policies."

ICE never found a way to define priorities so as to successfully map them onto individual equities. The complexities of criminal and immigration histories probably doomed such a mapping effort at its inception. Regardless, the administration began to search for other ways to structure administrative forms of relief. Such efforts began to gain traction after December 18, 2010, when the Development, Relief, and Education for Alien Minors (DREAM) Act, some version of which had been introduced by members of Congress repeatedly since 2001, again failed to clear the Senate. With this latest and very public congressional failure to pass legislation to provide a path to citizenship for long-time residents who had entered the country as children, the executive branch began to focus more intently on how DHS enforcement policy could cobble together some comparable form of relief for the DREAMer population. During the Morton memo years, the administration worked out the parameters that eventually defined the contours of the DACA program. Again, here's Edgar: "the DACA story really has to begin much earlier where . . . we were attempting to kind of shift ICE to focus on convicted criminals . . . and so it began with that, and really, I think the DACA story really begins in 2010 when we issued the civil enforcement priorities memo." When asked about when she first learned of the DACA program, Georgia responded: "I mean, probably in early 2010 I would say? Maybe 2009? You know, deferred action is not a new concept, it's been around for many years."

A third reason that the memo-led model of prosecutorial discretion failed was because of pushback by career ERO officials. Although ICE initiated a comprehensive review of hundreds of thousands of deportation cases for administrative closure, both frontline officers and pockets of agency leadership came to resist these broadly conceived efforts to protect segments of the undocumented population. According to Edgar, during President Obama's first term, "ICE at this time under [John Morton] generally took a very hard line and . . . resisted everything." This seemed to be a sentiment shared by those working in the White House as well. Again, as Georgia noted:

> 2011 through 2012 was a really difficult time. We had set up priorities for how we wanted immigration enforcement to take place. And, you know, our job was to set policy priorities, but I couldn't be a law enforcement agent all over the country. Neither could any of the headquarters people at DHS, right? So you know, it was the job of local ICE officials, thousands of them across the country, to be executing on the policies we had put forward.

More than anything, the model of government lawyering that the DHS embraced during the pre-DACA years bears shades of a key assumption that defines criminal law enforcement—namely, that the prosecutor is in a better position to judge the merits and equities of a case.[30] This might be one of the reasons some political appointees recoiled at the transition to the DACA model: it wrested the power to decide who "deserved" removal from the hands of immigration lawyers, modeled after prosecutors, and channeled that power into the hands of bureaucrats in USCIS.

Designing Discretionary Decision-making

DACA offered a set of benefits that relied on formulaic criteria: individuals must have arrived in the U.S. prior to turning 16 and before June 15, 2007; be under the age of 31 as of June 15, 2012; be currently enrolled in school, have completed high school or its equivalent or be a veteran; and have no lawful status as of June 15, 2012. They were also barred if they were convicted of a felony offense, a "significant" misdemeanor, or more than three misdemeanors of any kind; or if they posed a threat to national security or public safety.[31] While the age and presence determinations were formulaic, determinations as to whether an individual constituted a threat to public safety or national security so as to preclude DACA eligibility relied upon the discretion of the reviewing USCIS officials. Nevertheless, some of the government officials with whom we spoke contrasted this approach unfavorably as compared with the perceived flexibility, pragmatism, and common sense of the Morton memo approach. David, the senior ICE official, describes his reaction to the DACA program in terms of what was lost:

> [T]he idea of prosecutorial discretion or deferred action is not something uncommon in law enforcement. It's common in law enforcement at every level, but it more typically is applied to individuals on a case-by-case basis, you know, at the scene of the incident. You know, if two officers arrive at a bar fight just off campus, to put it in your world you know, they see two people standing there kind of bloodied, and the prosecutorial discretion process begins. They have to decide, you know, are they going to arrest one or both? What are they going to charge him with? They take him to some sort of a, a magistrate that decides whether or not this is worth the court's time, whether or not there's probable cause, are they going to detain them, are they going to set bond? A state prosecutor is going to decide whether or not to [offer a plea deal to end] the case. You know all of that is prosecutorial discretion. But it tends to be on a case-by-case basis. DACA was the first of a series of policy decisions that took large numbers of people off the enforcement table rather than considering them on a case-by-case basis.

Implicit in David's perspective are two interrelated assumptions. The first is that DACA did not involve discretionary decision-making. While establishing the factual basis for certain requirements were relatively straightforward, such as the age-of-entry cut-off at 16 years of age, other inquiries were much more subjective and open to multiple interpretations such as whether an applicant was convicted of a "significant misdemeanor" or posed a "threat to national security or public safety." Indeed, from the start, the administration insisted that DACA applicants would be reviewed by USCIS officials, and that relief would be issued on a case-by-case basis in accordance with their determinations. The second is the idea that prosecutors (here, OPLA attorneys) are in the best position to reconcile and prioritize the multiple factors that go into a charging decision than the USCIS officials reviewing DACA applications. In any given case, the underlying proof might be weak, there might be limited resources, or it simply might be unfair to pursue a case.[32] During the pre-DACA era, the driving philosophy of high-level DHS officials seemed to be that, just as prosecutors enjoy freedom from judicial interference in the realm of charging discretion,[33] so should OPLA attorneys enjoy similar degrees of autonomy. Yet there might be good reasons to doubt that prosecutors are necessarily better situated than other actors in the criminal legal system to evaluate whether or not charging a particular defendant would be fair.[34] As legal scholar Josh Bowers notes, prosecutors rely on police to gather the underlying facts, which can make it hard to determine whether a particular defendant is "deserving" of relief.[35] In many cases, a prosecutor's impression of a defendant relies on the record that police officers have built. While it is easy to lump prosecutors and police together into a single category, these criminal law actors are trained differently and tend to follow different career trajectories in terms of stature and culture.[36]

As others have pointed out, the pathologies of contemporary criminal law enforcement cannot be solved by noble prosecutors. Critical race theorist and legal scholar Paul Butler argues that while head prosecutors might have a great deal of discretion, the same does not hold for line prosecutors: "It's like working as an oil refiner because you want to help the environment. Yes, you get to choose the toxic chemicals. True, the boss might allow you to leave one or two pristine bays untouched. Maybe, if you do really good work as a low-level polluter, they might make you the head polluter. But rather than calling yourself an 'environmentalist,' you should think of yourself as a polluter with a conscience."[37] Unsurprisingly, some legal scholars have argued that prosecutorial offices should no longer hold a monopoly on the power to use state resources to punish Black and brown and often poor individuals.[38]

Still, the romanticized image of the powerful and benevolent prosecutor advanced by political appointees in the first part of the Obama administration helps explain why OPLA attorneys might have felt resentment toward criticisms that treated ICE as a monolithic agency. Many within and outside the government understood DACA as a repudiation of ICE as a whole. But OPLA attorneys may well have experienced that shift in policy as a kind of reprimand—one that penalized them for the overzealous and defiant enforcement practices of ERO. Senior DHS officials may well have been correct that OPLA was a more logical partner than ERO in their efforts to infuse immigration enforcement with greater discretion. Yet, as a result of that decision, OPLA attorneys may have felt that they lost authority when ERO was to blame for enforcement discretion failures.

Finally, this aspect of the Morton memo era also illustrates the depths to which criminal law norms informed immigration governance strategies. Obama administration officials viewed criminal law convictions and contacts as a tool to identify priorities for removal and attempted to infuse criminal law norms of prosecutorial discretion into the immigration enforcement system itself.[39]

DACA as a Discretionary Program

As noted earlier, the legal basis for DACA was a legal memorandum penned by Secretary Napolitano. DACA emerged out of the failure of the Morton memos approach, the growing political power and visibility of young immigrants who had resided in the US since childhood, and the coordinated efforts by a broader array of activists pressuring the White House. DHS modeled DACA on the failed DREAM Act, which would have provided a path to citizenship for childhood arrivals. What was innovative about DACA was its design. Unlike the Morton memos, which addressed ICE, the DACA memo tasked the USCIS with the goal of providing some measure of relief to high-achieving childhood arrivals. By the time Secretary Napolitano announced DACA's creation in 2012, the Obama administration had effectively abandoned the idea that OPLA attorneys could serve as the engine for far-reaching relief. DACA, in turn, represented a departure in the exercise of discretion in two ways.

First, DACA created a more clearly identifiable set of criteria upon which relief might be granted. While agency officials still possessed significant discretion to grant or deny applications, the program communicated to the public which types of applicants might be potentially eligible, thereby empowering them to make choices about how to manage the risks of engaging with a government agency tied to the DHS's removal engine. A number of legal scholars have noted that the move toward a DACA model for discretionary relief signaled the embrace of transparency as a mode of governance.[40] Generally speaking, administrative law—the area of law that most directly governs agency practice—has developed in a manner that seeks to minimize unfettered discretion exercised by government officials. As legal scholar Rachel Barkow points out, "[i]n a legal culture that is firmly committed to judicial review, wedded to reasoned decisionmaking, and devoted to a fair and regular process, there is little space for the exercise of unreviewable legal power that is dispensed without reason and without the need to be consistent."[41] By making the criteria for relief more visible, DACA brought immigration enforcement policy more in line with dominant legal norms.

This point about transparency and public input plugs into a broader critique of the deferred action programs more generally. While the DACA memo did spell out clear criteria that could help noncitizens decide for themselves whether to risk legal exposure, one way that critics of DACA have attacked the program since its inception has been to argue that the process creating DACA was flawed. By creating the program through an agency memo, the Obama administration did not go through the channels for policymaking known as "notice and comment" rulemaking, a process by which a government agency proposes a policy to the public and invites feedback, or "comments." The conventional wisdom is that policies generated through notice-and-comment rulemaking are less vulnerable to legal challenge because such policies formally have taken into account the views and preferences of the relevant stakeholders.[42]

Bert, a senior immigration expert, who joined the Obama administration after the DACA rollout, expressed surprise that immigration officials did not use notice and comment rulemaking for DACA. He notes:

I was surprised they didn't use notice and comment. Not because I thought it was clear that they had to, [but] because it was pretty clear that someone would challenge them on this ground, and why leave ourselves vulnerable to that possible lawsuit? It probably would have delayed things about a year, but at the time they had the year. And to this day I scratch my head and think why they didn't do it. I think part of it was they didn't want to create a precedent. I know the Department of Justice lawyers and DHS felt strongly that this is not something that required notice and comment, and they didn't want to deal with anything that might create contrary expectations.

Secretary Napolitano's public statements corroborate Bert's view. In a 2014 speech, former secretary Napolitano described DACA this way: "The law, we believed, was on our side. Bureaucratic momentum was not."[43] She describes the process of presenting the DACA program to the White House: "Our White House colleagues asked serious, tough questions along several dimensions. We had many conversations and went back and forth several times. Eventually, they reached a comfort level with our legal position— DACA was well within the legal authority of DHS—and with our preparations for implementing DACA across the country."[44]

The lack of notice-and-comment rulemaking for DACA did, indeed, lead to later litigation challenges, though not until the program had become a fixed part of the policy landscape. This delay perhaps gives credence to Secretary Napolitano's statements. Indeed, when President Trump's administration attempted to rescind DACA, the Supreme Court, even with its conservative majority, did not have enough votes to validate those efforts. Instead, the Court concluded, by a vote of 5-4, that the *rescission* of DACA likely required notice and comment rulemaking.[45] The Biden administration subsequently decided to reinscribe DACA as a fixture of immigration policy by promulgating it through notice-and-comment rulemaking, a sign that if DACA has any hope of living on it will be through formalizing the process generating the policy.

After sharing his concerns about the lack of notice and comment rulemaking in the lead up to DACA, Bert correctly prognosticated that legal challenges would be in some sense inevitable, even with a different approach to rulemaking: "Even if [government officials] use notice-and-comment procedure, all the critics would have to do is find a judge like

Andrew Hanen and go to court, and instead of arguing that they should have used notice-and-comment procedures, they would have said that the notice and comment procedures weren't fully complied with. They would say, 'Here's a comment we think is significant,' or 'Here is a reply they gave that was inadequate,' and then all Hanen . . . would have to do is just send it back saying, 'Nope, you need to do more work. Send it back,' and then that would delay things." The continuing history of DACA appears to be unfolding precisely as Bert predicted. Despite the Biden administration's adherence to notice-and-comment rulemaking, challengers have once against sued the president arguing that the program is unlawful and thus far, the Fifth Circuit Court of Appeals has (once again) agreed, leaving the Supreme Court poised to address the question at the time of this book's publication.

This shift to a front-end application program, rather than enforcement discretion exercised at the moment of an individual enforcement encounter, was accompanied by a change in the agency primarily vested with enforcement discretion. No longer would OPLA lawyers within ICE be making that call. Now it would be officials within USCIS—the arm of DHS that processes visa applications and is often identified as the agency's benefits arm. Georgia explained how the enforcement-benefits distinction that is often used to distinguish between ICE and USCIS undergirded a decision to put USCIS in charge of this program. Her words also reveal that the program retained its enforcement roots:

> The idea was, you know, DACA is a law enforcement policy, it's not a benefits policy. The idea is that these folks should be out of the enforcement process and . . . allow ICE to go after people who are priorities. So you know, let's not bog them down with implementing a program they have no expertise in. Let's give it to the agency within DHS, which is also, you know, an agency that cares about enforcement and does have enforcement as a part of their mandate . . . let's give it to them to implement it because we think they have the infrastructure to actually pull it together.

These comments reflect the ease with which officials can use terms like "enforcement" and "benefits" interchangeably, to mean the same thing or sometimes to mean complementary things. Because administrative law immunizes discretionary agency action, especially in the criminal realm against judicial review, immigration officials are incentivized to frame policies as exercises of enforcement discretion. At the same time, the demand by immigrants and their advocates for relief in the form of benefits unquestionably drove officials to seek alternatives to the traditional nonenforcement and deprioritization regime that the Morton memos offered. In many ways, Georgia's comments reveal the challenges that administrative agencies faced when seeking to address complex legal, social, and political problems with a limited set of legal tools.

Abandoning the "black box" of the prosecutorial model[46] in favor of DACA's relatively transparent model for relief presented new regulatory challenges. Because DHS could not grant deferral until and unless noncitizens affirmatively applied for such relief, USCIS officials focused their attention on ensuring that information on the content and parameters of the program was as accurate as possible.

Carl worked closely with the USCIS director during the DACA rollout and across two different presidential administrations. He began as a contractor and then eventually worked his way up to a senior level within USCIS. During our interview, his answers were littered with agency lingo describing different government officials as "principals" and "careers." Carl noted that after the program was announced in June 2012, but before USCIS began accepting applications, agency officials were reluctant to "go out with even a little bit of piecemeal stuff here and there" concerning the application process for fear of generating "confusion among advocacy groups or service organizations." To the extent USCIS communicated with the public, Carl noted, "[t]he message was, yes, we are working towards this, [but] don't prepare anything, don't give *notarios* anything. We are the official source. We will give things out on or about August 15."

Notarios in this context refers to immigration service consultants who erroneously hold themselves out as lawyers to noncitizen clients. In civil-law Latin American countries, *notarios* have legal training and are authorized to perform a number of legal functions, whereas in the United States, a notary's professional role is limited to validating signatures on documents. Nonetheless, some notaries (labeling themselves "*notarios*") and other so-called immigration "experts" advertise a range of legal services, charge exorbitant prices, claim to have special connections that will expedite cases, and promise positive outcomes when in fact, their clients may be ineligible for, or highly unlikely to receive, relief. In many cases, applying for status or benefits simply brings individuals to the attention of the government in ways that increase the likelihood of deportation. While some *notarios* arguably provide a cost-effective set of services for noncitizens, the industry as a whole has received harsh criticism for exploitative and predatory practices.[47] Misinformation spread by *notarios* combined with heavy-handed enforcement by ICE and other law enforcement officials can generate panic and misinformation. Carl's comments reflect the fact that there is a whole industry of private actors or brokers who enter this space and purport to fill gaps for noncitizens living in conditions of extreme vulnerability. In the case of *notarios*, brokering sometimes entails monetizing and exploiting fear, potentially leaving noncitizens even more vulnerable by drawing attention to their status.

A second way that DACA marked a departure from the Morton memo approach was its limitation on the discretion that immigration agents and officers could exercise over deferred action determinations. The self-selected nature of the DACA process created a pool of applicants that, on the whole, has a different legal history and profile than the larger pool of longtime immigrant residents. With clearly articulated criteria for eligibility, USCIS officials reviewed batches of applications that presented less variance and that largely met the defined criteria for deferred action.

Still, as discussed earlier, DACA did leave in place significant pockets of discretionary authority. Obama-era USCIS officials often insisted that the agency *did* adjudicate each DACA application on a case-by-case basis, especially with regard to crime-related criteria. A key criterion for DACA eligibility was not having been convicted of a felony, a significant misdemeanor, or three or more multiple misdemeanors. Individuals who posed national security threats were also barred. The process of deciding whether an applicant's prior record excluded from this program required the exercise of discretion within USCIS.

Felicia worked within USCIS during the Obama administration and she clarified that officials exercised significant discretion over crime-related criteria. A lawyer by training, Felicia came to USCIS from the law practice and advocacy world. After graduating from law school in the early 1990s,

Felicia spent many years representing immigrants in both private practice and with an immigrant-serving organization on the east coast before getting pulled into USCIS. At USCIS, she worked within the Ombudsman office, an office within the agency that reviewed denied DACA applications. Those whose applications were delayed or denied by USCIS could request "case assistance" from the Ombudsman office. Ombudsman officials followed up with USCIS officials to check on the status of an application or to request a refund. As she explained, "there were a wide range of actions that reflected poor quality in adjudications. Everything from . . . overly burdensome and inappropriate requests for additional evidence, to misinterpretation of policy, or just clear error in the way the case was handled. . . . Sometimes clients, or customers, came to us because USCIS owed them a refund and could not for the life of them get the agency to refund them for the application."

When asked to provide an example of USCIS officials exercising their discretionary authority to deny an application, Felicia said: "We saw issues regarding arrests in some cases. . . . There were perhaps, I think some juvenile dispositions, and some that should not have been . . . should not have cost denial. So there were discretionary denials that perhaps exceeded the agency's discretionary authority. . . . We saw requests for evidence related to juvenile records that applicants could not obtain." Felicia's observations reaffirm a broader point we have emphasized throughout this chapter, namely that despite popular perceptions about how DACA functioned, the program conferred onto agency officials important pockets of discretionary authority that could form the basis of a denial.

Mercy

In closing out the discussion on how discretion has informed Obama-era immigration enforcement policies, we offer one final reflection on the oddity of using criminal law both as a mechanism for control and punishment and as the basis for relief and safety.

Janet Napolitano's 2014 speech, given after she had already left the Obama administration to become President of the University of California (UC) system, provides a kind of oral history of the Obama administration's immigration enforcement policies. Much of the speech operates as a love letter to prosecutorial discretion, an attempt to collect both the Morton Memos approach and the DACA approach under the same broad rubric of prosecutorial discretion. Napolitano explains: "On a personal level, I myself had long exercised prosecutorial discretion—both as a former U.S. Attorney, and as a former state Attorney General. The Department of Justice, for example, does not focus on small bad check cases. It has bigger fish to fry. Prosecutorial discretion has a long and distinguished history in immigration law, and so we were confident that we were on solid legal ground when it came [sic] setting priorities for immigration enforcement efforts."[48] Though DACA remains a signature immigration benefits program, the broader enforcement legacy followed Napolitano into her service as UC president. Public meetings devoted to discussing Napolitano's candidacy faced interruptions from immigrant rights activists, and UC student regent Cinthia Flores voted against Napolitano's appointment, pointing to her role in deporting immigrants and noting that this record "produced insurmountable barriers to higher education."[49] Secretary Napolitano and other Obama-era officials often describe DACA in ways to suggest that the benefits created by that program "cancel out" or make amends from the deportation engine that drove the first part of the Obama administration, but it is clear that for many people, such programs cannot be so easily decoupled.

Edgar, whose story opened this chapter, expressed views of Obama-era policy that reflect the sort of discomfort and disconnect of incorporating principles of mercy into the immigration realm. The interview spanned two separate sessions. In the first interview, Edgar described the process of issuing the Morton memos this way: "I don't think people were feeling the change quick enough, and . . . we had talked about it, when we established the simple enforcement priorities, that we would also revise and issue a new policy on prosecutorial discretion. You know, who are you gonna show some, for lack of a better word, mercy towards."

He mentioned mercy reluctantly, almost in passing. In the second interview with Edgar, upon revisiting the topic of mercy, he expressed much greater resistance to that characterization. When asked to evaluate the extent to which the program was driven by resource management concerns as opposed to concerns with "clemency," Edgar quickly stated: "Uh, clemency I don't even think is the right word, and I don't like the mercy word, that's a really weird word for me to use. . . . Um, but it's more like this; I think it was like, well, this is the right thing to do. We shouldn't waste any resources on these people, right?"

After explaining the various benefits that qualifying immigrant residents could obtain through DACA, Edgar continued:

> You know, um, this is a population that shouldn't be touched. There was a lot of that, so that I wouldn't say mercy is the right word. It's not like, okay, we're going to show compassion to this population, I mean but it was more like, hey, this is a population that this country shouldn't waste any money or time deporting. I mean this was the kind of mindset we had, right? And we should just shouldn't waste time or money [or] energy on this population, and this is the best way to take care of it, so we're going to do it.
>
> Um, I, I don't think we were looking at it like a—I mean I think there was . . . certainly some sympathy for the situation these people find themselves in. There was a lot of sympathy, right? These—I think we—that's reflected in the [DACA] memo.

Not all of the government officials interviewed for this project expressed ambivalence about the equitable strains of DACA. Many fully embraced it. Others simply did not acknowledge it during interviews. But Edgar's struggle to land on a firm position on DACA's equitable dimensions once again reflects the limitations of the law's ability to meet the demands of immigrants and advocates. Despite the broad discretionary decision-making that administrative law doctrine affords, immigration officials still often struggle to provide relief on terms that matched the lived experiences of immigrants. These struggles continued as the administration engaged in thwarted efforts to expand deferred action with the DAPA and DACA+ programs, and those struggles are evident in the lives of immigrant residents.

THREE

Uncertainty

ALONDRA, A PERUVIAN WOMAN in her early fifties, immigrated to the United States legally in 1999 when her spouse received an H-1 employment visa reserved for highly skilled workers. When we met her in 2014 at a café in the San Fernando Valley, in the days before President Obama announced the DAPA program, Alondra regaled us with stories of the uncertainty and deprivation that she had experienced in the intervening years. Highly educated herself, Alondra's original goal had been to pursue graduate study in the United States and then return to Peru with an advanced degree in hand. Instead, she found herself trapped in the United States with few opportunities.[1]

When her husband's H-1 visa expired after six years, he entrusted his immigration case to a company representative who assisted with immigration paperwork but who was not an attorney. Alondra recalls that the company representative guaranteed that she would be able to secure her husband lawful permanent residency, claiming that she had never lost a case. Yet, Alondra believes this representative submitted incorrect paperwork on behalf of Alondra's husband. Meanwhile, he lost his job and then worked under his own social security number for another employer, thus unknowingly violating the conditions of his initial entry visa. Once their status lapsed, Alondra and her husband were unable to work legally, and so resorted to workarounds and subterfuge. They worked as independent contractors—a workaround that can avoid immigration-related consequences triggered by working as an "employee," a legally distinct category.

They also worked using social security numbers that did not belong to them—a form of subterfuge that is unlawful but not always detected. Alondra's educational goals fell by the wayside as she discovered that, without legal status, she lacked access to financial aid that would allow her to attend anything other than community college. There, she could study only English and office procedures, not graduate-level computer science. The couple considered returning to Peru, but their two children—a daughter, who had come with them when they first immigrated and so was undocumented, and a son, who was born in the United States and therefore a US citizen—excelled in school and had educational opportunities in this country. After winning a scholarship to attend a private high school, their daughter was admitted to a four-year university, also with a scholarship, and was able to obtain DACA. However, uncertainty always overshadowed such achievements. Would Alondra, her husband, and her daughter be able to regularize their status? Would Alondra be able to study? Would her husband be able to continue working? Would the family be able to stay together? Would DACA continue? Would she be able to obtain relief through DAPA?

Like Alondra, Julieta (first introduced in Chapter 1), a Mexican immigrant in her forties, had lived in the United States without status for many years, but unlike Alondra, she did not have children—a fact that, at the time of our interview, appeared crucial for her prospects of obtaining permission to remain and work in the country lawfully though the DAPA program. While sitting at a café at the Los Angeles Central Library, Julieta shared her immigration history with a member of our research team. Julieta originally left Mexico at the age of 18, leaving an unhappy family situation. After unsuccessfully applying for a tourist visa, immigration officials inspected and admitted her at the US-Mexico border, where she posed as a college student. Julieta had dreamed of becoming an actress and singer and had studied to be a nursing assistant in Mexico. But without a valid social security number, she worked in waitressing, in the garment industry, and as a house cleaner. Alongside her paid work, Julieta volunteered with an organization, where she informed listeners about immigration law over the air. Julieta's only hope of regularizing her status was to marry a US citizen,[2] but she would do so, she said, only if she were in love, and if the person she loved happened to be a citizen. As she was childless, she would not have qualified for DAPA if it had gone into effect. Having lived through multiple promises of immigration reform, including the DAPA announcement of a form of executive relief for which she could not qualify, Julieta was extremely frustrated. She explained, "I've been telling my family for years. 'This is the year. This is the time, you know. Obama won the elections. He's the new president. He's gonna change the system.' And every year, it's been probably like six years that I've been telling my family the same. And they tell me, nothing has changed."

Joonseo was in his early thirties when a research team member met with him at the office of a Korean community organization in Los Angeles. He also struggled with uncertainty and deprivation. Joonseo left South Korea at the age of fifteen because his parents wanted to protect him from having to assume an overwhelming business debt. In the United States, Joonseo lived with an aunt and sister while attending a predominantly Black and Latinx high school. He remembers peers bullying him for being Korean. Joonseo had entered the US on a temporary visa but could not find a way to regularize his status and could not afford to pay for legal assistance with the process. As an undocumented worker, Joonseo experienced abusive working conditions. Employers paid him at a rate below the minimum wage, passed him over for promotions, and did not pay him for overtime. Working nights as a dishwasher and attending school during the day, Joonseo became exhausted, leading school officials who saw him sleeping to assume he was taking drugs and report him to the police. Joonseo applied to and was accepted at a four-year university but was unable to attend because he could not afford the fees due to his undocumented status. At the time, California laws largely excluded undocumented students from tuition-related and funding-related benefits in the college admissions and enrollment process. Frustrated, Joonseo moved to New York, where, after a period of homelessness, he lived in a vermin-infested apartment while working fifteen-hour days and enduring police harassment. Joonseo had hit rock bottom.

But things turned around for Joonseo. A priest befriended and counseled Joonseo to improve his English by reading Hemmingway's *The Old Man and the Sea*. After doing so, Joonseo learned that in 2001, A.B. 540 had passed in California, enabling residents to pay in-state tuition regardless of immigration status.[3] He returned and became a legal and political activist, joining a lawsuit to compel his community college to comply with California legislation making undocumented high school students eligible for in-state tuition rates. He obtained DACA and participated in major national actions to support undocumented youth. Despite this progress, Joonseo worried about his future: "Even [though] I have DACA, how do you apply to companies that require legal documentation? I have to go through all this. It kind of like scared me you know? Ohhh they might find out that I worked illegally—fourteen years! They might like deport me or something like that!"

Alondra's, Julieta's, and Joonseo's experiences differ from the dichotomous narrative of "deserving" and "undeserving" immigrants that policy makers often articulate, a narrative that underlies both the enforcement initiatives and the discretionary relief discussed up to this point. Each of these individuals demonstrated the educational achievements, work ethic, and civic engagement that prototypical immigrant success stories feature, and each came to the United States out of a combination of necessity and the desire for opportunity. At the same time, Alondra, Julieta, and Joonseo also engaged in the sort of practices that enforcement rhetoric condemns, practices such as crossing a national border without authorization, overstaying the terms of their visas, and working with false papers. It is difficult to paint them as either innocent victims or as undeserving lawbreakers; instead, their narratives reveal them to be complex human beings who have contended creatively with exclusionary policies. Moreover, their experiences were shaped by race, class, gender, family status, country of origin, and immigration history. For instance, Julieta, who had completed high school in Mexico and had no family in the US, had fewer educational and employment opportunities than Alondra and Joonseo, whose educational level and business connections enabled them to enter the United States legally. Moreover, there are gender dimensions to their experiences: Joonseo, who was male-identified, experienced police harassment, which is consistent with policing practices that profile young men of color.

The gaps between each of these individuals' lives and societal measures of deservingness do not arise from individual failings but are generated by the operation of immigration law itself. Indeed, the federal government and popular discourse define categories of deservingness in ways that reveal fundamental contradictions that are at the heart of the US immigration system. For example, steady employment can be a measure of deservingness,[4] yet the undocumented are denied work authorization. In fact, recent Supreme Court decisions presage a threat to the work authorization held by those with deferred action, distinguishing as they do between forbearance—not deporting individuals as a form of prosecutorial discretion—and the conferral of work authorization, which the Court has characterized as a benefit.[5] Likewise, immigration policy and public rhetoric treat educational achievements as markers of merit, yet undocumented students may be ineligible for financial aid or in-state tuition, or even barred from state universities altogether.[6] Instead of being legally acknowledged, such contradictions are displaced onto immigrants who are forced to live with uncertainty, hoping to eventually sway US officials and policy makers to enable them to regularize. Yet, as the experiences of Alondra, Julieta, and Joonseo demonstrate, noncitizens can resist this uncertainty by moving forward with their lives regardless of US policy.

In this chapter, we analyze the complicated mismatches between the lives of the immigrants we interviewed and the forms of subjectivity created through enforcement initiatives and discretionary forms of relief.[7] Chapter 1 illustrates the many ways that enforcement initiatives have subjected unauthorized immigrants to *illegalization,* that is, to "the process of marking certain bodies, their practices and presence, as 'illegal.'"[8] Instead of being intrinsically illegal due to their own actions or behavior, unauthorized immigrants are constituted as "illegal" through historical processes that criminalize their movement[9] and through "surveillant assemblages"[10] of state and nonstate actors who request identity documents.[11] Furthermore, low-level policing activities have criminalized communities of color, including those of immigrant backgrounds. Indeed, the criminalization of individuals in these communities, also illustrated in Chapter 1, highlights the central role of criminalization in the illegalization process. Yet, because those who live in the United States without authorization become formally and informally incorporated into institutions, such as schools, neighborhoods, families, workplaces, and congregations, illegalization and criminalization are incomplete, giving immigrant community members opportunities to challenge the systems within which they are situated.[12]

A useful concept for understanding the material impacts of illegalization is precarity, which, in the case of migrants lacking lawful immigration status, may be defined as "vulnerability to deportation and state violence, exclusion from public services and basic state protections, insecure employment and exploitation at work, insecure livelihood, and everyday discrimination or isolation."[13] Clearly, the forms of precarity that unauthorized immigrants experience share commonalities with precarities that other marginalized groups face.[14] For instance, many in low-income and underrepresented communities experience housing insecurity, hunger, over-policing, underemployment, and labor exploitation.[15] At the same time, this definition highlights the fact that those who are unauthorized also face unique conditions, such as the denial of work authorization and the risk of being detained and deported.[16] As Goldring and Landolt note, "non-citizenship, by definition, is associated with limits in terms of voice, membership, and rights in a political community, and with social exclusion and vulnerability."[17]

Over time, individuals can experience precarity as a form of slow violence that can take high psychological and physical tolls. Chloe Ahmann describes slow violence as "a general wearing out . . . neither spectacular nor instantaneous, and often proceeding at a speed that decouples suffering from its original causes."[18] Individuals who are exposed to ongoing forms of violence such as family separations, uncertainty, labor exploitation, discrimination, and the risk of deportation may experience adverse mental health outcomes, chronic illness, and workplace injuries.[19] In response to such slow violence, many interviewees resisted illegalization and precarity, insisting on their deservingness, creating stability for themselves by remaining in the United States despite illegalization's harmful impacts, and seeking to regularize their status.

Those who hoped to qualify for deferred action experienced considerable uncertainty, which is itself both a form of social control and a source of negotiation and resistance. Imposed periods of waiting that are indefinite, such as at borders for permission to cross, or within a country for the opportunity to regularize, sap energy and initiative.[20] According to Ruben Andersson, in countries that police migrants, authorities engage in an "active usurpation of time for the purposes of migration control."[21] Many of the people we spoke to experienced such usurpation of time and energy given the need to plan for two different future versions of the same life: In one version, they are able to remain in the United States and secure work permits or permanent residence. In another version, they continue to lack work authorization and may even be deported. They shared with us how living lives that are contingent on political outcomes can be exhausting and deflating. For instance, during the period from 2012 through 2016, many interviewees experienced significant frustration and uncertainty over congressional inaction on immigration reform, exacerbated by rumors and reports that immigration policy would soon change, without specifics. Individuals and families worried about their own future prospects. At the same time, periods of uncertainty can give noncitizens the opportunity to attempt to redefine the significance of the time spent waiting, for example, as setting down roots or as evidence of connectedness.[22]

In a period when President Obama himself claimed that officials were differentiating "felons" from "families" to safeguard the latter, such uncertainty might appear to be misplaced in the lives of ordinary, working adults. Yet, as we saw in the previous chapters, immigration law's ability to meaningfully sort noncitizens into these categories is limited by the arbitrariness of distinctions based on entry dates, ages, family status, and—due to the over-policing of communities of color—race. The uncertainty experienced by immigrants whose ability to remain in the US depends entirely on executive forbearance brings particular sorts of quasi-legal subjects into being: transitory subjects who must attempt to sway authorities' exercise of discretion by documenting their lives in and contributions to the United States, even as the government retains the power to continuously redefine the terms upon which to grant relief and the nature of particular benefits. Our interviews with people who sought to regularize their immigration status detail the experience of *becoming* the subjects of discretionary power. Interviewees, for example, tried to gauge their chances of securing relief, even as they worried about revealing themselves to authorities. They also critiqued the boundaries that executive relief established between those who did and did not qualify. The legal injunction that prevented the implementation of DAPA and DACA+ exacerbated the uncertainty they experienced. This injunction demonstrated deferred action's instability, as well as the degree to which discretionary subjects, like disadvantaged groups more generally, can be mistreated: the government need not keep promises to them and can rescind programs designed for them.[23] There are no guarantees.[24]

Our interviews also reveal ways that individuals pushed back against the limitations of being subjected to discretionary power, both through activism and through their own life strategies.[25] The stigmatization of undocumented immigrants for allegedly undermining the rule of law differed sharply from interviewees' senses of their own merit. Despite uncertainty, many of the unauthorized immigrants we interviewed attempted to move forward with their life projects anyway: they established families, built social networks, moved through the various stages (school, graduation, parenthood, employment) that marked time, and practiced forms of integration, such as working, volunteering, organizing, and developing institutional connections. In short, interviewees resisted being consumed by uncertainty, even as they were also compelled to live with it.

Illegalization

In everyday discourse, many people casually refer to noncitizens as "illegal immigrants," but it is worth emphasizing that, as we have noted in earlier chapters, individuals are not intrinsically "illegal." Rather, they undergo a process of "illegalization" as they become subject to government policies that prohibit their presence, limit their work opportunities, shape their kin relationships, and restrict their movement.[26] Illegalization occurs through everyday interactions, such as when an individual applies for a job and the prospective employer asks for proof of work authorization; or when students wish to attend college but discover that only citizens and lawful permanent residents are eligible for financial aid; or when police impound the car of a driver who was unable to secure a driver's license without proof of lawful presence; or when a couple wants to go dancing at a nightclub but cannot provide IDs; or when a child wishes to participate in a school fieldtrip but cannot travel through local checkpoints.[27] In most cases, interviewees' experiences of dislocation began even before they left their countries of origin, as their lives were intertwined with the United States through drug wars, US military intervention, trade policies, family relationships, and labor recruitment. For example, Mireya told us that she was almost kidnapped by cartels in Mexico; Teresa, a domestic violence victim unable to secure protection from local police, went into hiding in Mexico before joining a brother in the United States; and Yupanqui related that NAFTA had exacerbated inequality in ways that forced laborers out of Mexico and into the undocumented workforce in Los Angeles. Therefore, one cannot separate "illegalization" from the transnational geopolitical relationships that displace people from their countries of origin and citizenship, in many instances plunging them into insecurity and quasi-statelessness.

Interviewees' journeys into illegalization create particular legal trajectories that, in turn, result in differential legal opportunities. Some interviewees, like Alondra and Joonseo, entered the country with tourist or employment visas and stayed beyond the expiration dates. Because border agents inspected and admitted them, they are eligible to adjust their status to that of a lawful permanent resident, should they ever qualify to do so, without having to exit the United States. Others, like Julieta, crossed the US-Mexico border without authorization. Therefore, even if they become eligible for lawful status via a family petition, they must leave the country in order to claim their visa. For those like Julieta with more than a year of undocumented presence in the United States, leaving the country to adjust status presents a huge obstacle to legalizing status because they are subject to a ten-year bar on legal reentry, a fact that deters some from even trying to qualify for a visa. In some instances, USCIS can waive this ten-year bar. But the question of whether a waiver will be forthcoming and whether advanced permission to reenter the country will be honored is yet another source of uncertainty and precarity. This is true even under presidents like Obama and Biden, who have overseen relatively generous uses of waivers. But it was a particularly acute concern when Trump was president. As we discussed in Chapter 1, if an individual had failed to attend a prior immigration court hearing, whether by choice or through no fault of their own, they may have been ordered deported in absentia and have an outstanding removal order. If ICE apprehends them, it can execute this order without going before a judge. In fact, if they had such a pending order and then left the country—for instance, to visit a sick relative—they unknowingly executed or effectuated their own deportation order. If they reenter the US without authorization, they are subject to prosecution for the crime of un-lawful reentry. In sum, the undocumented population is not positioned the same, legally. It matters how people entered; whether, when, and how they left; whether they were apprehended, whether they attended any applicable immigration hearings, and whether and how they came into contact with criminal law enforcement agents.

Moreover, differential legal opportunities are linked to differences in race, class, gender, national origin, dis/ability, and sexual orientation. Tour-ist and employment visas are typically only available to well-educated in-dividuals who have significant economic resources. As we saw in the sto-ries of Alondra and Joonseo, immigrants from distant regions, particularly Asia, Africa, and South America, were traditionally more likely to have ini-tially entered the country with a visa, traveling by air; those who crossed the US-Mexico border without authorization were more likely to be from Mexico and Central America. (These travel patterns appear to be changing as more individuals are traveling from great distances, such as from Venezu-ela and Haiti, to enter the United States through Mexico.) Gendered family dynamics may also inflect legal trajectories, with men traditionally immi-grating first, followed by spouses and children.[28] US citizens and lawful per-manent residents may also be indirectly subjected to immigration laws if their noncitizen family members are deported.[29] Until 2013, only marriages between one man and one woman were eligible for spousal petitions, creat-ing hardships for same-sex partners. Legalization processes thus privilege a particular profile: people who come from more distant lands and enter the United States in fewer numbers, who have economic resources and who are well-educated, who have family ties within the United States, and who have heteronormative family structures. Individuals fleeing persecution are also potentially eligible for asylum. However, historically, US asylum policy privileged those fleeing regimes that the United States condemns[30] and dis-advantaged those fleeing friendly nations, and these political preferences have racial impacts. During the Trump administration, the president and immigration officials dramatically curtailed access to asylum through mas-sive reductions in the cap on the number of refugees that could be admitted per year, restrictions on categories of eligibility, metering (that is, allowing only small numbers of would-be applicants to enter the United States at a time), and a "remain in Mexico" policy, which forces asylum seekers to live in squalid and dangerous camp conditions on the Mexican side of the US southern border while they await the adjudication of their asylum claims. Although President Biden campaigned on the promise to undo this damage and has walked back some of the most punitive aspects of these policies, it is unclear whether immigration officials even have a complete picture of the damage that has been done and whether those officials will have the will and resources to redress these harms once that picture is complete.

Legal trajectories also shape the material conditions of the undocumented population in the United States. Individuals who entered the country with tourist visas and who are well-educated in their countries of origin may have more employment opportunities in the United States, particularly if they are able to circumvent their lack of access to a social security number. Some, like Alondra's husband, might use a work authorization number that they were issued before their visas expired. Those who have parents, siblings, or children with lawful permanent residency or US citizenship[31] may eventually hope to qualify for status through these relatives—and may also have more resources because they live in a household in which some members can work legally. Some interviewees had started their own businesses and had employees themselves. Others had qualified for DACA and were pursuing educational or employment opportunities. Yet, despite these differences, interviewees overwhelmingly described frustration over unemployment, underemployment, exploitative labor conditions, lack of access to educational opportunities, lengthy separation from family members in their countries of origin, the inability to vote in the United States, insecurity, immobility, police harassment, and discrimination. Local policies adopted in the municipalities where interviewees lived and worked either exacerbated or ameliorated these conditions. As we will see in Chapter 5, Los Angeles County adopted more immigrant-friendly policies than did Orange County and jurisdictions within Orange County (with the notable exception of the city of Santa Ana), which largely collaborated with ICE in enforcing federal immigration law.

Just as the officials who were the focus of Chapter 2 developed executive relief in the absence of comprehensive immigration reform, so too did individuals who could have potentially benefited from immigration reform develop their own strategies in the absence of such a comprehensive measure. As we discussed in earlier chapters, the prospect of immigration reform almost became a reality when the US Senate passed the Border Security, Economic Opportunity, and Immigration Modernization Act of 2013. This legislation would have created an interim "Registered Provisional Immigrant" (RPI) status and, if key border and interior enforcement markers were met, would have enabled RPI recipients to apply for lawful permanent residency and eventually citizenship through a long and tenuous process over a ten-year period. The legislation included provisions of the DREAM Act, which the federal government would have implemented more rapidly, compared to the law's other provisions. The House declined to act on the bill, however, so it died at the end of the 2013 congressional session, shortly before we began interviewing immigrant residents for this book.

In 2014, rumors circulated that Congress might again take up immigration reform or that President Obama planned to announce a broad-based form of relief. Initial hopes that such an announcement would come early in the year were dashed when an influx of unaccompanied minors from Central America in the spring and summer of 2014 enabled restrictionists to criticize the president's handling of border security. The possibility of a new form of relief nonetheless raised expectations and was welcome to interviewees, who hoped that the country would recognize their worth and extend opportunities to them. Alondra, whom we quoted above, described what was at stake for her family: "If Obama does the Executive Action law, then our plan is to incorporate ourselves through this law, have a social [security number], get a work permit, and work. Because with that work permit, my husband would be able to work in California, he would be accepted at any job." For Beatriz, a full-time homemaker who like Alondra, had immigrated from Peru and become undocumented, the best possible outcome of executive relief or a reform would be "that my children could be legal."

In this context of prolonged uncertainty coupled with heightened expectations, misconceptions flourished. During a July 2014 interview, an immigrant rights advocate told us that many immigrants thought that immigration reform legislation that had passed the US Senate in 2013 had actually become law. As a result of this confusion, public notaries posing as immigration attorneys (*notarios*) were able to defraud immigrants by charging them to apply to a nonexistent program. Advocates also worried that any form of relief would come with trade-offs, such as increased militarization of the US-Mexico border and intensified interior enforcement efforts. Even so, interviewees conveyed a sense of optimism that administrative relief could lay the groundwork for broader legislative reform. Interviewees told us that they were gathering documents, seeking out legal advice, and saving money so that they would be prepared to apply for whatever opportunities arose. Key unanswered questions, however, were how many people—and who—would be included in any opportunity. Carla, a student activist and DACA recipient, worried, "I'm really hoping that what he [Obama] announces is Deferred Action for parents of DREAMers," while Josue, the policy director at an immigrant rights organization, speculated that "anybody that might be in the process pending a [family visa petition but without eligibility to adjust status in the United States]" might become eligible for relief. Perhaps the biggest question in the minds of many was whether Obama would act at all.

Categorical Deferred Action

On November 20, 2014, when President Obama announced DAPA and DACA+, he recalibrated, but did not eliminate, the uncertainty that unauthorized immigrants experience. DACA tried to distinguish high-achieving childhood arrivals from the broader undocumented immigrant community. To the preexisting differentiation within the undocumented immigrant community were added distinctions for DAPA eligibility based on whether someone had a US citizen or lawful permanent resident child and a clean criminal record. At the same time, DACA+ expanded eligibility for DACA, changing the date cutoff in ways that would have brought more people into the program. Immediately, the undocumented population was bifurcated between the estimated four to five million people who likely could qualify and the six to seven million who most likely could not, though the boundaries of this bifurcation were unclear, in sharp contrast to officials' predictions. Recall that, in Chapter 2, we quoted Bert, a DHS official, who commented: "I really did picture tears of joy just streaming down the faces of people in millions of immigrants' households around the country" once DACA was announced. Yet, some found this hierarchy of deserving- ness galling, both in the context of the original DACA program and in the expanded versions. Carla, a DACA recipient, complained, "There's a sort of hierarchy, when you think of undocumented people, in that DREAMers are the ones we feel sorry for and that deserve it, and everyone else is just kind of—of 'migrant' or of 'anchor baby' or something."

Eleana, the policy director of an API immigrant rights organization, pointed out that such distinctions were divisive. A lawyer by training, Eleana began her career in the late 1990s like many graduates of elite law schools, working at a large law firm in California. Even in those early years of her career, Eleana provided flashes of how her career would develop by devoting her pro bono time to issues, such as hate crimes and public ben- efits, that were relevant to API immigrant communities. After spending some time working on civil rights issues at a federal agency, Eleana joined an API-serving organization as a lawyer where she eventually moved into a leadership position. It was at this point in her career that our research team met with and interviewed her. Sitting in her dimly lit office surrounded by stacks of papers and folders, Eleana discussed the challenges of supporting and empowering immigrants to serve as their own advocates. Some of these obstacles stem from the limitations of the programs themselves. Many of the immigrant rights advocates at Eleana's organization are undocumented, and she noted that they did not qualify for even the expanded versions of executive relief. She said, "It's so heartbreaking and ironic when they have been at the forefront of the organizing and really pushing the [Obama] ad- ministration but now they're still left out." Some of the challenges relate to the social identities attributed to undocumented migrants. Eleana ob- served that "LA and Orange County have more undocumented APIs than anywhere else in the whole country, but people are so fearful and there's a lot of . . . stigma so we wanted to shift that paradigm." She continued, commenting that "there's a lot of internalization of the criminalization of undocumented immigrants." From her perspective, the API-serving media has not done as much to combat this trend as the Latinx media.

While President Obama tried to sell the expanded deferred action pro- grams as a pragmatic way of allowing unauthorized migrants to stay in the

United States temporarily with their citizen and green card holder family members, many of our interviewees did not see why such a bright line had to be drawn at lawful status. If the point was to keep family members together, many of our interviewees viewed DAPA as relying on arbitrary distinctions. Interviewees who did not believe they would qualify generally nonetheless saw themselves as equally deserving. For example, Graciela, a hairstylist, had entered the United States as an adult and her only son was undocumented. She commented:

> I had the hope that [Obama] would [authorize deferred action] in a manner in which those of us who are already here would obtain some permit. That was my expectation. We are citizens who are here. We don't do any wrong, right. We are people who work. We contribute by shopping here. They charge taxes on that so the economy will flourish, but unfortunately I wasn't within that package.

Graciela's comment, "We are citizens who are here," highlights ordinary understandings of citizenship-as-belonging, regardless of formal legal status, and presents a powerful critique of exclusionary practices.

In addition to those who were simply ineligible for reasons such as their lack of US citizen or lawful permanent resident children, there were others who worried that another aspect of their record would disqualify them. For example, Margarita, a housewife living in Los Angeles, feared that medical debt that she had incurred when being treated for cancer would be viewed negatively. She wondered anxiously, "I also have the whole debt that [the hospital social worker] already told me that that will impact me, because I don't know if [immigration officials] are going to approve me, because it is to the state that I owe the debt, so we will have to see." Logically, Margarita reasoned, if she owed the government money, she could not expect the government to approve her application. (In fact, such debts historically have not prevented individuals from qualifying for temporary programs such as DACA.) Erasmo, a construction worker whose son was a US citizen, was also concerned about his legal history. As noted in Chapter 1, Erasmo had a criminal conviction stemming from his arrest while driving under the influence and, after three months in jail, he had been deported. He had reentered the country and had no further criminal convictions. We met him when he approached a Los Angeles community organization in hopes of clearing his record so that he could apply for DAPA. "If I have to pay, then I'll try to pay. If I have to sign something, then I'll sign it so long as it's not another deportation because I won't sign. That's the only thing that's holding me back," Erasmo remarked optimistically. Erasmo did not appear to know that those who return to the United States without authorization after being deported can be prosecuted on felony charges and be permanently barred from the United States.

Not surprisingly, given the ways that the federal government's overarching enforcement focus limited forms of relief, interviewees also expressed concerns (rightly, as it turned out) about the instability of DAPA and DACA+ and the ambiguous nature of the status they could attain by applying. Nestor, a day laborer living in Los Angeles, had no US citizen children and therefore did not qualify, but even if he could, he said, the program wouldn't benefit him: "They say it's only temporary, [they] only are given for [a] three-year period. You don't know what's going to happen when Obama isn't there and a new president enters. Possibly they take it away." Carla worried that even with DACA, she was ineligible for healthcare coverage (though in 2022 California extended healthcare to those who are undocumented). Carla struggled to describe her status: "It is a form of documentation, but I am still not a legal citizen of the US or a legal resident, really. It's also a temporary relief, and that's emphasized in every paper I sign. 'Temporary Relief.' I am 'DACA-mented.'" Likewise, Sammy, who was affiliated with an immigrant youth organization, pointed out that "getting a work permit isn't the same as actually having your documentation or your status."

Fátima, who hoped to qualify for DAPA, noted the many obstacles that deferred action recipients face: not being able to study (due to tuition costs) or, at the time, obtain medical insurance. Regarding deferred action, she stated, "Only half [status, opportunity] is given, no more"—a striking contrast to the government official who was quoted in Chapter 2 as saying that DACA was not a half-measure. As a program grounded only in executive branch policy, not statute, deferred action was subject to "political maneuvering," to quote Alondra, and was particularly insecure.

Despite the shortcomings of deferred action, interviewees who thought they could qualify for DAPA or DACA+ placed great hopes on the program. Alondra hoped that she could return to school and her husband could obtain employment in California, instead of continuing to work out of state. Beatriz, the Peruvian homemaker mentioned earlier, wanted her college-age son to benefit from the expansion of DACA. She had some misgivings about the unstable nature of deferred action, but, she insisted, "hay que arriesgar"—one must take the risk. Margarita hoped to eventually qualify for residency through a petition that her fourteen-year-old US citizen son would be able to file for her at the age of twenty-one, but thought that DAPA would allow her to "at least breathe more easily" in the interim. With deferred action, she hoped to obtain a better job, earn more money, and travel to other parts of the United States. Alfaro, whom we met in Chapter 1, ran a small business and did not actually need work authorization. He described deferred action as "not indispensable to be able to get ahead, it is not indispensable to get work, but it is something that complements, it is like salt, a little salt that one puts on the food." Alondra was perhaps the most eloquent in describing what deferred action would mean for her family. In an email after the president's announcement, she told us, "Yesterday, I heard the message of President Obama. Finally, one feels relief, it is like being able to breathe after having been drowning. I believe that things will be different from now on. There are many projects in our minds, and an incredible optimism. We still are a little afraid, and that's normal, but the desire to fight for residency is huge."[32]

To "fight for residency," as Alondra put it, interviewees began preparing to apply for deferred action through DAPA and DACA+. The uncertain nature of the program seemed to make applying especially urgent, so that even if it were cancelled, those who had qualified for deferred action might be allowed to retain their work authorization and relief from deportation, if only temporarily. Interviewees began saving money for application fees, exploring the possibility of obtaining loans from relatives, and gathering documents to prove their physical presence in the United States for the requisite period of time. Some visited consulates to renew their passports so that they would have valid identity documents. Organizations began providing document preparation workshops, and some interviewees attended. Even those who did not qualify, such as Julieta, tried to assemble their paperwork just in case an opportunity to apply for status later arose.[33] Julieta told us:

> I've been saving everything. I have a . . . big suitcase filled with documents. My college records. My payment, check stubs. Letters. Everything. Even

my driver's license. My– in 1991 when I came I was able to get . . . a California ID. I have [had] that one since, as a proof, so . . . it's filled with documents already. I just need to organize it because they're all mixed, so I need to organize them by the years but I'm definite—I have everything that they may request. I've been paying my taxes, which I know it's the law. The Constitution says whether you are legal or illegal you have to pay taxes. I've been doing that. I have people, people in organizations who even would give me a letter of recommendation.

Such "hyperdocumentation"[34] was a creative response to indefinite waiting, remaining *pendiente* on the government, a wait that was to take new twists and turns as the legal battle over deferred action ensued.

Enjoined

On February 17, 2015, the day before the application window for the expansion of DACA was to open, Alma Garza, a member of our research team, was driving to Los Angeles to observe a community organization's staff training in preparation for the expected influx of new clients who would begin arriving the next day. On her drive in, however, she heard on the car radio that the previous evening, a federal district court judge in Texas had enjoined the implementation of DAPA and DACA+. The training went on as planned, but at the first break, Alma approached one of the presenters to ask about the judge's ruling. Alma's notes summarize the response:

> [The presenter] shook her head in disappointment and told me they were all well aware. I asked how this would impact upcoming day-to-day operations at [this organization] and she said that they were unfortunately unable to submit applications. Applications would need to be placed on hold until the issue got resolved. Hence, even though they expected an enormous turnout the next day, they would process applications meeting requirements of the old DACA but they would not be able to submit applications for DAPA or extended DACA. We talked about how an appeal would be filed but she believed it would take some time before any of it got resolved.

The injunction took would-be applicants by surprise. Many interviewees who had hoped to qualify for deferred action expressed bitter disillusionment. Herminia, who had hoped to qualify for DACA+, complete her education, and obtain a professional position, told us:

> When [DACA+] was suspended, all of my hopes fell. I felt very disappointed. . . . I was ready. I had gotten all of my paperwork in order and was preparing to apply as soon as the program opened. It is very, very frustrating! I had waited so long and then finally, there was a small light, and then it went out, suddenly. . . . We are just hit one way, and then we are hit another way, and then we are hit back. . . . When you are practically in the doorway and you see that something is possible and then the opportunity is taken away, it is really, really hard. Now, one can only wait.

Herminia's sense of extreme disappointment was echoed by other interviewees, who expressed frustration that their lives could be upended due to what they characterized as party politics. Ajira, a staff member at an API organization, pointed out that members of marginalized groups frequently experience broken promises: "As people of color, we're just used to things, like you have a step forward and you have a step back, multiple steps back sometimes." Oscar, a 35 year old restaurant worker from Mexico, broke down in tears describing the injustice of being unable to advance in the workplace without going back to school: "I am not a chef, not yet, with a diploma I'd like to be. That is why I want DAPA. The main difference if I get DAPA will be school. I want to study to be a chef and study English."

The state of Texas, on behalf of itself and several other states, argued that a sudden influx of deferred action recipients would strain their resources—introducing a questionable argument that would subsequently be repurposed to argue for standing in litigation over other executive actions relating to immigration, including DACA itself.[35] Within civil procedure doctrine, injunctions maintain the status quo for parties facing a significant and potentially costly violation of their rights. In this way, injunctions help minimize uncertainty. Yet our conversations with people experiencing the effects of the DAPA/DACA+ litigation painfully illustrate the very real costs of this particular injunction for affected individuals. Protecting the alleged interests of one party (such as the state of Texas) usually means displacing the interests of others (such as Herminia and Oscar). In this case, the injunction created extreme uncertainty, not only for federal immigration officials but also for potential applicants and their allies. In fieldnotes that he wrote for our project, one of our research assistants, Gray Abarca, described this uncertainty as a "limbo within a limbo." Like others who were living in the United States without legal authorization, potential applicants were undocumented. Unlike others, they could potentially apply for deferred action, yet they did not know when, whether, or precisely how they could do so.[36] Deferred action was tantalizingly within, yet ultimately beyond, reach. A few months after the district court judge issued the injunction, a member of our research team participated in a webinar that used a graphic based on the Chutes and Ladders board game to depict the legal uncertainty surrounding deferred action: one never knew when one would slide down a chute. At workshops that we attended in the wake of the injunction, advocates repeatedly stressed the limits of their own knowledge, telling participants that they did not know precisely how parent-child relationships would be defined for the purposes of DAPA, that DAPA did not actually exist as a program, that the information that they were presenting could potentially change, and that not even USCIS had a plan. As one workshop participant told us, "We are up in the air."[37]

The original DACA program was not at issue in *United States v. Texas*, the multi-state challenge to DAPA and DACA+ that resulted in this early 2015 injunction, but nonetheless DACA appeared more unstable after that injunction. At public presentations, advocates urged DACA-eligible individuals to apply soon, while the program still existed, reasoning that it would be harder to take DACA away from those who had received it than to prevent new applications. Interviewees who had received DACA expressed concern that whoever succeeded Obama as president could rescind the program. When asked about his future plans during an interview, Dean, a South Korean DACA recipient, replied, "Instead of looking at a—at a long term—ten years or five years. I look at my future in terms of two years and how I could make the best of two years." Lupita, a DACA recipient, characterized DACA as "not so safe. You don't know what's going to happen. I don't really trust them. Like, oh thank you we have it for now, but don't get too used to it because it might be taken away. I'm like, 'Don't take it away.'"

With the benefit of hindsight, we can see how justified these fears were, and we can also see the prescience of the advocates urging individuals to enroll while they could. President Trump ran on a promise to rescind

DACA on day one, and his administration formally attempted to do so in September of 2017, confirming fears that the program was politically unstable. But courts later enjoined the Trump administration's 2017 rescission of DACA, focusing heavily on the reliance interests of those currently enrolled in the program. After court intervention, new DACA applications were disallowed but renewals were permitted for existing DACA recipients. Advocates had been right to encourage all eligible people to sign up while they could. Unfortunately, individuals skeptical about the program's stability were also right. The Supreme Court's 2020 decision preserving the program did not end the legal fight against DACA. When President Biden assumed office with the promise to retain and stabilize the program, the state of Texas sued the Biden administration for its continuation of DACA. In 2022, the Fifth Circuit Court of Appeals signaled that the state of Texas was likely to prevail on this argument, casting deep shadows of doubt over DACA once again.

But in early 2014, there was no program for which intended DAPA and DACA+ recipients could enroll. Facing the prospect that potential applicants either would become discouraged and, if DAPA and DACA+ went forward, would not apply, or would be tricked into paying to prepare applications that could not be submitted, organizations urged community members to remain informed, hopeful, and ready. At a community presentation in Los Angeles a few weeks after the injunction, the presenter described "Obama's new programs" as "on pause for the moment." She confidently predicted, "it is not a matter of, 'will that program happen?' It is a matter of when. It could be weeks, it could be months, even a year. We don't know exactly but we have faith that it will go forward." This perspective was echoed by other advocates, who characterized executive relief as on a "hiatus" and contended that community members should not worry about the injunction.

In fact, some advocates adopted a "glass-half-full" attitude, saying that the injunction gave both community members and organizations more time to prepare: "We have to . . . take this . . . small moment, rest, and ramp up again." In public forums and at document preparation workshops, advocates urged community members to gather documents proving their arrival dates and continuous presence, obtain copies of their criminal records, consider filing FOIA requests to review their immigration records, consult with a reputable attorney or a Board of Immigration Appeals–accredited representative, and save money for application fees.[38] At one workshop that our research assistant Elizabeth Hanna Rubio attended, this advice extended to documenting one's present activities; as she summarized the advice: "If you go to the doctor, make sure you get a receipt of your visit with the date. If you go to your kid's PTA meeting, get a letter from the teacher saying you were there." Advocates encouraged community members to remain engaged, stressing that the Obama administration created DACA, DAPA, and DACA+ because community members demanded them and that attending rallies, speaking to the press, and being prepared to apply were ways to pressure the government to grant relief.

Some interviewees accepted the message that the injunction was temporary. For example, one month after the injunction, Reese, an Orange County college student and Chinese national from Hong Kong whose mother was likely DAPA eligible, told us optimistically, "that ruling's . . . highly going to be overruled. So I'm not too worried about it." Other interviewees reasoned that it was in the country's economic interest to extend work authorization to those who were undocumented. Oscar, the restaurant worker introduced earlier, hoped to apply for DAPA. He argued, "DAPA is not just relevant to immigrants; it actually will benefit the whole country." Margarita, who was DAPA eligible, had devised a complicated strategy to become eligible for lawful permanent residency by applying for DAPA if an application window opened. After gaining DAPA, she would apply for advance parole, exit the country, and be admitted upon her return, so that she could later adjust status without needing to exit the country again and facing possible entry bars. She explained, "I would apply [for DAPA], even if the program is only going to be in effect for a short time. My plan is to be able to enter the country legally. So if I am able to apply and I get a work permit, then I will ask to leave the country due to an emergency so that when I come back, I will have a legal entry. Then, when my son grows up, he will be able to petition for me, and I will be able to qualify." Many people who hoped to qualify for DAPA, DACA+, another opportunity, or even an eventual immigration reform, heeded the advice to be prepared. At document review workshops, we witnessed would-be applicants coming forward with binders, portfolios, and folders of documents.[39] Lucas, an interviewee who was not eligible for DACA or DAPA, told us:

> I have four, five boxes completely full of documents. I have like, I have all my tax returns from the time I came to the present time. I have each one of those documents. I have my check stubs from the day I started until this very day. I have the records of my kids when I took them to the doctor. You know, my signature and that of my children are on it. So I have everything. Whatever they want. Just try me. Were you here that year? Here it is mister, ready. Just test me, I have them all here. So I have everything, but yeah. I don't know. In my case I need, or I hope for a miracle from God that in the next few years the senate says, "Well, we're tired of working so much evil, let's do something good." You understand me?

Such preparations incurred costs, in terms of money, time, and emotional investment.

Not all interviewees or participating organizations were invested in the rollout of DAPA and DACA+. Some rejected the hierarchy of deservingness that undergirded both DACA and these proposed new programs, instead advocating a comprehensive approach to dismantling illegalization. For example, at a March 2016 conference that one organization held in Los Angeles, participants expressed cynicism about reform, treating this as merely reshuffling those who would be considered "deserving" and those who would be criminalized and subjected to deportation. Similarly, at the 2016 May Day rally held in Santa Ana, there were no signs regarding DAPA or DACA, even though the Supreme Court was set to issue a ruling in *United States v. Texas*. Some interviewees critiqued deferred action programs and other immigration reform proposals for being exclusionary. Reese, a DACA recipient herself, for example, told us, "It's time to move on from [protecting DREAMers] and, like, say what can we do about the undocumented workers, the laborers, like, the lower-class unskilled workers or their parents, you know? We've been talking about how, like, ... DAPA excludes nontraditional families like the LGBTQ immigrants, because most of them don't have children. Or they're not married." Nicolas, mentioned in Chapter 1, noted how an encounter with law enforcement might not only disqualify him from DACA but also make him a priority for enforcement under Obama's Priority Enforcement Program.[40]

Among interviewees, there were also some who stopped paying attention to the DAPA/DACA+ litigation not due to political considerations, but simply because they were demoralized or decided that they could make do without legal status. For example, Tomás had collaborated extensively with an immigrant rights organization, but had been unable to secure status himself. Dispiritedly, he told a member of our research team, "Nothing has happened that will help me. The president has made a lot of promises. And nothing." Tomás did appreciate local measures to assist those without documentation: "The only thing that has happened—thank God—is that is the legislation by that [Assembly Member Gil] Cedillo about the drivers' licenses here in CA. . . . This is the only kind of document I've gotten." But, regarding federal initiatives, Tomás remarked, "I am disillusioned. Demoralized." In contrast, Catalina, a DACA recipient, and her mother Bertriz, who was likely eligible for DAPA, were more upbeat, despite the injunction. During a joint interview, Catalina remarked of her mother, "Look at her. She got a [driver's] license, she's like, I'm good. Because they've kind of already been used to living with minimal resources and even what we have is just like, it's nice to have the ID . . . because in California you can get like your state ID." While Catalina had benefited from federal policy, her mother had benefited from state law interventions. Some interviewees developed strategies to cope with illegalization. Samuel, for instance, planned to open his own business, which would not require work authorization.

The injunction, and would-be applicants' varied responses, demonstrate the sort of subjects that deferred action creates: individuals in legally liminal states, who are physically present for substantial periods of time, but whose presence and time are legally ignored. Their demands must be made to the very state that illegalizes their presence and that always possesses the power to rescind promised assistance. They exist "in a limbo within a limbo."[41] Accumulating documents, pushing for legal action, critiquing standard measures of deservingness, and taking advantage of subfederal forms of inclusion are all ways to work against the limitations of this subject position.

The experiences of Sonya, a DAPA-eligible community member and activist, further illustrate how the putative subjects of deferred action countered their own illegalization. Despite being undocumented, Sonya took on important organizing roles in an LA-based nonprofit, traveling to Washington, DC to lobby for immigration reform and speaking to the media on multiple occasions. In recognition of her deep commitments, she was invited to Las Vegas along with other activists to stand with President Obama when he announced DAPA and DACA+. She recalled, "For me the main event was the announcement—it was the possibility of having a dignified life. It was not having to accept so much humiliation—being able to go outside, being able to know that your rights—that no one was going to be able to trample on them anymore. And something else that was even more important—was [ending] that the fear I felt, many times, innumerable times, that I thought I would have to leave my children behind." Sonya also fought hard against the injunction, participating in a nine-day hunger strike in New Orleans in order to pressure the Fifth Circuit Court of Appeals to promptly rule on the federal government's appeal of the district court's injunction of the DAPA and DACA+ programs. Sonya and other activists hoped that the Supreme Court would lift the injunction during Obama's presidency, allowing DAPA and DACA+ to be implemented before a new president took office in 2017. Sonya considered the hunger strike a success: "The Fifth Circuit [Court of Appeals] released the case." At the time of our June 2016 interview, Sonya was closely watching the Supreme Court for its ruling: "Every Monday and Thursday, at seven o'clock in the morning, we are ready in case we have to leave the house running" to attend a rally about the results. Succinctly describing the interdependency between the US government and its noncitizen subjects, Sonya explained, "The Supreme Court has us waiting on DAPA."

A few days after our interview, Sonya received her response. With only eight justices, due to the February 2016 death of Antonin Scalia, the court had deadlocked 4–4, allowing the lower court's ruling to stand. The injunction would remain in place.

Navigating Uncertainty Post-DAPA/DACA+

On June 23, 2016, the day of the Supreme Court ruling and a key turning point in the 2012–2022 period, two members of our research team went to downtown Los Angeles, assuming that there would be large-scale rallies in response to the outcome. But at a rally that evening at the Federal Building, fewer than twenty-five individuals stood, wearing T-shirts with the logo of a community organization, holding signs that read "Stop Family Separation," and giving speeches about the impact of the Supreme Court decision on their lives (see Figure 3.1). One speaker stated, "We were about to see the light, and we went back into darkness," while other speakers threatened that their voting-age US citizen relatives would be able to express their outrage at the polls. Those holding the rally were surrounded by journalists from both the English and Spanish press, almost equal in number to those who were rallying. Participants then lit candles of hope and put them in a circle, announcing that people would be available for individual interviews. As the rally concluded, some participants broke down in tears, while others hugged each other, and the media filmed. Participants stressed that they would not give up, telling each other, "la lucha continua," the struggle continues, and one woman pointed out to a colleague that she had stood with those who were eligible even though she didn't qualify, so the decision really just repositioned her colleagues in the same place that she herself was in already. This woman insisted that they could continue to work together for a more just future. Another activist pointed out that President Obama's announcement of DAPA and DACA+ had divided the undocumented community between those who were eligible and those who were not. "Now," he concluded, "we are united again."

The rally participants' defiant attitude echoed the sentiments of those we interviewed or re-interviewed in the months after the Supreme Court ruling. This was a heady political moment. With the 2016 presidential campaign underway, Republican Donald Trump and Democrat Hillary Clinton had made immigration policy a key issue. Trump campaigned on the promise to dramatically restrict immigration and legalization opportunities, expand interior enforcement, and build a wall along the US-Mexico border. Clinton, in contrast, favored broadening immigration and legalization opportunities. If she were elected, there was some expectation that she would support comprehensive immigration reform. The fact that immigration was a central election issue and that the candidates differed so widely increased immigrants' uncertainty in the wake of the Supreme Court's tied decision.

FIGURE 3.1. Rally and news conference following the Supreme Court decision in *Texas v. United States.* Photo by Elizabeth Hanna Rubio.

Interviewees generally feared what would happen to them if Trump was
elected. Some called him a racist, and worried, as Mauricio, a Peruvian
immigrant put it, that "[i]f Trump wins, he will cancel all these programs
that help our community." Alfaro, the undocumented business owner mentioned earlier in Chapter 1 and this Chapter, compared Trump to Hitler,
arguing that Trump's statements should not be dismissed as rhetoric: "They
allowed [Hitler] to exist, and look at what he did." Some interviewees hoped
for a Clinton win, reasoning that she could appoint a ninth Supreme Court
justice who would be more open on immigration issues, that she would fight
for DAPA and DACA+ in the courts, and that she would promote immigration reform. Others were more cynical, recalling that Obama had failed to
deliver on his promise of immigration reform and contending that Clinton
would likely do the same thing. As Esperanza, an undocumented homemaker, explained, "Obama had the chance to install another immigration
reform when he was elected the first time, but he didn't. He had enough

Democrats in Congress, but I feel like now, they are not going to do anything. I don't know if Hillary will actually do something to help the Latino community."

Interviewees' emotional reactions to the outcome of the Supreme Court case were also mixed. Some, such as Sonya, who was quoted in the previous section, were deeply invested in the legal process and had hoped that the Supreme Court would lift the injunction, allowing them to quickly apply for DAPA or DACA+. Such individuals were devastated by the outcome. During an interview in the days following the Supreme Court decision, Blanca, one of Sonya's colleagues, cried as she spoke of the case. Blanca said, "Oh my goodness, I was waiting for this permit! [T]hey gave you the option to go to Mexico, and my mom was very ill in the hospital. Many of my friends, their mothers have passed away and they weren't able to go see them. I had a lot of faith that this [program] would be accepted. . . . Our dreams were shattered." Similarly, at a "DAPA Dialogue" that a Los Angeles community organization held after the Supreme Court case, participants described to the group how they felt upon learning of the decision: disappointed, frustrated, hopeless, sad, as though doors had been closed, and in the shadows. In contrast, other interviewees, though equally disappointed not to be able to apply for deferred action, said they had already given up on executive relief at the time of the injunction. Esperanza, who was quoted above, explained, "I saw this coming, I knew that they weren't going to give anything." Similarly, Alondra, whose situation was described at the beginning of this chapter, complained that politicians were simply using immigrants for their own ends as toys in a political game. She commented:

> I remember when Texas did the suit, I remember analyzing [the] sequence of events and I saw that the judges that were going to analyze the situation, the courts where it was going to go forward, were ones where the judges were Republicans. It was not going to pass in any of these courts. And it didn't pass. Until it arrived at the Supreme Court. I also, I said, "I don't know whether Obama came to an agreement with Alito or with Kennedy." I think it was Kennedy. Maybe Obama pressured them and reached a political agreement with them. Obama could have done it. Because he did it for Obamacare. And he has done it for other points that have been debated by the Supreme Court. But he didn't push for it for immigration.

Again, recall that President Obama did not push for comprehensive immigration reform in 2009–2010 and spent much of his early presidency overseeing the escalation of enforcement initiatives, including Secure Communities. Alondra's comment suggests that the public, especially non-citizens, took notice. All of the programs he rolled out throughout the rest of his time in office, such as DAPA, were colored by his initial ambivalence toward inclusive policies. This quote further conveys Alondra's (and pre-sumably other noncitizens') suspicion that, in contrast to political party narratives about inclusion (on the part of Democrats) and restriction (from Republicans), governing elites were actually making backroom deals over things like immigration and healthcare.

Fátima, who would have applied for DAPA had the program gone forward, related that after the injunction, she no longer focused on litigation over deferred action. She said, "I was always glued to the news, but ever since . . . they canceled that executive action, that was when I said, no more. Enough. Enough. It was supposedly very solid that it was going to go through, and for something like that to be canceled it means that there isn't going to be an-other opportunity. And ever since then I gave up." Repeated disappointments made her and others resist feeling hopeful, as a means of self-protection.

Regardless of their frustration with the continued injunction, many interviewees, particularly those closely affiliated with the organizations in our study, were determined to continue to organize for immigration relief, though their strategies differed. (For a discussion of organizations' strate-gies, see Chapter 4.) Some interviewees focused on the political process, reasoning that registering more voters sympathetic to issues important to immigrants, especially within the Latinx community, would increase the likelihood of defeating Trump, protecting DACA, and electing officials who supported inclusive immigration policies. As Blanca commented, "We are going to focus on the elections because many, many Latinos, Mexicans, and [others] in general are not registered to vote." The goal of such efforts was not simply DAPA but rather a broader form of relief, as Marisol stressed to us that, "if we didn't get relief for five million [through DAPA and DACA+], we'd now fight for eleven million."

Other interviewees were more cynical about the political process and saw initiatives such as DAPA and DACA+ as distractions that dissipated community activism. In the days following the Supreme Court ruling, speakers at the Santa Ana March for a Moratorium on Deportations advocated organizing to dismantle ICE and end deportations nationwide, actions that one speaker said were especially important in the absence of more widespread deferred action programs. Likewise, in an interview, Carla, who was quoted above, compared executive relief to gaslighting, saying that such programs allowed President Obama to deceive community members into overlooking his abusive actions in deporting immigrants. Carla explained:

> [Gaslighting is] something that people do in abusive relationships. For example, somebody is cheating on his girlfriend. She comes home and sees that—"I know you were cheating! You didn't answer my calls, and there's lipstick on your shirt" and all of that. And he's like, "No! I didn't answer because there was no service. And this lipstick—it isn't lipstick, it's actually catsup." And he's telling her that she's hysterical and he's already done so much for her and all of that, because she doubts her perception of reality and doesn't know what to do and ultimately ends up forgiving him. It's an abusive tactic.
>
> The way that I see Obama enacting DACA and also deporting people, I think is gaslighting on a massive scale. Because he is kind of wanting to be like, "Yeah, look what I've done for you! How dare you call me deporter-in-chief." And then deporting millions of people! And it is kind of destabilizing the reality of people.

This skeptical, almost disdainful, view of DACA stands in sharp contrast to the full-throated idealism expressed by the government officials who conceptualized DACA. Interviewees therefore resisted federal inaction not only by organizing but also by simply moving forward with their life pursuits, regardless of whether or not they were able to obtain work permits or lawful residency. In so doing, some interviewees took advantage of state and local measures, such as California laws permitting individuals to qualify for driver's licenses, health insurance, professional licenses, and in-state tuition rates, regardless of immigration status. (See Chapter 5 for a fuller discussion of subfederal initiatives.) To our surprise, a number of interviewees informed us that, due to such measures—which, as will be discussed in Chapter 4, were the result of tremendous activism by immigrant rights organizations, immigrants, and their allies—their lives had improved between the time of our original interviews, shortly after DAPA and DACA+ were announced, and the Supreme Court ruling two years later that allowed the injunction to stand. Some interviewees had developed strategies that enabled them to work as independent contractors, thus avoiding the need for employment authorization. Such strategies included teaching music classes at a church, becoming a florist, starting a catering business, working in construction or gardening, becoming a cosmetologist, and obtaining a small cart to sell soft drinks in local parks on summer days. Access to driver's and business licenses facilitated these initiatives. Indeed, as we discuss further in Chapter 5, even if they did not work as independent contractors, many interviewees mentioned that obtaining a driver's license increased their mobility, decreased their insecurity, and enabled them to avoid having their cars impounded if stopped by the police for traffic infractions.

Of course, being an independent contractor has disadvantages, such as job insecurity and lack of access to employment benefits. Moreover, state and local measures did not and cannot remedy certain aspects of illegalization, such as family separations, the risk of deportation, and the inability to travel internationally. And not everyone's life circumstances allow them to take advantage of inclusive measures. Samuel, for example, hoped to become a private accountant, but was unable to obtain certification from the IRS. Patricia, who had survived domestic abuse, supported her family cleaning houses and was unable to volunteer at her children's school because doing so required submitting to a fingerprint check, and she was afraid of the potential consequences. Nonetheless, the fight to advocate for, and then take advantage of, inclusive measures was an important means of resisting government-imposed uncertainty.

Just as the undocumented community was internally differentiated prior to the announcement of executive relief, so too did the legal prospects of those who might have been eligible for DAPA or DACA+ differ after these programs were suspended. For many, DAPA and DACA+ had been the only means of obtaining relief, however temporary, so in the wake of the injunction, they had no opportunity to legalize. Others, in contrast, had legalization prospects, such as a pending family visa petition, or a relationship that could be formalized through marriage, thus giving rise to the possibility of a spousal petition. Some interviewees had visited the offices of community organizations to be screened for DAPA or DACA+, only to discover that they were eligible for something else. Teresa, for example, had planned to apply for DAPA, but learned that she likely was also eligible for a U visa for victims of crime. An attorney from a community organization was assisting her in getting a police report that she needed for her case. DACA recipients felt renewed vulnerability, due to both the election debates and to the litigation over DAPA and DACA+. Carla, a DACA recipient, told us that she had "a fear that they will discontinue it. If Hillary wins, we are safe. But there is a possibility that it won't pass. That will be one of the first things that Trump [ends]—because he is not going to maintain DACA." Likewise, Vanessa, another DACA recipient, expressed concern "that . . . they might stop DACA, and they might stop giving the work permits to all of those . . . people that have . . . been brought to the US as children."

In November 2016, interviewees' fears were realized when Donald Trump was elected President of the United States. Some organizations urged those who were eligible to apply for or renew DACA to do so right away, before the program could be rescinded, while others warned against giving information to the US government by applying. Some community groups immediately shifted to deportation preparation and prevention, holding "know your rights" presentations and explaining what legal provisions parents needed to make for their children if parents were apprehended by ICE and their children left behind. One organization compared such work to earthquake preparedness. Even a naturalized US citizen with whom we spoke expressed her fear that, as a woman of color, she would be discriminated against. "I'm in limbo right now," she told us. In June 2017, the new Trump administration rescinded DAPA and DACA+ via executive action, thus ending the *United States v. Texas* litigation over the legality of those programs. As noted in Chapter 1, in September 2017, the Trump administration also issued an order rescinding DACA, an action that immediately gave rise to widespread protests (see Figures 3.2 and 3.3). Legal action by DACA recipients and their allies has resulted in the DACA rescission being largely enjoined, meaning that while DHS would not accept new DACA applications, existing DACA recipients were eligible to submit renewals. As litigation proceeds and as immigration reform bills (including permanent solutions for DACA recipients) have stalled in Congress,

'DREAMERS' CRUSHED

Trump to phase out protections for 800,000 young immigrants

President speaks of 'love for these people' and, with little guidance, gives Congress a deadline to help them.

BY BRIAN BENNETT
AND JOSEPH TANFANI

WASHINGTON — President Trump on Tuesday took action to strip away protections from deportation for roughly 800,000 people brought into the country illegally as children, giving Congress six months to write a law to resolve their plight.

Trump's long-awaited decision to get rid of the Obama era program for so-called Dreamers fit a pattern of his young presidency: As with other signature campaign promises on infrastructure, overhauling taxes and health insurance, he offered little guidance on what exactly he wanted done and left it to a polarized Congress to fill in the details.

If Congress fails, and the Dreamers are put in jeopardy of being deported to countries they know little of, if anything. Trump and

GLORIA MENDOZA demonstrates outside New York's Trump Tower against the president's decision. Protests broke out in many cities.

FIGURE 3.2. Front page headlines regarding the DACA rescission. Photo by Carolyn Cole of the *Los Angeles Times*. Reprinted with permission of the *Los Angeles Times*.

FIGURE 3.3. Photo of rally in Santa Ana protesting the DACA rescission. Photo by Susan Coutin.

uncertainty about the future of undocumented community members intensified. Meanwhile, restrictions on refugee admissions, enhanced interior and border enforcement, the separation of parents and children by ICE officials, detention of juveniles, and metering policies that force asylum applicants to remain outside of the United States created an increasingly hostile climate for immigrants, including those who could have obtained work authorization and temporary relief from deportation had DAPA and DACA+ been implemented. These developments, and the later pendulum swing toward less extreme immigration policies under President Biden, are explored in greater detail in later chapters.

Phantom Programs

DAPA and DACA+ were never implemented, but in some ways, this is precisely why they are worth examining. Both programs died an unceremonious death at the feet of a short-staffed Supreme Court and have largely been forgotten by the American mainstream. But as our findings demonstrate, the announcement and then retraction of these programs had a huge impact within the undocumented community. Expectations were raised, criteria for determining deservingness were articulated, some five million people were told that they could potentially obtain work authorization and temporary relief from deportation, another six million were told that they could not do so, and many who were potentially eligible to apply invested time, money, and emotional energy in preparing to apply. Yet, deferred action was an unstable form of relief, "only half" a measure, as Fátima put it.

The experiences of potential DAPA and DACA+ applicants provide insight into the nature of discretionary power and the state-noncitizen relationships that it brings into being. Individuals are "illegalized" through everyday practices, such as being fingerprinted before volunteering at a school or having one's car impounded due to lack of a driver's license. Such illegalization stems from racialized relationships that grow out of US intervention abroad and enable the exploitation of undocumented workers at home. Fundamental contradictions, such as that between the key role that immigrant labor plays in the US economy and the denial of work authorization to immigrants, are displaced onto immigrants themselves, making their labor and presence illicit. Such power relationships are naturalized through discourses of merit that mark noncitizens' lives according to their age at the time of immigration, the date that they immigrated, whether they have children, whether children were born in the United States or outside of the country, and whether individuals have been formally admitted to the country (which enables status adjustment without subjecting individuals to the ten year entry bar) or not.

Yet, immigrant communities fight back against the power relations within which they are enmeshed. Unauthorized immigrants and their allies have formed their own ideas of merit, critiquing state narratives of deservingness, drawing attention to the political nature of what are allegedly lawful processes, and denouncing policies as "evil," as Lucas put it, or as racially motivated. Interviewees resist uncertainty by moving forward with their lives anyway, working with and through local institutions where possible. Some interviewees are also activists, working in collaboration with community organizations. Applying for deferred action also was a means of resistance. DACA recipients used the relative stability of their status to force authorities to comply with their promises, and to render these material (through the issuance of work permits, for example). Through their visibility, DACA recipients made the underlying program more difficult to rescind, even as they highlighted the overly narrow criteria for deferred action relief.

DAPA and DACA+, though significant, are also ghost-like programs. Like a phantom, DAPA and DACA+ continue to haunt both immigrant communities and advocacy organizations, and court decisions regarding these programs continue to be cited in subsequent cases. Individuals who potentially could have qualified for relief know that an opportunity was created for them and then snatched away, while advocates experienced the challenges of gearing up for, and contending with the aftermath of, programs that did not go into effect.

Even if DAPA and DACA+ been implemented, their protective capabilities would have been phantom-like. DACA is illustrative. From the moment it went into effect in 2012, notwithstanding its concrete effects, it has felt somewhat ephemeral. It may soon disappear. In July 2021, a US district court enjoined DACA. That court temporarily suspended the injunction for those who had received DACA, but prohibited new applicants from receiving DACA. DACA easily survived early litigation challenges in 2012, but ten years later, the reasoning of the courts in the states' successful DAPA/DACA+ litigation challenge has been repurposed and turned on the DACA program. This is yet another iteration of the haunting phantom forms of DAPA and DACA+.

The mobilizations that have resulted in phantom programs are nonetheless significant, as shown by the remarkable longevity of DACA in the face of extraordinary political countermobilization by parties and interests with far more power than the DACA recipients themselves. What happens in the aftermath of DAPA, DACA+, and DACA itself will also depend on activist strategies, as we will see in Chapter 4.

FOUR

Advocacy

Sameer M. Ashar is a co-author of this chapter.

THERE IS NO SINGLE community of advocates and organizers but instead a mix of lawyers, organizers, activists, and leaders who engage in immigrant rights advocacy in Orange County and Los Angeles. Some are focused on individual cases (especially the lawyers) and others on local, regional, and national policy. Advocates did not see themselves as part of a single formation. Many were themselves of immigrant backgrounds. At times, some organizers and organizations collaborated; at other times, they remained separate, and perhaps even in competition for philanthropic and government resources. They had differing ideas regarding the sites and methods of effective advocacy, from electoral to legislative to direct actions and protests. They all experienced varying degrees of ambiguity, contradiction, and confusion as to how the state saw them and their clients/constituents. They grappled with aggressive frontline ICE agents, distant and sometimes unreliable allies within government, and judges and justices up and down the federal court system.

In the late years of the Bush administration and the early years of the Obama administration, as the enforcement regime came down upon the communities for which they advocated, the immigrant rights advocates we interviewed fought to protect individuals and keep families together. They exploited fissures within the immigration enforcement regime, and between levels and departments of government. They generated a rhetoric against the reality of enforcement through creative data gathering and media advocacy.

During the 2012-2022 period covered by our study, the entities and individuals engaged in immigrant rights advocacy have experienced legal liminality in different ways. Legal liminality—living in a state where one's presence is subject to temporary, discretionary, and easily revocable forms of official forbearance—is a tax. It casts a pall of existential dread on individuals deprived of permanent and lasting legal status, and also on their families and communities. But ambiguity, contradiction, and confusion also create openings for especially creative advocates who placed themselves in the gears of the deportation machine, nurtured solidarities, and forced alliances. The need to support, enact, and expand various forms of legal liminality put pressure on advocacy systems and forced changes in the ways that legal services were provided. The proliferation of individuals in liminal legal categories fostered new relationships between legal services and immigrant activist formations, especially in the more fluid advocacy environment in Orange County as compared to the more entrenched and better-funded Los Angeles context. This proliferation created new pathways of learning across localities.

To be clear, the expansion of legal liminality that occurred over the past decade is not a boon. Legal liminality in the enforcement era is unrelenting and existential. It compromises one's ability to learn, to imagine, and to provide. It has the potential to make travel treacherous and to keep one pinned in place, away from homes and families and nourishment. But legal liminality created new realities that some advocates were able to read, understand, and exploit. In so doing, advocates fought to preserve possibility and create moments of respite for immigrants and their families. This chapter focuses on their story in the context of the larger picture that this book presents.

Organizing in Spaces of Liminal Legality

As they work with clients and constituents in the immigration arena, advocates face legal uncertainty themselves. The programs they seek to implement may suddenly evaporate, as occurred with DAPA and DACA+. Policy changes may make the legal tools at their disposal slower and more precarious, making it difficult to advise their clients with certainty. In recent years, these constraints have forced advocates to develop creative approaches to working within the existing legal system even as their commitments to social justice have pushed them to imagine alternative, more just worlds. At the same time, their connections to people who are subject to illegalization have shaped the conditions experienced by advocates. As discussed in Chapter 2, the government officials trying to craft and implement programs like DACA sometimes worried about misinformation that some service providers (particularly *notarios*) might disseminate. In the same vein, advocates also expressed concern about having to compete with *notarios*, fearing that some *notarios* might take advantage of immigrants' desperation for immigration status.

This chapter draws on the theory of movement law developed by legal scholars Amna Akbar, Sameer Ashar, and Jocelyn Simonson. Movement law is "an approach to legal scholarship grounded in solidarity, accountability, and engagement with grassroots organizing and left social movements."[1] A key goal of this approach is to produce legal scholarship that is inspired by the vision of movement actors, rather than scholarship that reproduces conventional accounts of law and of social institutions. This approach is appropriate for our analysis of organizing. We have noted policy makers' *lack* of imagination when it comes to immigration reform. In contrast, the ways that organizers, like their clients and constituents, are impacted by legal liminality leads them to envision alternative, even abolitionist (or "protoabolitionist") social orderings. Akbar et al. identify four moves as core components of movement law: (1) paying attention to the forms of resistance employed by social movement actors; (2) "understand[ing] the strategies, tactics, and experiments of resistance and contestation" in order to "engage with new pathways to and possibilities for justice"; (3) shifting focus from courts to the tactics and knowledges produced by social movements; and (4) writing in solidarity with movements and recognizing movement actors' expertise.[2]

We complement our exploration of movement law with the notion of "shapeshifting" developed by anthropologist Aimee Cox, who describes the ways that Black girls living in a Detroit homeless shelter reinterpret the institutions and discourses that shape their lives. Cox writes, *"Shapeshifting* most often means shifting the terms through which educational, training, and social service institutions attempt to shape young Black women into manageable and respectable members of society whose social citizenship is always questionable and never guaranteed, even as these same institutions ostensibly encourage social belonging."[3] Shapeshifting entails reimagining these institutions through Black girls' accounts of their own lives and treating these accounts as sources of theory. For example, Cox pays attention to the ways that one of her interlocutors—Janice—defines the "missing middle." Cox quotes Janice's observation about "the way we always have to think about how other people see us and compare it to how we see ourselves. . . . They [TV, papers] miss the middle because they are always focused on the outside and making assumptions about who we are. There's a lot in the middle, but who's trying to hear that?"[4] In that example, Janice "shapeshifts" news media by defining these as institutions that see only external characteristics and that make assumptions, thus missing the "middle" that reflects these girls' self-understandings. Similarly, we identify examples of *legal shapeshifting*—the ways that organizers and advocates envision and enact law, legal institutions, and social justice. Treating their accounts as a source of theory also aligns well with the exhortation of Akbar et al. to recognize movement actors' expertise.[5]

Adopting a movement law perspective to study legal shapeshifting reveals whether and how advocates' strategies transcend the constraints that immigration law imposes on the imaginations of reformers and activists. As legal scholar Leti Volpp notes in an essay critiquing the Biden campaign's immigration platform, "Without critique, our vision is cramped: we naturalize subordination in the name of accepting what is pragmatic or reasonable, limiting the possibility for transformative change."[6] The organizations in Los Angeles and Orange Counties that participated in our study developed advocacy strategies in this imaginatively cramped environment. Attorneys and organizers had to respond to the enforcement dynamics that they encountered in Orange and Los Angeles Counties as Secure Communities came into full effect in California by 2011. Over the decade that followed, the expanse and pervasiveness of immigration enforcement methods—coupled with uncertain and easily reversed forms of executive relief like DACA, Temporary Protected Status (TPS), and the thwarted DAPA and DACA+ programs—gave rise to a "protoabolitionist" campaign (Not1More) that both energized and split the immigrant rights advocacy community.

Our analysis draws most heavily on (1) our fieldnotes regarding the rallies, "know your rights" presentations, document preparation workshops, and legal consultations that we observed; and (2) the interviews we conducted with thirty-nine advocates, six of whom were interviewed multiple times over the period from 2014 to 2018. The advocates we interviewed included executive directors, organizers, attorneys, policy analysts, paralegals, and youth activists, including those in organizations that did not have paid staff. These advocates worked for, or were affiliated with, twenty different organizations from Los Angeles and Orange Counties ranging from newly formed grassroots groups to established nonprofits with local, statewide, and national reputations. Reinterviews were conducted with a subset of organizations with which we had the most contact and where we had also been given permission to make observations. Interviews focused on the mediating role played by civil society groups in helping communities cope with a high degree of legal uncertainty and personal risk. We asked about the positions advocates held within organization, the nature of their work, their interactions with clients or constituents, their legal and political strategies, the coalitions they worked with, the local political environment, and their analyses of existing immigration law and policy. We also spoke with them about how their organizations were impacted by developments like the DACA program, changes in TPS programs, evolving narratives of "crisis" at the Southwestern border, the DAPA and DACA+ announcement (along with the injunction and rescission of those programs), the shifts in immigration policy as the nation was led by Presidents Bush, Obama, and Trump, and their plans for the future. Because interviews were conducted over the four-year period from 2014 to 2018, they provide an in-depth picture of how organizations were situated within the development and suspension of DAPA and DACA+ and the dramatic transformations wrought by the Trump administration. Strikingly, they also reveal continuities in the uncertainty of immigration law and the precarity of immigrant communities across this time period—continuities that we are able to contextualize in the broader temporal scope of our study.

Our dataset allows us to analyze how organizers, activists, and attorneys advocate around phantom programs with and on behalf of legally liminal clients and constituents. We found that the precarity experienced by those with uncertain legal status impacted organizations as well, in that they had to contend with a shifting legal environment, resource scarcity, rising anti-immigrant sentiment, and the ways that intensified enforcement harmed their clients' lives. Yet, the uncertainty served not only as a form of social control but also as a source of openings and an opportunity for redefinition. Organizations responded by developing at least three distinct strategies that varied depending upon the degree to which they preferred to work within or sought to transform existing legal structures. First, many organizations provided free or low-cost legal services to help individuals regularize their status when possible. These strategies helped individuals but generally worked within existing categories of deservingness, perhaps even reinforcing the broader immigration system, to some degree, by presenting well-documented and normatively appealing cases that immigration authorities could process efficiently. Second, organizations performed important policy work promoting legal reforms such as the DREAM Act, comprehensive immigration reform, and a wide variety of state and local measures. Reform work sought to move the boundaries of deservingness to make them more inclusive while largely accepting the notions of citizenship and alienage that undergird existing law. Third, organizations critiqued the legal order built around dichotomies between "deserving" and "undeserving" immigrants. Pivoting away from these false binaries, some organizations advocated for abolitionist futures, alternate universes that attempted to denaturalize the idea that banishment might be fit for anyone. Such critiques were made through direct actions that challenged both criminalization and racial hierarchies, thus creating opportunities for solidarity between immigrants and others who have experienced precarity. These strategies were not mutually exclusive, and in fact, many organizations pursued all three, but with different emphases. Collectively, these strategies shapeshifted existing legal and social institutions based on understandings grounded in immigrants' lives.

Mapping the Organization Landscape

The organizational networks in Southern California are spatialized in multiple senses. First, they span geographic locations. We focused on Los Angeles and Orange Counties, but each of these counties is part of broader jurisdictional networks—the state of California, the federal government—even as there is variation across neighborhoods and cities within these counties. Second, advocates' strategies are forged in relation to spatialized enforcement tactics such as checkpoints, detention centers, or roving police patrols. While some localities have embraced immigration enforcement and others have sought to protect immigrant residents, any policing activity can potentially impact noncitizens, who may have their cars impounded due to driving without a license, or who may face heightened police scrutiny due to race.[7] Indeed, bordering practices create racialized boundaries, making some appear "out of place" and therefore suspect in particular communities.[8] Advocates' work is performed in relation to these dynamics. Third, those who advocate with and on behalf of liminal legal subjects also occupy an interstitial domain in that they must devise legal and organizing tactics in a context characterized by uncertainty, resource scarcity, and unlicensed practitioners who take advantage of immigrants.[9]

Approximately half of the twenty-one organizations that participated in our study had offices in Orange County and half were based in Los Angeles, though in some cases, organizations had offices in both counties. Organizational reach varied. Some had a national or statewide presence, even though we met with them in Southern California, whereas others served only local communities. Organizational structures differed as well, and included established nonprofits, grassroots groups of student activists, and other recently founded groups. We interviewed advocates at organizations that had a broad mission, such as providing legal services to low-income people, as well as organizations that focused specifically on immigration. Nine of the groups that were part of the study prioritized serving API communities, four prioritized Latinx communities, and the rest served populations defined by other criteria such as income, refugee status, students, union membership, or being an immigrant regardless of ethnicity or nationality. As we detailed in Chapter 1, geography mattered for the organizations' work. Los Angeles had a more established network of immigrant-serving organizations than did Orange County, as well as a political environment that was more welcoming to immigrants. Spatialized enforcement tactics were pervasive in both counties. As detailed in Chapter 1, these included police stops, checkpoints, immigration raids, targeting of street vendors and day laborers, and surveillance at bus stops and on public transportation. (Chapter 5 provides further nuance regarding the distinct nature of enforcement in Los Angeles and Orange Counties.) Organizations were also differentially impacted by the liminal legality of the constituents they served. Some groups provided deportation defense and therefore had to provide legal representation in the adverse conditions associated with detention and imminent removal. Others supported the DACA application process as part of their broader mission of providing services to immigrant communities. And still others were made up predominantly of immigrant youth and engaged in direct actions with a goal of transforming policy.

The group of organizations that we observed fell on either side of a fairly straightforward divide between those that are primarily legal service providers and those that are engaged in various forms of community organizing. Yet all of the organizations that we profiled had in common—to varying degrees—certain kinds of services and modes of advocacy. Direct services typically were offered for free or at low cost, and due to resource constraints, organizations and groups prioritized types of cases that could be served at a high volume. In other words, working with readily identifiable segments of the undocumented or temporarily authorized population enabled advocates to maximize their reach with a limited investment of service providers' time. Such "simple" cases, as an attorney put it, included DACA, naturalization, immigration relief under the Violence Against Women Act (VAWA), U visas, family petitions, and green card renewal. A more limited number of organizations within our sample concentrated on time-intensive services in areas that were deemed high priorities for humanitarian reasons, such as asylum, deportation defense, and Special Immigration Juvenile Status (SIJS). Organizations generally did not work on employment visas, which were often out of reach of the low-income clients they served and were considered something that eligible individuals could afford to pay for by hiring private attorneys. In addition to providing individual assistance on the immigration matters listed above, these organizations engaged in organizing work, which included capacity-building activities (such as recruiting immigrant community members to take on leadership roles), providing legal education to clients, participating in advocacy coalitions around key policy issues, meeting with government officials to advocate specific policy reforms, and spearheading or participating in impact litigation, voter registration drives, media work, and direct actions such as protests and sit-ins. These activities engaged policy at the local, state, and national levels, and sometimes occurred in conjunction with other issues, such as parents' rights, unionization, or campaigns to raise minimum wage. Funding was also a consideration in service provision and organizing, as local, state, and foreign governments provided resources to subsidize certain services, while private foundations and individual donors supported some organizing work.

While organizations differed in their emphases, it was also the case that organizing groups generally gravitated towards the provision of direct legal services, and the legal service providers generally moved to support more grassroots advocacy and bottom-up policy initiatives. Marge, the executive director at a Los Angeles–based organization that focused on Central American migrants, explained this connection: "We continue to be an immigrant rights organization, and I think that the way that we have defined it for ourselves is that we have to do a little bit of everything. Right? That that's our model. That we're not just a policy organization that then has no connection to the community. But then we're not just a service organization that then doesn't really kind of change policy for long-term. You know. That we're all of that." This particular organization provided an extensive array of legal services but also was involved in campaigns to remove ICE from East Los Angeles and to stop deportations. Within our sample, even grassroots antiestablishment organizations were generally aware of the role and benefits of lawyers, even when organizations were ambivalent about the prospects that providing direct services could bring about meaningful change. Some organizations had extensive legal departments, others had only a handful of attorneys, and still others had no attorneys on staff but collaborated with other groups to hold citizenship fairs and other document preparation workshops.

Both service provision and organizing had to navigate the complexities of their clients' liminal status. For example, one attorney highlighted the need to combine legal services with social work: "You can't help when a client is living on the street and doesn't have enough food to eat, you have to deal with that need before you can provide legal services, and that is a real challenge in our work." Similarly, a Los Angeles–based organizer indicated that mobilizing community members required overcoming the internalization of criminalization advanced within the larger culture against communities with significant undocumented populations. Advocates agreed that the need for services vastly exceeded what they were able to provide. In the words of Gerarda, an attorney located at a Los Angeles organization, "The need is bottomless."

One key factor that shaped the relationships between organizations and constituents was the precarity that constituents experienced. Their prior immigration histories sometimes made them vulnerable to being deported if they applied for status. A speaker at a public presentation on immigration law told audience members (in Spanish), "If you have a deportation order after January first of 2014, you should not apply for deferred action. You would be a priority for deportation." Attorneys had to decipher clients' immigration and criminal histories by questioning clients and checking immigration and criminal court records. Many of their clients had experienced traumas that made them distrustful of the government and fearful of submitting applications for status, which further complicated this work. One attorney commented, "My clients are by definition traumatized, by the time they have gotten here, they have been through hell and back. Often times, I am the first person they have even told about the trauma that they have experienced. There [are] a lot of challenges relating to the role they play and trying to provide an effective legal service and helping them manage their other needs." In the period beginning with the initial DAPA/DACA+ announcement, and extending throughout the year and a half of litigation over the program, attorneys were also operating in a particularly uncertain legal environment with respect to potentially DAPA/DACA+ eligible clients. They practiced law in a domain filled with liminal clients and constituents.

To address the clients' and constituents' vulnerabilities, organizations sought to forge meaningful relationships with them. The director of an

Los-Angeles-based organization told us, "I think that people see [our organization] as a safe space, where they're protected, that is theirs." Advocates stressed that they tried to help clients and constituents overcome fear by educating them about the workings of immigration law. An attorney explained that her role consisted partially of translating legalese into understandable language: "It's also helping people understand what their conviction even is to begin with, and then how that may impact their case. There is a lot of translation between the legalese of the criminal documents, the impact for immigration purposes." Organizers claimed that such direct service gave their groups on-the-ground knowledge that more distanced organizations lacked. According to one attorney, working "on the ground" allowed her to build rapport with clients: "I try to calm their fears and clarify any confusion and just be accessible in that way. I don't think that I have the demeanor of a traditional corporate attorney and I think that helps to bridge the gap between their experience and my own." At the same time, as brokers who translated immigration law, advocates also in some ways served the government's interests, for example, telling clients to pay back taxes and to police their own behavior in order to avoid criminal convictions. That role, coupled with the uncertain legal environment in which they operated, sometimes complicated and strained advocates' relationships with clients and constituents.

A second factor informing organizational strategies was the scarcity of qualified service providers. At a public forum on human rights, an advocate at one organization estimated that in Los Angeles, there is one immigration attorney for every ten thousand immigrants. This speaker stressed that when qualified legal representatives are not available, unqualified ones fill the void. "They outnumber us," this speaker commented. Advocates who offered direct services adopted practices, such as giving their clients contracts describing fees and services, providing copies of all documentation submitted, and not guaranteeing results, to distinguish themselves from fraudulent providers. Organizations nonetheless had to take measures to manage the high demand for their services. One Los Angeles–based organization only offered consultations to a limited number of clients each morning on a first come, first served basis. At this organization, would-be clients regularly got in line outside the door at 5:00 a.m. in the hope of being seen.

This reality of the endless need for legal services provides context for how legal shapeshifting unfolds within these communities. Central to Cox's theory of shapeshifting is the concept of the middle—that space in which individuals must reconcile how they view themselves with how others view them. Our data expand on this idea by illustrating the complications associated with shapeshifting within an organizational context. In the context of immigrants' rights advocacy in Southern California, the organizations we interviewed aim to serve overlapping communities to which many different entities (including, as we mentioned above, *notarios*) offered services. Several advocates that we interviewed elaborated on the appeal of *notarios* to immigrants, most notably that *notarios* offer a simple message of hope grounded in promises of regularization that are difficult if not impossible to keep. By contrast, the advocates we spoke to often described the challenges of having to describe the nuances and contradictions of immigration policy such as DACA and other deferred action programs. Our point here is not that all *notarios* provided false promises about legal relief (though some did), but rather that the legal-services space that advocates occupy is filled with competing entities with different sets of motivations.

Unable to provide tidy and easy answers, advocates had to find other ways to assuage concerns and anxieties among constituents in the hopes of forging "meaningful relationships" and opening "safe spaces." Our team interviewed Pascuala, an advocate who works in Los Angeles and whose work includes expanding healthcare benefits to unauthorized migrants. When asked about the challenges of organizing immigrants, she explained, "You build and you build and you motivate and you motivate and you inspire. You need to have some type of victory at the end." She then went on to explain the challenges of motivating and securing victories within a community that struggles due to a lack of economic security. As she states: "We have to be very sensitive about how we organize those folks and how we engage them. We provide childcare. We provide translators and we try to make it as easy as possible. Meals, what have you. But a serious challenge is the struggle that people are facing." For many of the advocates, a defining feature of trying to reorient political struggles and social movements was to embrace rather than avoid the messy and difficult realities facing constituents. Many made efforts to see constituents not just as clients paying to file an application, but rather as individuals facing a range of challenges, and with a spectrum of skills that might be brought to bear to address those challenges. This orientation opened a range of organizing capabilities that organizations tried to support.

Many of these organizations were in formal and informal coalitions or networks with each other as they strove to meet community needs. Los Angeles has more direct legal service providers than Orange County. Generally, the Los Angeles organizers also have more experience. This is consistent with our assumptions at the start of this project—namely, that there is a much higher volume of need in Los Angeles, but also a developed nonprofit infrastructure and a variety of service providers to whom immigrant communities could turn. But we were struck by the networking and communication across the two geographic areas, particularly among the organizing groups. The diffusion of expertise and insight through these networks was complicated and circular. Orange County groups came to share the sophisticated policy goals and organizing methods used by the Los Angeles groups, mitigating the differential with regard to resources and advocacy experience, while Los Angeles groups learned from Orange County organizers who had to develop expertise on how to operate in hostile local environments, at some distance from like-minded organizations, and in contexts of great ethnic and national diversity among key constituents. Further, Orange County community organizers learned how to have statewide influence, so as to bypass the local political infrastructure that was largely hostile to immigrants. And groups from both Los Angeles and Orange Counties worked collaboratively at the state level. As noted above, some of the organizations that were part of our study spanned geographic boundaries, with offices in both counties (usually a primary office in Los Angeles and a satellite office in Orange County).

There were clear differences in the ways that the governments in Los Angeles and Orange Counties responded to immigrant community members, and this had implications for the way organizers worked. Los Angeles has an Office of Immigrant Affairs that provides services to immigrants in the county. Its website projects a welcoming attitude, stating, "The Los Angeles County Office of Immigrant Affairs helps all immigrants learn about available services for them and their families. We always help you with a

smile, speak your language, understand your culture, know your immigration concerns, and safeguard your information."[10] Consequently, some of
the organizations that we observed collaborated with Los Angeles County
and city government. For example, an API-serving organization had developed a youth empowerment program through the Los Angeles Unified
School district. Los Angeles had also established a Justice Fund to provide legal representation for Los Angeles residents who were in deportation proceedings. Despite this officially supportive attitude, however, Los
Angeles–based organizations sometimes complained about encountering
anti-immigrant attitudes on the part of officials. The Executive Director of a
Latinx-serving nonprofit told us, "on the surface [Los Angeles is] a lot more
friendly and a lot more warm but when you get down to the nitty gritty details, that there's still a lot of things to be worked out, and unfortunately
people still . . . are still deported and there's still hostility and issues, and
what happens is that the already fragile relationship between local law enforcement and the undocumented communities and immigrant communities, it breaks."

Los Angeles was also known for having a strong network of immigrant-
serving organizations. An Orange County advocate who was tasked with
developing such networks there commented: "In Los Angeles, there are
larger, more established organizations, many, there's actually like a sat-
uration of nonprofits doing a lot of different work." The presence of these
groups was important given the significant presence of immigrants in the
county. In fact, one Los-Angeles-based advocate referred to Los Angeles as
"a city of day laborers" where people performed "disposable work."

In contrast, Orange County was known for being less welcoming. At
the time of our research, the county had no office of immigrant affairs or
justice fund, though the City of Santa Ana, located in Orange County, had
declared itself a sanctuary for immigrants.[11] During the period of our research, foundations had provided funding to organize Orange County
coalitions of immigrant-serving organizations, a topic we return to below.
Politically, Orange County was more conservative than Los Angeles, even
though the number of registered Democrats has now surpassed registered
Republicans.[12] An Orange County advocate described the challenges that
this political context created for her work: "Orange County is a really

conservative county, and so the undocumented are not popular. The rhetoric is very strong. We can see that in the current political landscape. And that translates into services and funding, availability of funding . . . the ability to do work here in Orange County regarding these issues."

When compared to the Los Angeles–based network of established immigrant-serving organizations, Orange County had fewer such groups. César, an organizer at a labor organization that had taken on immigrant rights advocacy, explained why they had done so: "in Orange County, we have less nonprofit organizations providing services, so we have felt compelled to fill a void." Yet, changing demographics were beginning to cause these political winds to shift. An Orange County activist commented, "Orange County was always known as very conservative. It was always perceived as very white, so we do a lot of education—saying, 'No, no, no, it's actually, you know, majority minority. It's actually, people of color are the . . . majority.'" Nonetheless, Orange County was also known for local collaboration in immigration enforcement. César, who was quoted above, emphasized to us that "Orange County deported more young men than any other county in the state of California."[13]

Despite these contrasting organizing environments, the organizations that participated in our study also collaborated across county lines—and some organizations had offices in both counties. When we asked advocates to describe their organizational networks, they frequently mentioned organizations in other counties. Furthermore, from the point of view of advocates, Southern California was seen as a leader within the state of California and within the nation on immigration issues, and immigrants from other parts of the state sometimes traveled to Los Angeles or Orange County to seek services. Yet there were still county-level organizational disparities. We heard Los Angeles advocates discuss the need to expand their services to Orange County, but Orange County advocates did not mention a need to expand to Los Angeles. Staff at the Orange County offices of larger organizations sometimes mentioned feeling that they were underfunded compared to their Los Angeles counterparts. One such organizer related, "Sometimes I call the Orange County office, like the neglected younger sibling. They [the larger organization] didn't really invest in strategically planning or thinking about how different Orange County is from Los Angeles.

They would just kind of come down and do legal clinics and workshops. They had some staff, but they weren't really tasked to kind of raise the presence or to really build the capacity of the office." Despite these differences, advocates in both counties developed innovative strategies designed to address the needs of the particular communities they served.

The racial, ethnic, nationality, and language communities served by the organizations that participated in our study shaped the forms of advocacy that they practiced, too. The people served by these organizations differed in how and when they entered the United States, their eligibility for particular forms of immigration status, their historical relationships with government authorities in their countries of origin, their vulnerability to racial profiling, and their access to and consumption of various forms of media. Organizations designed their services, outreach, and policy work with such distinctions in mind.

The most salient distinction to which advocates drew our attention was that between Latinx and API immigrant communities. The different needs of each community shaped outreach and targeting efforts, and organizations often expressly organized their identities around these differences. Often, organizations were clearly marked as either Latinx-serving *or* API-serving organizations, but usually not as both. Organizations that targeted particular communities prided themselves on having on-the-ground knowledge and awareness of heterogeneity among the immigrant groups that they served. The director of an LA-based organization told us that in contrast to national immigrant-serving organizations, "We talk to people every day. We know exactly what the issues are. We know the diversity among the immigrant communities and so a lot of times the people that are debating in Washington, DC . . . [t]hey don't even know what they're talking about because they don't deal . . . with the undocumented population on an ongoing basis or ever. And they are leaders. They are the people that the president invites to the White House for advice and you think, oh my God!" API-serving organizations faced unique challenges that, according to advocates, were not always fully appreciated in broader immigrant rights coalitions. The most fundamental challenge was the linguistic diversity of API communities. Outreach efforts and service provision always had to take linguistic diversity into account. One organization developed a hotline to answer questions in different languages. This organization's vice-president of communications explained:

> I think we actually did an analysis in late 1999, early 2000s, because we actually had a great demographer who's been on staff that whole time. Looking at where or, you know, which languages, Asian language, ha[ve] the highest levels of poverty, highest levels of limited English proficiency where they focus in Los Angeles County. So we started, I think, with—I think it was Vietnamese and Chinese, and Chinese is both Mandarin and Cantonese. And then I think maybe two or three years after that started, we added Cambodian and Korean, and so those four have been the mainstays. We actually added Thai a few years ago in part because the Thai consulate came to us and says "Why aren't you helping our people? We need someone to help the Thai community." . . . We have kind of intermittently had a Tagalog speaker.

The quantity and quality of media coverage of immigration issues also varied depending on language. An advocate at an API-serving organization noted that, "When DACA broke, we did not have a fluent Chinese speaker who was experienced in immigration or [could] keep track [of] what was going in that community so that we would know, like, what the Chinese community [was] saying about that issue. We were just, you know, 'send stuff to Chinese media, work with them to get it out' but it was sort of one-way, like, we're broadcasting information but not in a certain position to really get a good sense of what the Chinese speakers are . . . saying, [or] the questions."

At the same time, this broadly conceived Latinx/API distinction obscured important nuances. For example, organizations reported that regardless of whom they targeted, they in fact served immigrant community members outside of their intended clientele. Marge—the executive director of the LA-based organization serving primarily Spanish-speaking migrants—emphasized the broad and diverse nature of her organization's constituencies: "All people are welcome here. I mean, I think that in some of our programs we've had Korean immigrant families that have participated, I think that in some of our youth groups, we've had African American families that have participated, and everybody's welcome." Likewise, an LA-based organization that directed services at API residents informed us that most of their DACA clients were Hispanic.

Assumptions about language and identity also shaped and limited advocacy efforts and efficacy, but not always in ways that mapped onto broad, stereotypical assumptions. For example, there was a common assumption that Latinx immigrants speak Spanish, while API groups speak many languages. This assumption, in turn, painted a picture of Latinx-serving advocates as moving through a unified and uniform linguistic environment while API-serving advocates had to navigate a more diffuse and resource-intensive polyglot landscape. While there was some truth to this generalization, it nevertheless obfuscated the fact that some immigrants from Latin America speak indigenous languages or Portuguese. The more extensive focus of resources on Latinx and API immigrants also erased the distinct experiences of Black immigrants, including, but not limited to, Afro-Latinx immigrants. Indeed, while the organizations that were part of our study fought against racism, xenophobia, and nationalism, these groups sometimes also reproduced stereotypes in their own rhetoric, as well as in their silence regarding the vulnerabilities experienced by Black immigrants. Some advocates' arguments regarding deservingness reproduced comments about immigrants' law-abidingness and self-sufficiency, tropes that appeal to respectability politics and that are steeped in anti-Black racism.

We also observed that API-serving organizations sometimes compared their own experiences to those of organizations that served Spanish-speaking immigrants, but the reverse was seldom true. Moreover, organizations that did not have a particular ethnic or nationality focus told us that the majority of their clients were Spanish-speaking or Hispanic. This is not surprising given that Mexico and Central America are the largest sources of immigration to Southern California. Yet, according to the Public Policy Institute of California, the majority of recent arrivals in California are from Asia.[14]

The extent to which the stigma associated with undocumented status posed an obstacle to organizing and legal service outreach also varied among communities. Organizations reported that in API communities, there was more stigma regarding being undocumented than in Latinx communities. A staff member at a Korean-serving organization stressed, "We're firm believers in the fact that you need folks in the community doing this work. Because the stigma, shame, some of the cultural nuances, you just can't go in no matter if you speak the language. You really have . . . to be a trusted community kind of presence."

The histories of particular API communities—such as Cambodians who were persecuted by the Khmer Rouge—produced heightened levels of distrust of government officials among their community members. One of our research assistants summarized her conversation with staff at a Cambodian-serving organization: "During the genocide, speaking out against the government meant torture and death. People bring these fears with them over the border and harbor a similar mistrust of the US government. Thus, for many people, signing up for DACA/DAPA/DACA+ essentially means exposing one's name and the details of one's life for a malicious force to do whatever it wants with that information."

Finally, ethnic diversity could be layered onto geography in ways that impacted outreach. A staff member at the Orange County office of an API-serving organization explained:

> In Orange County, like, you're holding something in Fullerton/Buena Park, like, not necessarily people from, you know, Garden Grove or Westminster are going to come. Like the—even the ethnic communities themselves are more kind of geographically sprawled out. And [they] don't necessarily kind of intermingle, and so there's a need for us to think strategically about that, right? So instead of holding one thing in the middle of Orange County where some people are for sure not going to come, like maybe we need to be more geographic and ethnic-specific, so hold multiple events or, you know, days of providing legal services.

These broad contrasts associated with serving API or Latinx community members hid other sorts of variation. As previously noted, they obscure the linguistic diversity of immigrants from Latin America, particularly those who speak indigenous languages. Undocumented Black immigrants were underrepresented within our study, which is partially a function of the nature of the organizations that agreed to participate in our initial organizational studies, but it also reflects a broader invisibility and racial silence within the immigrant rights movement.[15] As a self-identified "undocu-Black" participant observed at a student event attended by one of our research assistants, "Undocumented Black people get picked up twice as much by ICE than non-Afro-Latino people, yet I didn't get an invitation to this [student] summit until the last minute." While our study deliberately sought out API-serving organizations, we also observed a broader silence regarding the undocumented members of this diverse set of communities. The policy director at an API-serving organization commented, "A main challenge has been, how do we raise the visibility of API immigrants, educate the general public as well as elected officials and decision-makers, that not only are APIs the most diverse immigrant group in the US as well as California, but that there are 1.4 million undocumented APIs nationally, with the largest number being in LA and Orange Counties." Muslim immigrants have also been the targets of virulent policy initiatives, which ramped up visibly during the Trump administration. The bans imposed under President Trump on travel from certain Muslim-majority countries, built upon and extended the excessive policing and surveillance of Muslim travelers and immigrant communities that have been a pervasive feature of post-9/11 life in the United States.

Given such silences and invisibilities, it is not surprising that we encountered instances of anti-Black racism, stereotyping, and respectability politics on the part of some of the advocates we interviewed, even though these advocates largely fought against racism, nativism, and xenophobia. For example, as part of their efforts to help constituents develop strong immigration claims, advocates sometimes urged clients and constituents to police themselves in ways that conformed to dominant notions of respectability. An organizer affiliated with a Latinx-serving organization told us, "We [Latinx immigrants] are living with the African Americans in our neighborhoods, we are living with the Asians in our neighborhoods, we are there, the whites are there, so we are all together. So we need to follow the good examples, and to spread the good examples for the people to know how's the way to survive as an undocumented in this country and not having problems with the police or with ICE." This interviewee criticized African American neighborhoods for being "disintegrated" in contrast to "Asians," who, the interviewee said, were a better example to follow. These comments perpetuated the "model minority" myth of API success as well as anti-Black racism. While this was an extreme example, and was not at all typical of our interviews with advocates, these comments reveal ways that, by drawing on dominant notions of respectability and law-abidingness, the traditional immigrant rights movement narratives have reproduced notions of criminality that are grounded in anti-Blackness, as we saw in Chapter 3. Fortunately, the rejection of these narratives, and new efforts to build solidarity across racial justice and immigrant rights movements, grew over the period of our study.

Changes over Time

In addition to being a spatialized practice, advocacy and shapeshifting in this context is also a temporal one, impacted by the complex temporalities associated with undocumented and precarious legal statuses. In contrast to linear notions of time, in which actions or events produce predictable consequences, legal shapeshifting takes place in an overarching context of *uncertainty*: it is unclear whether existing programs will endure or be rescinded, whether proposed legal and policy changes will come to fruition or fail, and whether courts or policy makers will alter standard practices in ways that open doors or suddenly make advocates' recommendations obsolete.

Such uncertainty has two seemingly contradictory effects: on the one hand, there is a sense that nothing changes, that people simply have to wait in hope of a day when immigration reform will be approved by Congress or when a program will be allowed to go forward. Advocates often urged their clients and constituents to prepare for such a day by gathering paperwork, saving funds for application fees, and living in a way that produces a record of law-abidingness, financial solvency, and aspiration for a better life. On the other hand, there is a sense of continual change, that the laws and policies relied upon by advocates may shift at any moment and in unpredictable ways, or that events on the ground—such as a new influx of refugees or migrants—may require organizations to reprioritize. Both of these effects are visible in the way that organizations have operated during the DACA program, and even more acutely, during the attempted establishment and injunction of DAPA and DACA+, and the attempted rescission of DACA and various forms of TPS during the Trump administration. These forms of deferred action were designed to confer temporary stays of deportation and work authorization, thus putting a temporary end to the limbo of living as an undocumented immigrant. Yet the very name of this form of relief—*deferred* action—highlights the degree to which, even when these programs go forward, recipients experience continued uncertainty. At the same time, the various steps involved in creating these programs created a sense of legal flux. This was particularly true of DACA+ and DAPA. These programs were announced, a start date was identified, the programs were enjoined prior to the start date, the government and various advocacy groups appealed the injunction, but ultimately the US Supreme Court allowed a lower court's injunction to stand. DACA+ and DAPA thus never became concrete programs. They existed only as phantom programs. Yet, advocates had to adapt their organizing and legal strategies to each stage in the process through which DAPA and DACA+ did not happen. And these developments took place in a broader context of intensifying enforcement, local and state resistance, and shifts in migration patterns. Even as they were haunted by what might have been, advocates and constituents had to contend with the almost continuous enforcement and policy changes that were put into place.

The advocates and organizers we interviewed described immigration enforcement during the Obama years, particularly the 287(g) and Secure Communities programs, as pervasive and as having "really changed the DNA of our community." There was a realization that even in the absence of an enforcement spectacle, as in Arizona,[16] the effects were devastating for community members. Marge, the executive director of a Los Angeles–based organization reminded us: "[T]he sheriff department of the county of LA has deported more people than Sheriff Arpaio." In Orange County, advocates were particularly concerned about the ways that school discipline policies fueled a school-to-prison-to-deportation pipeline. As noted in Chapter 1, César—the director of the Orange County–based labor organization focusing on immigrant rights—laid out the discretionary moments in criminal and immigration enforcement wherein residents were given the harshest possible treatment: "at every single step where a kid would be processed, they would get the highest maximum sentence." One clear effect was that Orange County had the highest rate of juvenile referrals to ICE in the state in this period.[17]

In this heightened enforcement context, fear of the government became part of the DNA of communities. For example, a group of young organizers in south Orange County reported on their unsuccessful efforts to gather people for a "know your rights" session at a local church, a place that community members likely would have considered "safe" during earlier decades:

> We canvassed in the neighborhood. Like we were going door to door and letting people know. Um, and the day of the event, no one showed up, except the—because it was at a church—except the mass that had just happened before. Some of those people stayed, so that was our audience. But nobody from the neighborhoods where we canvassed at came out. So you know, then we had to process that experience.

Likewise, one interviewee said in 2015, "We're still not at the point where you can say an undocumented person can really be just calling the police and not fear for any repercussions."

Meanwhile, the lawyers with whom we spoke discussed structural injustice and disaggregation of federal responses during the Obama administration: "[ICE agents] remain just as aggressive as they have been, and they will fight every case. . . . I don't think most immigration judges are impartial. They can just side with the government, and you are having to sway both of them. So I don't appreciate and I find it really upsetting when the judge will play both the prosecutor as well as the adjudicator. It is really unfair." Another lawyer cast doubt on the application of the prosecutorial discretion regime unveiled by the Department of Homeland Security in this period: "There's a lot of rhetoric about them just targeting people with violent or serious crimes but that's not the reality. The reality is that the way they're going after our clients is pretty ruthless and they don't care. They're just targeting people for pretty minor offenses, even misdemeanors that aren't serious or violent." Further, protective state laws, such as California's TRUST Act, which prevents local law enforcement referrals to ICE for all but more serious crimes, were implemented in an uneven manner. Implementation often depended on local and even individual decisions, and state-level oversight of compliance was imperfect. Even as the wave of children arriving at the border from Central America in this period received media focus, an organizer commented on how this sort of attention was "criminalizing." For one advocate, the injunction of DACA+ and DAPA actually "wasn't much of a surprise. But it was still a letdown. We have to just, have to find a strategy now like we have in the past, through actions to coordinating the 'Shut

Down ICE' actions throughout the country, so it's just finding what do we do next?" Though the intensity of federal enforcement varied, and though state and local policies developed over time in ways that modulated the effects, the fact of enforcement was a constant.

In 2016, an organizer in Orange County talked about the context in which they did their work, "[L]ike a lot of what happened in 2012, 2013, 2014 . . . [A] lot of, like, the policies [locally in Santa Ana] and on the state level [were created] with, like, Secure Communities in the background, and Secure Communities in mind." Another organizer in Los Angeles said, "So that's the forever campaign, you know. Prepare against deportation, the forever campaign, never stop." The Obama administration modulated the operation of Secure Communities in the period from 2014 to 2016, ushering in the era of the "Priority Enforcement Program," which purported to give local governments more of a say in setting enforcement priorities in their jurisdictions. The number of people removed through the program did drop significantly during this time. But advocates continued to observe individuals who seemed low priority for enforcement getting caught up in the enforcement system. They also began to push harder against the priority frame itself, and particularly its adherence to criminal convictions as a sorting mechanism for prioritization.

The modest gains that advocates had made against the Secure Communities program under President Obama were reversed when the Trump administration restored the program to full operation and kept it in place through the end of his administration. To this day, the complete integration of immigration enforcement with criminal legal systems throughout the country continues to shape the conditions under which immigrants live and advocates operate.

Against this enforcement backdrop, the priorities of immigrant rights organizations shifted repeatedly in response to crises and potential opportunities for regularization. From 2012 through late 2013, organizations anticipated that the Obama administration would launch a legislative effort to pass a comprehensive immigration reform (CIR) bill that would have created a slow pathway to citizenship for many of the undocumented. In preparation, advocates analyzed draft bills, developed recommendations and critiques, and considered how to revise their services in light of this new opportunity. By the summer of 2014, immigration reform efforts had been derailed by bad-faith political messaging regarding an increase in the number of unaccompanied children arriving at the US-Mexico border from Central America. Although the overall numbers of unauthorized entrants during this period were at levels that were extremely low when compared to those of recent decades, restrictionist members of Congress and their allies in the anti-immigrant media system, particularly Fox News, cynically pointed to the swell in the number of unaccompanied minors as evidence that the border was "out of control."[18] Members of Congress used the manipulated data to justify their opposition to legalization opportunities, which restrictionists falsely but successfully framed in the public discourse as magnets for migration.

As the media largely amplified the restrictionist framing of the arrivals of Central American children at the border, some of the organizations that were part of our study prioritized providing services to these children. Marge, the director of an LA-based organization referenced earlier, told us, "Now this drastic increase in [unaccompanied children] this year has—and this drastic attention to the issue—has definitely affected our work. And again, it's an issue of, do we go into it and work on it? . . . We couldn't not work on it. If we'd not worked on it, we would not be fulfilling our mission." Prioritizing services for unaccompanied children required hiring staff with relevant expertise, visiting detention facilities (or collaborating with groups that did) and assisting children in being released to family members or guardians. Marge's organization works with a limited budget, so devoting resources to these activities inevitably risks taking resources away from other programs. Reflecting on her organization's experiences preparing for the DACA rollout in 2012, Marge describes it this way: "I mean, we had to hire people. We had to buy equipment. We had to, you know [order] supplies, etc. And so we have a model where we charge for services. That helps but it doesn't pay for everything. It's a gamble because you don't know what's going to happen—if people are gonna come, if they're not gonna come, if they're gonna end up paying what you're asking them." Given these resource constraints, the arrival of unaccompanied minors combined with the continued rollout of DACA and the pending rollout of DAPA created a kind of "perpetual crisis" for advocates and their organizations as they attempted to fulfill their missions without abatement.

In the fall of 2014, as the prospects for immigration reform faded, the organizational challenges became particularly acute. Organizers were aware that the Obama administration planned some sort of expansion of the type of enforcement forbearance it had initiated with DACA, but they were unsure of what the contours of that program would be. Facing needs for services on many fronts, organizations had to reprioritize in the face of uncertainty. Marge described such reprioritization: "We can do as much as we can to prepare, but [the DAPA/DACA+ rollout is] going to be overwhelming and we know that, you know, we're nonprofits and we survive through the kind of diverse way of fundraising, one of which is foundations, and foundations move really, really, really slow even in a crisis."

Between 2014, when DAPA and DACA+ were announced, and 2016, when the US Supreme Court allowed the injunction of these two programs to stand, the organizations that participated in our study were in limbo, but they were still faced with the need to make resource allocations in a fast-changing environment. From November 2014 when the program was announced to February 2015 when it was enjoined, organizations hired additional staff and, in some cases, opened new offices in an effort to expand services in anticipation of the deluge of new applicants seeking services. The DAPA/DACA+ injunction caught organizations off guard. One of our research assistants was on her way to observe a staff training on DACA+ when she learned the news: "On my drive into the training, however, I learned a federal judge had just (the night before) ruled against the enforcement of these executive actions." The training went forward as planned, but speakers were uncertain about what would happen next. Advocates reported that the injunction sapped the momentum that the DAPA/DACA+ announcement had generated. As an advocate explained during a March 2015 interview, "It kind of took the fire away." Programs, such as DACA, that were not covered by the injunction nonetheless slowed down, as immigrant community members feared that they would not see any form of deferred action. The spaces were advocates had to work were haunted by phantom programs.

In these haunted spaces where law remained unsettled, advocates had to contend with uncertainty and unpredictability. As one attorney explained, "I think the uncertainty is really hard. It's hard for us as providers to not be able to give answers to our clients, and it is hard for the community to not know what is going to become of their families and to feel like in the interim that they are being targeted, which they are." This attorney added, "It feels like a big scramble constantly to catch up with ever-changing potential policies." Once DAPA and DACA+ were enjoined, advocates placed their hopes on a successful appeal, which would allow the program to go forward at least as long as there was a Democratic president in the White House. At a 2016 public presentation on immigration law, a speaker from one organization described their strategic thinking this way: "Obama is president only until January, and the administration indicates it is ready to start the program as soon as it goes through, but even if the Supreme Court says it can go through ; if we get a new president, they may not be willing to do this program." This quote demonstrates the tenuous nature of the relief offered by DAPA and DACA+ and deferred action programs generally. In the case of DAPA and DACA+, the Supreme Court would have had to rule favorably, the Obama administration would have had to act quickly, and then the Democrats would have had to win the White House in 2016. Everything needed to break the same way, and in the absence of clarity regarding whether this path was feasible and whether existing programs like DACA were also in jeopardy, attorneys were not certain how to advise their clients. For example, in an interview in March 2016, a few months before the Supreme Court decision in *United States v. Texas*, an attorney told us that she had become reluctant to assist DACA recipients with advance parole applications, through which DACA recipients received official permission to leave the country and return. She worried that an adverse decision concerning DAPA while they were out of the country might complicate their efforts to reenter. While these programs arose from distinct executive actions as a matter of law, for many advocates it was hard to separate that fact from the grim political reality that the challenge and defeat of DAPA and DACA+ may well portend the same outcome for DACA.

During this interim period, when the fates of DAPA and DACA+ were unclear, one certainty was continued enforcement. In the spring of 2016, when immigration from Central America increased again, the Obama administration launched raids that targeted undocumented Central Americans, effectuating the administration's decision to prioritize recent entrants for enforcement. Evelyn, an advocate at an API-serving organization in Orange County, drew attention to the contradictory nature of such tactics: "I feel like DACA/DAPA was huge and so I'm very happy that he [Obama] did that. I know that he, despite that executive action, has done some of those, like, raids and stuff, so I have found that to be very conflicting. I feel like the immigration landscape is just a hot mess." Given this continued "hot mess," advocates sometimes shifted their focus from federal reform to local initiatives, such as sanctuary declarations, even as some organizations held vigils and hunger strikes to exert pressure for a favorable court decision regarding DAPA.

When there was still a possibility that DAPA and DACA+ would be implemented, advocates developed strategies to cope with uncertainty. One was to prepare for an application window that would open up between the time of a favorable Supreme Court decision and a new president taking office. To do so, some organizations held document preparation workshops, in which they prescreened clients for DAPA and DACA+ eligibility. In theory, if the window opened, workshop participants would be ready to apply immediately. A second strategy was to maintain hope and interest in DAPA and DACA+ as time passed. We attended multiple presentations at which attorneys stressed to potential applicants that executive relief was simply "on pause." Our fieldnotes include a summary of a training session led by a staff attorney at one of the organizations we were following. At the beginning of her presentation, she described the DAPA/DACA+ program as "in a pause," and reassured everyone that it was only a matter of time— and not a matter of whether—those programs would go into effect. She said, "Tenemos fe que esto va pasar." ["We have faith/hope that it is going to happen."] Here, the word *fe* has dual meaning: both faith and hope. Our fieldnotes continue:

> Though she made it explicit that it was not a guarantee, she still seemed confident that the new DAPA/DACA+ program would begin, perhaps in several weeks but definitely within a year. One of the attendees asked: *"Entonces seguimos arreglando nuestros papeles?"* ["So we should continue

organizing our paperwork?] to which she replied: *"Es buena idea que se preparen,"* ["It is a good idea to be prepared,"] and explained that since the program would allow relief to a limited pool, those who were more prepared had a better chance of obtaining DAPA/DACA+ quicker.

In advising constituents to continue preparing and in insisting that the program would go forward, attorneys and organizers staked some of their own social capital on the outcome of pending court cases. They did so despite their awareness that, as an immigrant rights litigation director at an API-serving organization put it, "as we've seen with admin relief, I mean it's just continuing, to change every day. Like one day there's an injunction, the next day there's a stay or whatever." Advocates had to develop the ability to adapt to such changing circumstances by encouraging constituents to maintain hope, even as the injunction demobilized would-be applicants.

In June 2016, the deadlocked Supreme Court decision allowed the lower court injunction of the program to stand. Though litigation over the program continued, the Supreme Court's decision to maintain the injunction strongly suggested that arguments about the legality of the program would be unavailing in the next stage of the litigation.[19] Facing indefinite limbo and likely litigation defeat of DACA+/DAPA, the organizations that participated in our study once again reprioritized.

By summer, the US presidential election campaigns were in full swing, and it appeared that Hillary Clinton, who favored DACA and supported more comprehensive immigration reform, and Donald Trump, who disfavored DACA and strongly espoused restrictionist policies, would receive their parties' nominations. Many of the advocates we interviewed threw their energies into naturalization campaigns and voter registration drives, in hopes of swaying the election outcome and securing immigration reform. Advocates pointed out that however disappointing it was, the outcome of the Supreme Court case realigned the interests of those who were and were not eligible for deferred action: both needed new legislation. Our fieldnotes at a Los Angeles rally denouncing the Supreme Court outcome summarize this voter outreach strategy. Members of a large Los-Angeles-based organization spoke at one of these rallies, using it as an opportunity to galvanize constituents for the purposes of punishing elected officials who opposed the deferred action programs:

Come November, we'll remember. The message that [this organization] is clearly putting forward is only a slightly veiled threat: US citizen children of all the parents who were denied DAPA will be voting in the upcoming elections and they will not be voting for the Republicans who are at fault for shutting DAPA down (whether you consider them at fault for bringing the suit in the first place or for denying Merrick Garland the possibility to be considered as a nominee for the vacant seat.)

Our fieldnotes go on to record how two other women in the community who would have been beneficiaries of DAPA reiterated this message. They said that the next few months would be committed to registering all eligible voters and to getting those who have the privilege to vote to get out to the polls in November.

In contrast, other organizations that were part of our study eschewed voting- and reform-focused strategies to instead prioritize more transformational approaches. For example, one youth organizer stressed to us that their goal had shifted to "social justice" rather than "citizenship." She explained, "In a lot of ways we identify with the African American movement for, you know, what is social justice? What does it mean to be a citizen when people are still getting profiled?"

In the fall of 2016, when Donald Trump won the US presidency, organizations found themselves in a transformed policy environment. Trump banned immigration from certain Muslim-majority countries, freely used xenophobic and racist rhetoric, encouraged police violence, launched an effort to build a border wall, reduced refugee admissions, promised intensified interior enforcement, promoted a widely unpopular policy of intentional separation of parents and children at the border, detained minors in cruel conditions that were denounced as "cages," and forced asylum applicants who presented themselves at the US-Mexico border to remain in Mexico while awaiting their court appointments. The Trump administration also backed away from deferred action as a temporary remedy, first rescinding DAPA and DACA+, then attempting to rescind DACA, as well as various TPS designations, before the courts enjoined these rescissions. Organizations that had prioritized naturalization and voter turnout confronted white supremacists, racialized and anti-immigrant violence, and a fearful community. The executive director of an Orange County group described how his organization shifted gears in this context:

> I think many immigrants, most, a lot of people of color, just woke up [after the presidential election] completely scared that their life is now in danger and that of their families, and although under previous administrations, like say, Mr. President Obama's administration, there was tons of people living in fear because he deported a lot of people, the way I've defined it is: there is undocumented folks, then there's like DACA, then legal permanent residents, then there's those of us that were born in the US but our parents were not, right? And the conversation that Obama had was in this spectrum, around undocumented folks, but now Trump is talking about, all the way over here, of people that—one thing that they were mentioning was the natural birthright [citizenship],. . . . The conversation ceased to be on this side [of the spectrum between undocumented folk and everyone else] and now it's all the way over here.

Organizations quickly launched "know your rights" workshops so that undocumented community members would know what to do if ICE came to their door, and assisted with deportation preparation planning, so that custody arrangements for US citizen children of deported parents would be in place. Sanctuary efforts intensified in order to prevent local law enforcement agencies from collaborating with ICE and to protect residents' personal information. Solidarity between immigrant rights and racial justice movements increased. And immigration lawyers continued to provide representation, but in a depleted legal context. During a 2017 interview, one attorney told us, "Things have changed and the things that we used to rely on as advocates don't work anymore, so I'm having less stuff in my toolbox to work with." These legal changes also reshaped organizations themselves. This perspective highlights that there are limits to the holistic approach described by Pascuala earlier, in which organizations provide constituents with translation services, food, and childcare to facilitate organizing efforts. Many of the advocates describe their work as resource intensive. As more legal challenges arise, the resources begin depleting. As legal terrain shifts, legal remedies are harder to find.

The shifting institutional landscapes and changing organizational priorities had implications for the staffing and structure of the organizations that were part of our study. Many of the organizations that participated in our study had pivoted to providing DACA services in 2012, and then continued to do so thereafter, but also spent the fall of 2014 and winter of 2015 gearing up to provide low-cost or free legal services to an anticipated onslaught of DAPA and DACA+ applicants. Organizations hired additional legal staff and organizers, opened new offices to expand their geographical reach, encouraged their existing staff to become accredited by the Board of Immigration Appeals so that they would have greater legal capacity, held training sessions for volunteer "community navigators" who could support the application process, and opened satellite offices to expand their reach to underserved areas. Additional support staff and media expertise were also organizational priorities within this preparation environment.

Organizations made huge efforts in a very short amount of time. During a January 2015 interview, Marge described these changes: "We are tripling in size over the next six months, which is a little overwhelming. Last year we had a budget of two million dollars. This year we're going to have a budget of six million dollars. . . . We are going from about thirty-plus staff to about seventy-plus, plus about forty temporary positions." This organization planned to open satellite offices in the San Fernando Valley, Inland Empire, and South Los Angeles while also partnering with other organizations to increase its capacity to support applicants for administrative relief. Marge explained, "We're really focusing on churches and schools and unions—anybody and everybody [including]consulates—that could really be key partners in this effort so that we could help even more people in some ways." We found similar patterns at other organizations, though the scale of such expansions differed. For example, one organization tripled its legal staff from two to six.

Not all organizations chose to work on administrative relief, however. One organization that participated in our study decided to continue to focus on detainees and unaccompanied minors, primarily because it was already at capacity with such work and could not take on anything else. The increase in arrivals of unauthorized migrants at the southern border at the time of the anticipated DAPA/DACA+ rollout put organizations in the position of making choices about which constituencies to serve.

For those organizations that did gear up for the new programs, the extensive preparations were something of a risk. Organizations were expending resources that they did not have in anticipation of a program that did not yet exist. Organizations had different funding models to support these efforts. Some planned to obtain grant funding in order to offer free services, others planned to offset costs by charging a low fee plus obtaining grant money, and still others—primarily those that did not anticipate preparing DAPA and DACA+ applications—recruited attorneys who would take cases on a pro bono basis. In August 2014, before executive relief had been announced, our research team interviewed a staff attorney at a well-known Los Angeles organization that did not focus its resources on one specific racial or ethnic community. This attorney described her worries about providing DAPA/DACA+ assistance: "I don't know where the resources are going to come from. . . . It's going to be really hard to do, so I am not sure where we'll fit in." Similarly, during a retrospective interview in 2018, a lawyer in Marge's organization recalled this time period: "There was nervousness on the board [of directors], some people got a little scared that we're going to bankrupt the organization by having stretched ourselves too thin for this thing that might never happen. It was scary."

Luckily for organizations, the state of California, some local cities, and certain foundations made funding available. The advocate quoted above explained, "Everything we do is contingent on funding and resources, so the fact that the state of California has been so generous and so effective in reacting to what is happening now with the new priorities and policies in DHS has really made it possible for nonprofits to step up and do a whole lot more." This perspective was echoed by Marilyn, whom we first introduced in Chapter 3 and whose voice has appeared throughout this book. From her vantage point as an advocate and lawyer at an API-serving Los Angeles-based organization, she explained:

> We got the funding from California, so that has helped a lot. I think without that, it would have been pretty tough just for the service provision, so we saw a good, steady increase in funds—a combination of foundation and government support from the Department of Social Services. It made a big jump, actually. We went from almost nothing—just grassroots fundraising—to about half a million dollars. I think Governor Brown,

advocacy groups, were saying we have to have this for immigrants; there needs to be some sort of funding to provide these services. And there was, back before Arnold Schwarzenegger, there was funding for citizenship. There had always been support for social services. So based on that argument, right now there's even more immigrants in California, so the big funding to support social services and legal services came about in 2015.

Funding supported not only individual services but also community partnerships and coalition-building. For example, the Orange County Community Foundation provided approximately fifteen small community organizations with funding in order to increase their services for specific immigrant communities, such as Vietnamese or Cambodians.

After this outpouring of energy, the suspension of DAPA/DACA+ and then the anti-immigrant policies of the Trump administration caused organizations to regroup. Changes were sudden and unexpected. An attorney recounted the way that the injunction disrupted his organization's efforts:

> We decided to launch this Valley office, primarily to do expanded DACA processing, and then later be in a position to do DAPA. And that was going to be the legal service that we provided indefinitely there. And then we would consider when we get back to providing the, you know, variety of services that we provide there. And we broke ground, literally opened the doors the day before the injunction! Literally! It was like, "Wait, wait, what?"

Organizations that had expanded their staffing and geographic reach had to repurpose these resources for ongoing work that had long been underresourced. An attorney described this process: "We just had to redirect them to doing everything else. More family-based immigration. We just really expanded our general intake capacity." The new office remained open. Another attorney told us how, during the Trump administration, when DACA was suddenly rescinded and the lawsuit challenging the rescission was filed, the focus of her own work shifted. She recounts the moment she learned that the district court had denied the government's motion to dismiss, effectively allowing the lawsuit challenging the DACA rescission to proceed:

> Our nature is to like, as soon as something happens, we pivot, we switch gears like the next day or the day of. Right? When we hear something. So I was focused primarily on family unity cases and, like, [the district court

issues its order allowing the lawsuit against the DACA rescission to pro-
ceed], and I remember, I was in the restroom when it happened, and I was
like, "Oh! Okay! I guess I'm switching gears!" I got out of the restroom and
started talking to [the policy director], and he was, "Okay, let's do this,
this, this."

The Trump years brought unprecedented levels of private and foundation funding to immigration serving organizations, but also required advocates to confront continuous adjustments to an unsettled legal landscape.
The constant legal flux and the surrounding political context unsurprisingly took a toll on advocates. First, advocates had to confront rising hate
crimes and racial violence. During a 2018 interview, Marilyn—the lawyer
at the Los Angeles-based API-serving organization—shared how she had
been affected by seeing white supremacists at rallies and protests: "Well in
one way I think it's important that we see that, so we know it's real, it's not
[just] a concept. Like white supremacy and white supremacists really do
exist, not just in like [a] faraway place, but actually in our community. So
that we are able to think of ways to combat that and also understand that
umm, this is what we need to work with. I'm scared." As Marilyn indicated,
organizing strategies were one way to overcome such fear.

Once the COVID-19 pandemic hit in March of 2020, conditions de-
teriorated even further. Attorneys already strained to the breaking point
now confronted border closures, a chaotic revision in administrative procedures, new challenges to maintaining contact with clients, and the need
to try to get clients out of detention facilities that had quickly turned more
deadly than usual.

Community Resistance

Through community-based resistance to both immigration policing and to
legal and policy reforms that left noncitizens in vulnerable circumstances,
advocates practiced legal shapeshifting to transform legal and social institutions. As we noted earlier, advocates who developed initiatives to resist
and challenge immigration enforcement have exhibited greater political
imagination than have the officials who merely granted undocumented immigrants a temporary reprieve from deportation through deferred action,

or who proposed comprehensive immigration reforms with slow and unwieldy pathways to citizenship, or who reinforced narratives of deservingness that left criminalization unchallenged. In contrast to these officials, advocates who worked closely with immigrant community members, including many who were themselves of immigrant backgrounds, were able to envision alternative worlds, in which the government's role in illegalization would be acknowledged, and in which government institutions would decriminalize communities of color.

There was sometimes a mismatch between advocacy efforts that sought to secure legal status and the social realities in which over-policing, labor exploitation, racism, and financial precarity were pervasive and could not be overcome through legalization alone. Nonetheless, community-based resistance sought to alter the legal landscape and historical context that otherwise situates illegalized residents in a spatial and temporal void, present but absent, participating in social life but cut off from desired futures by continued uncertainty. Community resistance has several characteristics that distinguish it from other organizational tactics: such forms of resistance are collective, they transcend distinctions between advocates and constituents, they combine lawyering and organizing, and they are shaped by tensions between reformist and abolitionist approaches. Above all, they are imaginative in envisioning that families could stay together, that local governments could push back against federal policies, that noncitizens could access justice, that individuals' multiple identities could be recognized and celebrated, that committing a criminal offense would not eclipse all other aspects of personhood, and that justice could be restorative.

A foundational facet of community resistance during this period was an evolution of advocacy norms from notions of deservingness grounded in a politics of respectability to protoabolitionist analyses that critiqued criminalization and sought to dismantle the immigration enforcement apparatus. Sammy, an undocumented migrant from Guatemala, grew up in the United States. He became an organizer for an Orange County–based group focused on immigrant rights issues. Sammy explained how his support for comprehensive immigration reform shifted throughout the process. He reported: "[Our organization was] very much in favor of CIR until the bill actually came out and we read it and we saw everything that was added into it. We had already been involved with Not1More [deportation], but after the senate bill came out, that's when we went head-on and we started getting very involved with it."

The "Not1More" campaign ties immigration enforcement to a broader history of institutionalized racism. This movement aims to eliminate deportations, incarceration, and the criminalization at the heart of immigration policy. Movement activists espouse these positions not simply as bargaining chips in a political process. They are not interested in advocating for reforms that might grant relief to some migrants and not others, thereby legitimating the suffering in immigrant communities. Sammy's perspective illustrates how some organizers shifted their focus from reform packages that included pathways to citizenship for *some* migrants to halting deportations altogether against *all* migrants. For people like Sammy, whatever benefits CIR offered came at too high a cost, excluded too many people, and simply perpetuated the broader systems of subordination and inequality that would continue even if large segments of the undocumented community could get on a path to citizenship.

Advocates at other organizations echoed Sammy's sentiments. Marc, an advocate at an API-serving organization in Los Angeles, told us, "When we saw immigration reform not happening around late 2014, we jumped onto the Not1More campaign. Immigration reform, it's not going to move forward, and that's how our members felt." A thread connecting both Sammy's and Marc's experiences with shifting toward more radical positions like Not1More was the recognition that effective advocacy required a negotiation within a fluid political environment. For Marc, some of the shift toward supporting Not1More was practical in nature. He explains that some in his organization "saw the need to have the API voice included in that as well as seeing the [fight for CIR] not necessarily going in our favor." Marc described the floundering of CIR as a "valid argument" that he could make to constituents as to why they should support Not1More. Sammy highlighted some of the concrete benefits that members of his organization would have to stop pursuing in order to embrace a Not1More platform:

> For every person, it's a different thing. For example, we used to have a member who moved to Chicago, so he hasn't been involved for a while. But when we decided that we no longer want to pursue CIR, and we are going

to go with Not1More, he was very conflicted. Not1More or getting a work permit isn't the same as actually, the same as having your documentation or your status, which is something he very much wanted, to have his status fixed. It had a lot to do with his career and he studied to be an accountant, but he couldn't actually get a job as an accountant, and had he actually had at least a [social security number], he could have actually had a good position, so for him it was conflicting personally, but he did understand[.]

As at least some advocates became disillusioned about the prospect of meaningful reforms, they became more committed to direct actions grounded in their connections with constituents. Indeed, organizers had a theory for why the administration was unable to end the enforcement assault on immigrant communities: "the president hasn't met with those personally affected, those that are personally persecuted by programs that are put in place." Organizers contrasted the distanced position of policy makers, such as President Obama, President Trump, and many of their advisors, with their own deep collaborations with undocumented community members. Amaru, an organizer in Orange County who focuses on faith-based collective action, put it this way: "We have people who are directly impacted by the structure. Because of the structure they have no voice. People who are undocumented can't participate in the system. They have a God-given right to participate. The fact that they don't have the documents or a path to it, that is not their fault. They are being directly left out and marginalized by the system."

Organizers' concern that policy makers were too distant from immigrant communities extended to incumbent nonprofit policy advocates. Here is Sammy again: "In the end these nonprofit organizations are funded, and they do have political ties. So they're not going to go up to the president and directly say, this is what you need to do. They are going to try to push something that could benefit, and then whatever comes up is going to be called a victory. As opposed to if there was actually people that are in these processes, having those conversations and leading those conversations." This account was consistent with the way that some government employees described their approach to immigration enforcement during the Obama administration. Recall David who joined ICE after spending a number of years in the Federal Bureau of Prisons. During the Obama administration, he explained, ICE's approach was to connect with organizations in different regions: "At the local level we made a real effort to make sure that our Field Office Directors would hold regular meetings with local NGOs [nongovernmental organizations] and that the NGOs could have the Field Office Director, the Deputy Field Office Director, the Assistant Field Office Directors. They had my phone number, they had my email address. You know, we didn't hide from them." These perspectives shared by advocates and government employees illustrate the complicated political economy in which advocacy unfolded. Stopping or curbing immigration enforcement policies involved a range of actors from the president to nationally identifiable political officials to field office directors and all those who worked within Southern California organizations. The individuals who were most system-impacted usually were not the ones at the table with government officials.

The interviews we conducted with policy advocates help round out this picture. Their comments demonstrate that advocates within organizations valued the access they had to government officials. Indeed, the access itself was an organization resource. But like any resource, it came with constraints, the kind that could have the effect of deterring some well-connected organizations from embracing overly oppositional tactics in galvanizing community resistance. Other organizations within Southern California did not feel so bound. Based on changes in grassroots sentiment about federal enforcement, many of the organizers with whom we spoke made a turn toward "protoabolitionism." One organizer indicated that this shift was responsive to "the demands of membership, the things that membership demands of the organization," Another said that their constituents "are not going to just take any small thing as a victory. It has to be something that will not further criminalize people. And again, that conversation started within the Not1More internal conversations and how do we have that impact?" This skepticism of the background hum of the Secure Communities/287(g) enforcement machine led to critiques of executive relief programs: "He [the president] can put a moratorium on deportations, they can stop the S-Comm, which would ... actually have more of an impact than just starting some program that would give some sort of relief. . . . Even though there is relief, certain people aren't going to benefit from that, and it's just with the deportation quota that is already set in place.

Once people are given relief, those that aren't are just going to be persecuted even more." Nicolas, an undocumented organizer who is a part of the same Orange County–based organization as Sammy, explained their internal prioritization of advocacy efforts: "That's why we are focusing a lot on campaigns like ICE Out of OC, because those are the types of programs that are going to start affecting those who are left out." The highly conditional and, in any event, failed efforts at passing CIR combined with the cramped visions underlying the various deferred action programs seemed to undergird a turn among organizers and their constituents against the acceptability of compromises on enforcement in exchange for legalization programs.

There was also a clear turn toward the logic of prison abolitionists, particularly on the part of grassroots organizations and youth. Reese, the DACA recipient from Hong Kong attending college in Orange County, put it this way: "I really want to see . . . no deportations. Like, just stop, and . . . just abolishing detention facilities. The prison industry is making a lot of money, but it's only because more communities are being criminalized. It's actually possible that we don't need prisons or detention facilities, and we find another alternative."

This protoabolitionist logic played out in Orange County in the debate among advocates regarding the shutting down of a detention pod for trans women. The lawyers at one organization that we studied had been instrumental in pushing, over the course of about a decade, for improved conditions for trans women detainees in the Santa Ana jail. This had the effect of markedly improving conditions for trans women in detention. But they were still in detention. During the period of our study, other organizations we were following began fighting to shut down the detention center in which the pod existed, rather than focusing on conditions. An organizer explained, "[Santa Ana was] the model facility for detaining trans women. So if we legitimize this project [and the resulting DHS memo citing to the facility as a model of "best practices"], then they're going to be creating detention centers across the United States like the one in Santa Ana." The pod ultimately was dissolved when Santa Ana ended its contract with DHS and declined to house immigrant detainees. Some of the detainees in the trans pod were sent to other detention facilities around the country which lacked protocols. While the shutdown of the facility was a victory for abolitionist organizers, one attorney expressed concern that some detainees were worse off on an individual level after the transfer.

This fight raised the fundamental challenge of abolitionist advocacy: assessing reforms to determine which advanced long-term goals and which sustained the system that advocates hoped, ultimately, to take apart. Jaime, a Latinx advocate at an Orange County–based organization, reflected on the tradeoffs involved with going after ambitious policy goals. Here is what she said about the trans care memo and universal defense proposals, "Sometimes you don't know what you've lost and sometimes you do. And sometimes you don't know what you lost until way later." Jaime was referring to an effort to convince local officials to support universal representation. After an extensive and heated political battle, a universal representation program was created as a part of a budget plan. She notes: "So we get universal representation. We allocate the sixty-five thousand dollars. In that same budget the police union got three million dollars." She continued "So that always struck me in terms of, like, was it worth it? The police union got so much money and so much more of the budget, so I don't know if it was a good trade-off."[20]

Efforts to dismantle the detention and deportation apparatus led advocates, organizers, and community members to devise extralegal forms of defense. That is, instead of merely providing legal representation and "know your rights" workshops to individuals who were in detention, organizers launched political and social media campaigns to pressure ICE to release individuals who were in detention facilities so that they could fight their cases from outside. Marc, an advocate at an API-serving organization told us of one such case in which a Sikh man had an interview with USCIS in order to obtain a green card, but unbeknownst to him, he had an outstanding Notice to Appear in immigration court. Because of that notice, he was taken into custody at the interview and was placed in detention. While he was in detention, his green card was approved, but he could not move forward in adjusting his status because he was detained. Marc stressed that his organization approached this case "in a more organizing way where we support . . . folks who are in deportation proceedings." To do so, Marc's organization worked collaboratively with the Sikh man's family, and "his children became organizers and his family became organizers to get him out of detention and, and figure out how to provide him a more sustainable relief." An attorney at another organization stressed to us that her organization had to exert political pressure to overcome family separations that resulted in children being placed in foster care. She told us, "Many local agents are not even familiar with the ICE directive on families [which sought to preserve parental rights][21] so people are being wrongfully detained, and release generally requires going all the way to Washington, which they do routinely and successfully." By organizing in collaboration with detainees' family members or "going all the way to Washington," advocates went outside of formal legal channels to exert political pressure and to transform the broader social discourse.

In addition to advocating outside of formal legal channels, advocates practiced community resistance through policy advocacy outside of the federal immigration law system. These policy initiatives are addressed in more detail in Chapter 5, but here, we provide some examples to illustrate how advocates creatively pushed to open state, county, and city doors when the door of federal immigration relief closed. One Los Angeles organization proposed state legislation—which went into effect on January 1, 2016—to extend eligibility for in-state tuition to undocumented students. Numerous organizations that were part of our study both advocated for, and helped to implement, A.B. 60, the legislation allowing undocumented noncitizens access to driver's licenses. To do so, attorneys and organizers advocated with relevant state agencies and participated in community forums organized in conjunction with state legislators who helped ensure passage of the bill. Organizations were also influential in shaping implementation of the California TRUST Act, which prohibits local law enforcement from honoring ICE detainer requests for immigrants who have committed low-level crimes. These organizations also successfully advocated for legislation limiting misdemeanor sentences to 364 days—a significant legislative victory for immigrant-serving community organizations because it allows immigrants with these misdemeanor convictions to avoid the severe immigration consequences that would otherwise attach to some of these convictions as "aggravated felonies."[22] Relatedly, they convinced the California legislature to create forms of post-conviction relief that allow immigrant residents to vacate their old criminal convictions—and eliminate related immigration consequences—where they were not properly advised about immigration consequences when they pled to the crime.

These state-level initiatives were combined with city and county-level work, for instance, to change LA County sheriffs' perceptions of immigrant community members, to secure legal representation for local residents who were in removal proceedings, to close local detention facilities, to obtain healthcare and medical insurance for undocumented community members and their families, and to pass city-level sanctuary resolutions. Advocates also supported initiatives that would improve immigrants' quality of life, such as increases in the minimum wage and support for victims of wage theft. State and local advocacy was carried out through partnerships between advocates and community members, and in solidarity with other groups, such as parent groups and organizations for low-income workers. Through this work, advocates sought to build a future in which distinctions based on legal status would cease to be meaningful.

The interviews we conducted with advocates suggested that authority to shape legal and political strategies did not reside exclusively, or even primarily, in the hands of lawyers and other elite organizational members. Indeed, one LA-based organization's decision to push for A.B. 540, the legislation allowing undocumented California residents to pay in-state tuition at state colleges and universities, was informed by the experiences of an undocumented intern who finished high school in less than three years and was ineligible for in-state tuition under prior law. In Chapter 3, we highlighted Joonseo's struggles to survive in the United States as an unauthorized migrant. He joined a lawsuit to force a community college to comply with California laws that provided unauthorized students with access to in-state tuition rates. But his story provides further insights into the advocacy landscape in Orange County. He shared his legal problem with a lawyer during a pro bono consultation service provided by an Orange County–based non-profit that serves the Korean community. Because of this conversation, that lawyer eventually reached out to the Los Angeles office of an elite and well-resourced national organization. Joonseo's inability to access in-state tuition benefits led to litigation that eventually was settled outside of court. This is a story about a resource-rich organization in Los Angeles lending support to a resource-poor Orange County organization, but this is also a story about how Joonseo's experience as an unauthorized migrant drew attention to access issues that might not register at a national level but affect a hugely important resource at the local level, namely access to community college.

This bottom-up approach to advocacy is at the heart of a movement law orientation. As articulated by Akbar et al., "grassroots contestation at the local level is central to the shape of law and legal entitlements" and stands as a response to a reality defined by "the limits of formal political and legal processes to represent the needs and preferences of working-class people, and the people of elites and corporations in defining the terrain."[23] Some of the people at the organizations we interviewed explicitly mentioned the value that unauthorized immigrants brought to the task of identifying problems and setting organizational priorities. Earlier in the book, we discussed the experiences of Eleana, a longtime advocate at an API-serving organization in Los Angeles, who noted the importance of empowering immigrants in organizing and advocacy efforts. In her experiences working with youth organizations, for example, Eleana observes that youth "really are engaged, like when we were discussing administrative relief priorities, the members were so engaged and they were picking up technical points. I think it's because of their lived experiences, things like parole-in-place or the three- or ten-year bars, I mean things that their families experienced, so they were totally picking up on that and offering really great suggestions." Although DACA and the other deferred action programs draw significant attention, Eleana's comments suggest that immigrants shaped advocacy around a broad range of legal issues that needed attention in order to improve the daily lives of undocumented residents.

Given the shortage of qualified attorneys and the dearth of immigrant-serving organizations in some areas, creative approaches to broadening access to justice were a key focus of the advocates we interviewed. Of course, organizations sought to increase the number of attorneys by hiring additional staff and training volunteers to be community navigators. As discussed above, this became more common as government support for these organizations increased during the Obama administration, and as private support increased under Trump. As mentioned earlier, some organizations supported universal representation initiatives, in which cities and counties funded legal representation for individuals in removal proceedings. These efforts to increase the availability of legal representation helped individual migrants but left institutional structures intact.[24] In addition, however, advocates pursued more transformational strategies including empowering immigrant community members by creating space for them to use legal tools to their own strategic ends, and dismantling systems that subjected noncitizens to surveillance and detention.

Strategies pursuing legal empowerment ranged from community-based education regarding immigration law to "know your rights" presentations that coupled information with consciousness-raising and organizing. Yupanqui, a staff member who focuses on organizing day laborers at a Los-Angeles-based organization described how this approach was implemented: "We modify the structure, like being an open, horizontal structure, so nobody is being less, nobody is being more, they are having their responsibility, their own power." Political organizing gave people access to justice outside of legal structures, enabling community members to participate in direct actions (such as lobbying, rallies, and sit-ins), regardless of legal status or citizenship. Sammy, the Orange County–based youth organizer, explained that in his view, even the act of immigrating without authorization could be considered a form of civil disobedience: "A CD [civil disobedience] is basically knowing that legally, there could be repercussions. But deciding that it seems, that for you, it's worth, like, as an undocumented immigrant just making that travel from your country to here, that is CD. They've already partaken in this kind of CD."

Restorative rather than punitive approaches to social justice and immigration experiences were at the heart of community resistance. Rodrigo, an Orange County–based youth organizer, told us, "With everything that we do we try to address the personal, and the individual healing that the person has to go through, but also the systemic transformation that has to happen so that the trauma doesn't happen again." Promoting systemic transformation took the form of protoabolitionist approaches that sought to counter criminalization, to build solidarity across movements, racial, and ethnic groups, to dismantle violent institutions, and to promote social integration regardless of immigration status. As noted above, efforts to remove ICE facilities from particular communities or to stop deportations were key to these efforts.

Protoabolitionist approaches sought alternatives to proposals such as comprehensive immigration reform legislation rooted in selective legalizations obtained at the price of greater enforcement, and deferred action programs that excluded many community members. One of our research assistants summarized the attitudes expressed by participants in a youth panel at a 2016 API conference in Los Angeles: "They were all very cynical about 'reform' and understood that it merely meant a reshuffling of who are the new deserving immigrants and who will be demonized and removed. Most had nothing good to say about DACA, and they didn't seem to care at all about whether or not DAPA would happen. They didn't mention it." Indeed, legal setbacks fueled efforts to look for solutions beyond conventional ideas of reform like CIR. At a rally on the evening that the Supreme Court delivered its deadlocked opinion in *United States v. Texas,* according to our fieldnotes, "The crowd cheered as [the speaker] said that the struggle to end the *polimigra,* to dismantle ICE and end deportations nationwide needed to continue." These protoabolitionist approaches both affirmed community understandings of the law—the term *polimigra* combines the Spanish term for police (*policía*) and the derogatory nickname for immigration enforcement officers (*migra*)—and promoted restorative justice by ending the distinctions that harmed noncitizens and communities of color.

Finally, community resistance enacted forms of intersectionality that transcended divisions between citizens and noncitizens, and between different racial and ethnic groups. Intersectional approaches developed for multiple reasons, including a convergence of interests between communities targeted by policing, proximity of members of these groups in the same neighborhoods, and solidarity born out of having common opponents. Marilyn explained, "the education that [our organization] tried to do with our youth, and even like older people, is, like, to understand the struggles of Black Americans, the civil rights movements." Overcoming these distinctions and owning these histories required questioning received categories such as "refugee," "economic immigrant," and "Dreamer." Sammy described how his Orange-County-based group was trying to redefine the criminalizing terms used to discuss unaccompanied minor children without recreating distinctions between deserving refugees and undeserving economic immigrants:

These children at the border, it is still a very real issue, right? But how do we take off the attention that they have? Because a lot of that attention is very criminalizing attention. It's that very narrow-minded thinking that they are coming here to invade when really, for the most part, they're coming here to reunite with their families or they're escaping that high crime and mortality rate that is in Central America. So it's just redirecting [the attention] in that way, and as well, combining both issues, that issue and Not1More, and make [them] into the same thing. You know, these kids are seeking asylum. And we, internally, have been speaking about maybe making the argument that . . . everyone is a refugee, you don't just decide, 'I am going to leave my country'. So making that argument and combining it, to make it just one issue. That is the way [that evolving events have] affected, not negatively, but . . . affected . . . how it is we . . . talk about it.

Sammy's comment that "everyone is a refugee," like calls for "citizenship for all," refuse the distinctions on which both criminalization and illegalization are grounded.

Conclusion

This chapter describes forms of advocacy devised by organizations that serve immigrants with liminal statuses in a legal landscape of great uncertainty. The imaginative nature of these advocacy efforts sharply contrasts with the proposals developed by officials who simply and almost imperceptibly shift the boundaries of the "deserving" and "undeserving," without dismantling the systems of criminalization and illegalization that make these community members' lives precarious. These advocates "shapeshifted" existing institutions by envisioning a world in which distinctions between citizens and noncitizens would become insignificant, and in which a criminal offense would cease to define individuals' futures. Just as the immigrant community contains a diverse range of individuals, these organizations vary by geographic location, community served, and advocacy goals. Not all organizations embraced protoabolitonist strategies, but there was a clear trend. The anti-enforcement approach embraced by a segment of the advocacy community during the Obama administration was extended to a much wider swath of immigrant rights advocacy during the Trump administration. This approach was exemplified in the growing criticisms of legislative deals involving the criminalization of many immigrants and the militarization of enforcement in exchange for legal status for a subset of the undocumented population.

One effect of the broad and creative mobilizations during the waning years of the Obama administration was the creation of coalitions that were able to hold on to narrow policy gains during the Trump administration, even in the face of an administration that had made it a priority to end these programs. DACA, though frozen in a form that permits no new applicants, has nevertheless survived for ten years, despite mounting legal challenges. Individuals with TPS also organized and litigated to preserve their liminal status under both presidents Trump and Biden, though the courts have been only sometimes protective of the rights of these liminal legal subjects. The community groups that participated in our study have also mobilized in support of state and local immigration defense programs, including the provision of legal counsel and bond funds, and in the closing of immigration detention sites. In addition, we found continued subnational experimentation on immigration enforcement issues, including the development of restorative justice programs in schools and localities and the development of rapid response infrastructure. The forms of advocacy analyzed in this chapter exemplify movement law in that they "offer hopeful visions for a more equal world, a theory of change aligned with engaging and enfranchising the grassroots, and a meaningful set of experiments and demands to move us toward those visions."[25]

FIVE

Location

DURING THE ADMINISTRATION OF President Donald J. Trump, the state of California was often portrayed as the vanguard of the "resistance." Over the course of Trump's presidency, California Attorney General Xavier Becerra sued or joined other states' lawsuits against the Trump administration more than one hundred times, including numerous challenges to President Trump's border and immigration policies.[1] On October 5, 2017, California's governor, Gavin Newsom, signed S.B. 54 (known as the California Values Act), limiting state and local cooperation in federal immigration enforcement efforts.[2] Numerous jurisdictions within the state of California also declared themselves immigration "sanctuaries."

Given the highly publicized efforts by and within the state in response to President Trump's immigration policies, one might surmise that residents of California who lacked US citizenship—even those who were undocumented—would not feel vulnerable on account of their immigration status. Yet, based on the interviews that we conducted in the years immediately preceding and at the beginning of the Trump administration, the experiences of residents in some California localities reveal a much more nuanced picture. Residents of Southern California navigated a variegated enforcement landscape. With federal immigration enforcement and immigration consequences tied so tightly to state and local criminal laws and policing practices, states and localities have significant influence over the implementation of federal immigration policy within their jurisdictions.

Even when those jurisdictions put distance between their own law enforcement goals and federal immigration enforcement efforts, residents still worried about policing practices that they often perceived as discriminatory, violent, and unjust.

In May of 2016, we interviewed Coni, a thirty-eight-year-old Guatemalan national and a resident of Los Angeles County's San Fernando Valley, who was undocumented but who had applied for a U visa based on her cooperation with the government in a criminal investigation relating to crimes committed against her. Though she had worked with a lawyer to file the necessary paperwork, at the time of our interview, she still lacked legal immigration status as she awaited the approval of her visa. A little more than two years earlier, in January 2014, California's TRUST Act went into effect. The law prohibited local law enforcement from detaining noncitizens based solely on a Department of Homeland Security request or detainer notice.[3] The state had also enacted A.B. 60, legislation that allowed for the issuance of driver's licenses to undocumented residents.[4] But Coni still expressed significant concerns about interactions with the police. She was not worried that encounters with police would lead to her deportation. Rather, based on numerous past experiences, Coni feared that police would profile her as undocumented based on her appearance, the kind of vehicle she drove, and her neighborhood, and that they would subject her to the humiliation and expense of impounding her car during a traffic stop.

Coni described several incidents when she was stopped by the police—supposedly for traffic violations, but in her view, due to her appearance and related factors. During several of these stops, the police impounded her vehicle because she did not have a driver's license—an inevitable byproduct of her undocumented status in the pre-A.B. 60 era.[5] She describes how these encounters have shaped how she talks about the police with her children:

> [My children have] seen how they've taken my cars away from me. How they've left us on the streets. And I've cried in front of them. And so that affects them as well. . . . I've tried to tell them about the police, that they do their job, that they don't kill us, that they don't hurt us, simply that they discriminate against us, or they stop us because we are Hispanic, but they aren't going to do anything to us. They aren't going to do anything

bad. Because it isn't good for [the children] to grow up with the fear that police are bad, or that they are going to kill them[.]

In Los Angeles County, Coni lived in fear of racial profiling and racial harassment by the police before Trump came to office, and despite immigrant-protective state and local policies. She recounts having to tell her children that, while the police will harass them, the police will not "do anything bad"—that is, "they don't kill us." Notably, Coni did not express fear that she would be the victim of unjustified use of deadly force by the police, in contradistinction to many Black residents of Los Angeles. Nor did she express fear of deportation at the hands of police—even before California and Los Angeles County adopted more stringent anti-cooperation measures during the Trump presidency. Her fears of deportation centered on federal immigration officers, and she avoided places where she might encounter an "immigration squad," but otherwise she did not seem to harbor constant or daily fears about deportation. Her fear of local police was real, and her experience legitimated that fear, but this was different in her mind from her fears of deportation.

The story was different for Imelda, an Orange County resident and college student with DACA, whom we interviewed in August of 2016. Even though she had a driver's license, she said that when driving around Orange County, she worried that she would "get pulled over . . . [and] if you get pulled over and you don't have your license, they assume you're undocumented. . . . I'm scared that that's going to happen. And then it's just going to ruin all my future plans . . . for grad school. I really want to go." Her fear was not only that she would be pulled over by police, but that police would assume she was undocumented and turn her over to immigration agents. In other words, her concerns were not just with discriminatory policing (though she shared those concerns as well); Imelda also worried about deportation as a consequence of ordinary interactions with police.

This difference between Los Angeles County and Orange County residents appeared throughout our interviews. Individuals whose lives straddled the county line observed the differing enforcement climates too. Mireya, a twenty-year-old Mexican national and DACA recipient, attended college in Orange County when we interviewed her in August of 2016. But she had grown up in Los Angeles County, where her mother and father still lived. Mireya, fair-skinned and college-educated, described herself as "white" in appearance. This was not true of her father, she said. He was also a Mexican national, but darker-skinned and not proficient in English. She spoke of her fears for him when he drove her to school in Orange County:

> My dad, whenever he's able to, he drives me here. So that worries me because whenever he leaves me here, I am calling like an hour later to figure out if he already got home. So I don't really like that. I have that whole stress, really, and then it's frustrating because I wish I could just be okay, you know, he just came, left me and now I can go about doing my own things, without having to look at the clock.

When we asked her why she worried, she said, "I fear him just doing something wrong [that would get him pulled over] . . . and I also fear profiling, especially when he goes to Santa Ana."

Imelda expressed the same fear for her parents, who were also residents of Los Angeles County. In her experience, "driving over there [in Los Angeles], it's like, if they pull you over, you just call someone that has a license. They pick up the car, and then they take you, and that's it. But here [in Orange County], it's like you don't have a license, then . . . they're supposed to arrest you."

These anecdotes highlight several themes that recurred in our interviews with Southern California residents in the mid-2010s. First, residents of both Orange County and Los Angeles County expressed concerns that police would target them or their loved ones for investigative stops based on race. Second, while residents of both counties expressed concerns that the police might give them erroneous tickets or impound their vehicles, residents of Orange County were, on balance, more likely to be concerned that these stops could lead to arrest and deportation than were residents of Los Angeles County. Third, the people we interviewed frequently expressed the view that the passage of California's A.B. 60 had made them less fearful and more protected from abusive policing practices. Fourth, no one that we interviewed felt that local policies could protect them from the direct actions of federal immigration officers. Finally, and consistent with the findings of other scholars,[6] we found that fear of deportation was often not the most salient concern that undocumented residents had when interacting with public officials. Concerns about mistreatment and discrimination were more routine. Sanctuary policies, which prohibit the sharing of information about immigration status, seemed to decrease residents' fears that contact with local police would lead to deportation, but these residents still felt vulnerable to local police due to their immigration status. Policies like California's A.B. 60—which allowed undocumented residents to apply for driver's licenses, thereby removing one of the most significant status vulnerabilities of Southern California residents—were at least as important, if not more important, than sanctuary policies in providing security for immigrant residents. But even A.B. 60 protections did not eliminate residents' perceptions that police unfairly targeted them for enforcement actions, particularly around traffic infractions.

These findings have both theoretical and policy significance. The findings confirm that local governments and other subfederal entities (from college campuses to tribal governments to states) have substantial capacity to affect the quality of lives of their immigrant residents through their choices around policing and crime. Scholars have documented the uses of state criminal laws to target immigrants.[7] In recent years, the Supreme Court has decided a number of cases that have allowed for substantial state-level variation in policies that indirectly shape federal immigration enforcement.[8] On the flip side, some legislatures have used their power to decrease unnecessary police interventions in certain communities by providing illegalized immigrants with access to documents such as driver's licenses. Such legislation removes incentives for law enforcement agents to pursue low-level, revenue-generating policing activity against residents they perceive as potentially undocumented. Some prosecutors have also used their charging discretion to avoid imposing harsh collateral immigration consequences on immigrant residents accused of crimes. Just as state criminal law can be used to target immigrant communities, state criminal law is a powerful lever for decriminalizing immigrant communities.

Similarly, because arrests by state and local police became in the mid-2010s the most common way that DHS identifies immigrants for enforcement, attention to policing practices—and the incentive structures around them—has the ability to transform the daily experience of immigrant residents. Because state-level convictions are now frequently central determinants of whether noncitizens face the immigration consequence of removal, state legislators can protect long-term immigrant residents from removal through recalibrations of their laws, including through decriminalization of offenses, adjustments to sentencing requirements, and creation of targeted forms of postconviction relief.[9]

The benefits of such state-level efforts extend far beyond immigrant residents for two reasons. First, since policing practices that target undocumented residents spill over to others—most often Latinx residents—who are more likely to be perceived as undocumented based on their race, neighborhood, and language or accent, both citizens and noncitizens benefit when law enforcement agents have fewer incentives to engage in racialized policing. Second, because Black and Latinx residents are often targeted for low-level, revenue-generating policing, any legislative or administrative efforts to decrease incentives for such policing can benefit these communities of color. The same is true with decriminalization and sentencing reduction efforts, which benefit everyone who has been targeted for these prosecutions and sentences.

This chapter illustrates these points through a narration of the experiences gathered through our interviews with Southern California residents. The chapter first describes the immigration enforcement regime in place in the jurisdictions covered by our study. Because the book's introduction provides a detailed account of federal immigration enforcement efforts, this chapter only briefly summarizes those efforts, and then turns to describing in greater depth the changes in law and policy at the state level and at the level of county and city governments in Los Angeles and Orange Counties. The chapter then explores how these laws and policies shaped the lives of immigrant residents of these counties.

State and Local Immigration Law Choices

The shifts in federal immigration enforcement policies that are mapped out in the introduction of this book form the backdrop for, and did much to shape, the experience of people living in immigrant communities in Southern California. Federal officials made significant shifts in enforcement policy in the period from 2013, the highwater mark of interior enforcement in the Obama administration, to 2017, when Trump took office and immediately began to follow through on his pledge to more aggressively enforce immigration laws both internally and at the border, to 2021, when President Biden assumed office on a promise to reverse Trump-era policies but proceeded much more deliberately (and at times, far too slowly and with significant state-level resistance) to do so.

In 2013, just one year after the Obama administration rolled out DACA, the Secure Communities program was operating nationally for the first time. The number of people removed from the interior of the country hit a record high, and many of those removed did not appear to fall under the umbrella of the administration's defined priorities. Some states and localities, including the state of California, sought to increase the distance between their own law enforcement agencies and these federal efforts by placing limits on information sharing and cooperation between their own agents and ICE.

In the period from 2014 through 2016, facing criticism from immigrant rights organizations both for detaining and deporting individuals who did not have criminal convictions and for the high levels of deportation more generally, the Obama administration began to modulate its interior enforcement efforts, shifting its enforcement resources to the border, even as DHS officials gave localities greater input in setting and implementing interior enforcement priorities. In November 2014, DHS secretary Jeh Johnson issued a new enforcement priority memo strongly reiterating the need to exercise discretion in enforcement and to deprioritize agency actions against individuals who did not fit the department's stated priorities. President Obama simultaneously announced the department's intention to expand DACA and to extend similar protections to some parents of citizens and lawful permanent residents. Even so, removals from the interior of the country remained high, and federal prosecutions of immigration crimes continued to set records.[10]

President Trump assumed office in 2017 with a promise to implement more aggressive immigration enforcement than his predecessor. Interestingly, during his first year in office, the federal government deported fewer people and prosecuted fewer people for immigration offenses, than it had every year under President Obama. Even after restoring Secure Communities to its full strength, attempting to rescind DACA, and revoking other enforcement priority systems, the Trump administration never matched Obama-era deportation numbers.[11] This counterintuitive result was largely the product of growing state and local resistance to the federal government's enforcement initiatives, though bureaucratic ineptitude may have played a role as well. The policies of the Trump administration brought new fear to noncitizens throughout the country, but the administration's anti-immigrant stance also prompted significant resistance from many pro-immigrant states and localities. This undoubtedly undercut the efforts of newly empowered federal officials to deport as many people as possible. And while the federal government could control the volume of federal immigration prosecutions, it had less control over how states and localities shared information and resources with the federal government. This turned out to be a crucial damper on Trump-era interior enforcement. (At the same time, the Trump administration was much more successful in its effort to implement harshly restrictive policies at the border, all but shutting down asylum processes and refugee resettlement systems through a combination of programs, and setting new records for the prosecution of misdemeanor entry at the southern border.)

California responded to shifts in interior federal immigration enforcement policy with significant laws and policy changes in the period from 2014 to 2017.[12] First, from 2013 onward, the state of California pushed back against full cooperation with the Secure Communities program in a variety of ways. On January 2, 2014, the previously mentioned California TRUST Act went into effect.[13] The TRUST Act limited the information shared by state and local police with federal immigration enforcement officials. Federal law forbids state and local laws that "prohibit, or in any way restrict, any government entity or official from sending to, or receiving from, [DHS] information regarding the citizenship or immigration status, lawful or unlawful, of any individual."[14] However, the California law avoided conflicts with this federal law by restricting state and local officials' efforts to investigate immigration status. Rather than limiting communications about immigration status, this law limited other kinds of information that could be shared about any individuals in state and local custody, such as their release date. Coupled with limitations on state and local compliance with detainer requests, these efforts substantially reduced state cooperation with federal immigration enforcement efforts. But the law contained numerous exceptions, most notably, allowing information sharing and detainer request compliance for individuals accused or convicted of a wide array of criminal offenses.

After the election of President Trump, the California legislature enacted additional immigrant-protective measures aimed at further short-circuiting state and local collaboration with federal enforcement efforts. These included A.B. 450,[15] which limited federal immigration enforcement agents' access to private workplaces, and A.B. 103,[16] an omnibus budget provision which imposed on immigration detention facilities certain requirements concerning conditions of confinement and attorney access. But the most significant law was S.B. 54, which imposed greater limits than the 2014 TRUST Act on state officials' coordination with federal immigration enforcement efforts, applied to a broader array of officials than the TRUST Act, and eliminated many of that Act's loopholes.[17] Under Attorney General Sessions, the federal government sued California's Governor Brown and Attorney General Xavier Becerra, alleging that S.B. 54 violated federal law and the constitution. A federal district court and the Ninth Circuit Court of Appeals rejected their claims, and the Supreme Court ultimately declined to hear the case.[18]

On July 21, 2014, Governor Brown also signed S.B. 1310, a revision to the California Penal Code limiting misdemeanor sentences to 364 days.[19] Among other things, this new law ensured that affected California misdemeanor sentences would no longer trigger the numerous negative consequences (including deportation and a lifelong ban on return) associated with an "aggravated felony" in immigration law.[20] A second law aimed at mitigating the immigration consequences of criminal justice contact required prosecutors to take into account the immigration consequences of plea bargains.[21] A third, A.B. 60, allowed for the issuance of driver's licenses to individuals present in the state without legal immigration status,[22] removing a significant incentive for police stops of immigrant drivers on the streets of California. These and other immigrant-protective measures initially emerged as a result of strong grassroots organizing and activism in opposition to Obama-era enforcement policies but were expanded with great urgency during the Trump administration. This collection of immigrant-protective measures marked a significant shift in California state politics. In the 1870s and 1880s, California led the way in anti-immigrant policies aimed at Chinese immigrants. In the 1990s, California was at the forefront of restrictionist activity with the passage of Proposition 187, which aimed to disqualify undocumented immigrants from state benefits, including public schools. By 2017, however, the politics of the state had shifted such that California was a leader in resisting aggressive federal enforcement efforts.

While California was developing legislative responses to changing federal immigration enforcement policies, many localities within the state crafted their own immigration enforcement agendas. Sometimes these complemented the state's more welcoming efforts, and sometimes they cut against those efforts.

Los Angeles County Policies

Los Angeles County is home to more than ten million people, which means that it has a population larger than forty of the fifty US states. Almost four million of those people live in the city of Los Angeles. Los Angeles County is a county of immigrants, where about a third of the population was born outside of the United States,[23] and more than half of the children reside with at least one foreign-born parent.[24] It is also a racially diverse county, with over half of the population identifying as "Hispanic" or Latino, and another 16 percent API, 9 percent Black, and under 2 percent American Indian and Alaska Native. Only about a quarter of the population of the county identifies as white.[25]

Given the diversity of the county's residents, it is unsurprising that Los Angeles has developed a reputation as immigrant-friendly. But Los Angeles County is also complicated. It is made up of 88 different cities, with hundreds of local governing entities. These cities are diverse in their sizes, demographics, economic profiles, and politics. The various political entities within the county, not to mention the various immigrant communities within it, have different views concerning the appropriate approach to the question of immigration enforcement. Jurisdictional fragmentation and political diversity, which complicate governance in Los Angeles County, prevent the formation of a unified, county-level policy with regard to immigration enforcement (or almost anything else).

The county's reputation as immigrant-friendly is partially due to the policies of the county's largest city: Los Angeles. In the 1970s, Los Angeles was a politically conservative city—its white elite dominating the city's political and economic scene. But during the latter part of that decade, a significant number of Central American refugees moved to the city. Many were left-leaning students, labor organizers, religious leaders, and others who had been persecuted for their political views and activities in their home countries.[26] The activism of these refugees, along with the city's Black and Chicano residents, helped generate a leftward shift in Los Angeles politics. One resulting policy was the Los Angeles Police Department's (LAPD) Special Order 40, which went into effect on November 27, 1979. This was one of the earliest "don't ask, don't tell" policies around immigration enforcement, instructing police officers not to investigate immigration status or "initiate police actions with the objective" of discovering an individual's citizenship status.[27] The policy also limited the occasions on which LAPD officials could communicate an arrestee's immigration status with federal immigration enforcement. The policy pre-dated the city of Los Angeles's brief declaration of its status as a sanctuary city in 1985 in response to sanctuary activism on the part of religious organizations—a choice that the city quickly reversed.[28]

But these protective policies and labels belied complexity below the surface. A great deal of collaboration persisted between the LAPD and federal immigration enforcement agents. In the wake of the 1992 uprisings that followed the police violence against Rodney King, for example, LAPD officials raided the homes of Latinx residents under the guise of investigating "looting." In reality, LAPD was operating in cooperation with the then-INS, turning over residents arrested for violating the proliferating and shifting curfew laws and other violations.[29] The investigation of the late-1990s Rampart scandal, which pulled back the curtain on the LAPD's racist and abusive practices, involved "incidents of corruption, intimidation and other police misconduct" that often included "exploitation of the legal vulnerabilities created by federal immigration regulations."[30] A special report commissioned in the wake of the scandal found that individual officers circumvented Special Order 40 "by either working closely with federal agents stationed around their field office, or simply calling in federal agents when they wished to intimidate a witness or make them 'disappear.'"[31] All of this occurred at a time when migration from Asia was increasing the size of API communities in Los Angeles. These communities were often more likely to be ignored rather than targeted by police,[32] but ignoring these communities carried its own costs. Notably, Los Angeles's Koreatown became what one scholar has called a "battlefield" in the "war" that broke out in the aftermath of the violence against Rodney King,[33] and API communities frequently became wedge communities in the city's fraught racial discourse. That experience shaped how API immigrants to the area navigated their relations with police, and with other racial groups in the city, in the decades that followed.

In recent years, however, and particularly in response to the election of Donald J. Trump, the city of Los Angeles renewed its official commitment to the protection of its immigrant residents. On March 21, 2017, in direct response to the restrictionist policies and rhetoric of President Trump, Mayor Eric Garcetti issued Executive Directive No. 20 with the subject "Standing with Immigrants: A City of Safety, Refuge, and Opportunity for All," in which he noted that "1.5 million residents of our city are foreign-born, and nearly two of every three Angelenos are either immigrants or the children of immigrants."[34] The Executive Directive lists many of the existing immigrant-protective measures operative in the city, including the LAPD's Special Order 40, a 2014 LAPD directive of noncompliance with ICE detainer requests in the absence of judicial warrants (issued in anticipation of the TRUST Act), and the LAPD policy against participation in the 287(g) program.[35] The mayor's March 2017 directive called upon the LAPD to reaffirm these orders, and also upon the "Fire Chief, the Chief of Airport Police, and the Chief of Port Police" to issue consistent policies and procedures.[36] The directive also made clear that city employees acting in their official capacity are prohibited from cooperating with, or using city resources or dollars to assist, civil federal immigration enforcement.[37] All managers and department heads are required to report on any efforts by CBP, ICE, or USCIS to enforce federal civil immigration laws with city support.[38] The order prohibits the unnecessary collection of immigration status information, directs the promotion of the work and resources made available by the city's Office of Immigrant Affairs, and requires each general manager and department or office head to designate an "Immigrant Affairs liaison."[39]

The actions of the LAPD, however, did not consistently reflect the city's, or the department's, official stances of noncooperation. Though the city's policy cited Special Order 40, that policy has always been imperfect in preventing police cooperation with ICE. For example, on June 24, 2016, the LAPD conducted a controversial joint operation with ICE, targeting underground nightclubs supposedly suspected of involvement in human trafficking. When these actions drew public criticism, the department issued a memo requiring that any coordinated enforcement with ICE receive prior approval from the bureau commanding officer and clarifying that all such cooperation (with the exception of existing joint task forces governed by written agreement and emergency efforts) "must be limited to the investigation of criminal activity, not immigration violations."[40] After the passage of S.B. 54, the LAPD issued a memo describing how their policies comported with the elements of the new, broader noncooperation law, though later reporting found problematic examples of continued cooperation.[41] While implementation may be imperfect, generally speaking, the trend at the city level has been in favor of noncooperation in federal immigration enforcement efforts.

Many other cities in Los Angeles County have taken immigrant-protective stances similar to that of (and as internally imperfect as) the city of Los Angeles. Cities including Culver City, Glendale, and Long Beach adopted immigrant-protective ordinances in the early days of the Trump administration, albeit with flawed implementation. The cities of San Gabriel and Santa Monica ended their contracts with ICE. But this protective stance is not universal throughout the county. The cities of Beverly Hills, Glendora, and West Covina, for example, took actions to oppose or contest California's noncooperation laws.[42] The patchwork of city policies complicate the enforcement climate on the ground in Los Angeles.

Further complicating the picture, the Los Angeles County Sheriff's Department (LASD) has a long tradition of official cooperation with federal immigration enforcement efforts—a tradition that continued throughout the period of our study. In 2005, the LASD entered into a 287(g) agreement with ICE that allowed ICE agents to screen inmates in county jails for immigration violations. That policy remained in place through the initial rollout of Secure Communities and was only rescinded when the Los Angeles County Board of Supervisors voted 3–2 on May 12, 2015, to end the county's contract with ICE.[43] In September 2015, the LASD's Manual of Policies and Procedures was updated to ensure compliance with the state's TRUST Act and other county-level restrictions on civil immigration cooperation.[44] But the Los Angeles Board of Supervisors continued to allow ICE to access county jails in order to identify individuals who were priorities for removal under the Obama administration's Priority Enforcement Program (PEP).[45] Therefore, county-wide policy changes left room for LASD collaboration with ICE. Only as the federal enforcement pendulum swung away from PEP back to Secure Communities at the beginning of President Trump's administration did the board of supervisors announce an end to this cooperation.[46] Throughout this time, LASD had law enforcement authority over tens of thousands of immigrant residents through their jurisdiction in unincorporated areas, their operational control of the county's jails, and their policing of Los Angeles Metro transit services.[47]

Even as LASD officially began to participate in the state's and county's implementation of protective measures in response to the Trump administration's policies, LASD's implementation of these measures was imperfect. In December 2016, the Los Angeles County Board of Supervisors passed a motion entitled "Protecting Los Angeles County Residents Regardless of Immigration Status" to address postelection fears in the immigrant community.[48] An October 2017 report from the county's Office of the Inspector General (OIG) identified several instances of LASD information and resource sharing with ICE that violated county policy and the LASD's own stated policies. The OIG's report found, for example, that ICE continued to occupy space in an LASD-run jail, notwithstanding the policies to the contrary that had been enacted by the board of supervisors in 2015.[49] OIG staff also observed LASD officials communicating with ICE regarding release dates, contrary to written policy and the LASD's public statements about its policy.[50] The office recommended better training and compliance with existing immigrant-protective policies.[51]

In the meantime, LASD exerted political pressure on California's legislature to narrow state-level noncooperation legislation. Following the 2016
presidential election, as the state legislature sought to enhance protections
for immigrant residents through S.B. 54, Los Angeles Sheriff Jim McDonnell actively opposed the broadly protective legislation originally proposed
and pushed for carve-outs to the legislation's noncooperation policies that
would allow for greater collaboration with federal immigration enforcement
agents. That law went into effect on January 1, 2018, with many of the carve-
outs advocated by McDonnell and other county sheriffs; McDonnell issued
a public statement of support for its passage.[52] On March 8, 2018, LASD circulated a memo detailing the changes of practice necessary to comply with
the terms of the new law,[53] but the department still faced regular criticism
from advocacy groups for failing to adhere to its written policies.[54] Indeed,
immigrant rights activists' opposition to McDonnell may have cost him
reelection in 2018.[55] These groups wound up deeply disappointed by Mc-
Donnell's successor, Alex Villanueva who had campaigned on a promise to
end LASD cooperation with ICE, but moved slowly on those efforts once
in office.[56] Many people who had previously supported him quickly became
frustrated by this, by his unwillingness to address problems of racism in
the Department, and by his exceptionally antagonistic relationship with the
Los Angeles Board of Supervisors, the Civilian Oversight Board, and other
governance entities. County voters replaced him with former Long Beach
Chief of Police Robert Luna in 2022.[57]

Orange County Policies

If Los Angeles County can be characterized as a county with many official
immigrant-protective policies, undercut by imperfect implementation and
cross-cutting city prerogatives, Orange County, on the whole, has favored
immigration enforcement cooperation to the fullest extent possible under
state and federal law. Yet, there have been some important, countervailing
trends in some of the county's largest cities, and those trends have shifted
the politics of the county as a whole.

Orange County is much smaller than Los Angeles County, but still
large, with more than 3.2 million residents in 2018, approximately 30 percent

of whom were foreign born.[58] Non-Hispanic whites are the single largest demographic group, making up about 40.5 percent of the population, Latinos are 34 percent of the population, API residents make up just under 24 percent of the population, and only 1 percent identify as Native American or indigenous.[59] As continuing evidence of Orange County's legacy of anti-Black racism, Black people make up a mere 2 percent of the county's population.[60]

Demonstrating their support for policies that maximize immigration enforcement cooperation, county officials entered into a 287(g) agreement in 2006.[61] Although the county sought broad policing authority, the federal government limited the scope of the agreement to a small number of officers in the county jail.[62] In 2017, when S.B. 54 passed, Orange County was the only California county with a 287(g) agreement still in place; the remaining counties had ended them in response to earlier statewide noncooperation policies.[63]

As California passed successive laws limiting enforcement cooperation, the county largely attempted to resist these restrictions. For example, while detainer holds in the county dropped after the passage of the TRUST Act, those numbers began to tick back up after 2015.[64] After California enacted S.B. 54, the Orange County Board of Supervisors initially passed a resolution stating that it would comply with federal law and encouraged cities in Orange County to do the same. Several months later, the board did an about-face, voting to direct county counsel to intervene in the federal lawsuit against the state of California on the side of the federal government.[65]

The sentiments of the Orange County Board of Supervisors, which long favored cooperation with federal immigration officials and opposed the state's efforts to decouple state law enforcement from immigration enforcement, were mirrored and amplified by the Orange County Sheriff's Department (OCSD) during the period of our study. Like the LASD, the OCSD polices a number of the county's cities under contract. Due to those contracts and its policing of unincorporated areas, OCSD patrols almost half of the geographic areas of the county, including almost all of the southern part of the county.[66] OCSD also has jurisdiction over the Central Men's and Women's Jails, the minimum security James A. Musick Facility, and the maximum-security Theo Lacy Facility. The latter two facilities housed ICE detainees pursuant to a contract with the federal government well into

2019.[67] The OCSD has a long history of collaboration with ICE and has tended to favor maximizing federal immigration enforcement cooperation whenever possible. Because this approach aligns with that of the majority of the Orange County Board of Supervisors during the time of our study, the board did not provide the same institutional check on unlawful collaboration as does the Los Angeles County Board of Supervisors over the LASD.

The pro-federal-enforcement-cooperation views of these key county actors mirror the pro-immigration enforcement policy responses of many Orange County cities. In early 2018, several cities in the county voted to join a federal lawsuit seeking to enjoin California's enactment of S.B. 54, and two others voted in symbolic opposition to the law. In Huntington Beach, not only did the mayor condemn S.B. 54,[68] (something that also occurred in Tustin[69]) but the city filed its *own* lawsuit against the state in opposition to the bill.[70]

In contrast, on December 6, 2016, the City of Santa Ana passed a resolution declaring itself a sanctuary city.[71] The resolution stated that Santa Ana "is a sanctuary for all its residents, regardless of their immigration status." Under the terms of the ordinance, city officials, including law enforcement, were instructed that they "shall not administer federal immigration law which is the exclusive authority of the federal government" and that they "shall not take any direct action against an individual solely because of his or her immigration status."[72] The ordinance outlines various policies the city will implement regarding immigration. As discussed earlier, one controversial consequence of the ordinance and related activism was that the City of Santa Ana phased out its jail contract with ICE.[73] Less boldly, and with some internal criticism for the unclear legal significance of the move,[74] the City of Anaheim declared itself an immigrant welcoming city in 2017.[75] But, as our conversations with residents of these cities revealed, these policies did not eliminate the negative effects of other policing policies and practices that increased the vulnerability of immigrant residents to fines, fees, arrests, and in some cases, even deportation. As our study came to a close, the politics of Orange County continued to exhibit notable shifts, and in the 2022 election cycle, Democrats gained control of the board of supervisors for the first time in 40 years.[76]

Experience of the Residents of Two Counties

How do people experience immigration enforcement policies on the ground? Our interviews with residents of Los Angeles and Orange Counties revealed how local immigrant residents perceived and experienced federal, state, and local immigration enforcement policy shifts. The interviews illuminated several themes. First, no matter where they lived, fear of deportation was only one of a long list of concerns that shaped immigrant residents' perceptions of their own safety and security in the place that they lived. Other factors that were repeatedly mentioned included the availability of work, the presence of community members perceived to be welcoming, and the attitudes and practices of local police during ordinary policing activity, particularly traffic stops. We find, consistent with other scholars, that undocumented status operated not as a distinct "master status" but as a status consideration that interacts in complex ways with other factors like place of residence, English language ability, race, class, gender, and dis/ability in shaping how secure undocumented residents felt in their neighborhoods at particular times.[77]

Some of our findings were predictable based on the account of changes in law and policy that we have already described. Many residents reported greater concern over the possibility of being targeted for immigration enforcement in Orange County than in Los Angeles County—and within those jurisdictions, expressed the greatest concern over being in places policed by the Sheriff or governed by more conservative leaders. But we also heard from residents in jurisdictions that were officially sanctuaries who continued to fear interactions with local police because they had experienced policing in these jurisdictions as racially biased, unnecessarily heavy-handed, disrespectful, and personally costly. Often, race was an important factor in determining how secure people felt in their homes, workplaces, and when moving about in public, with Latinx residents more likely than API residents to express concerns about being stopped on the basis of race, but with most nonwhite residents expressing concerns about how racial stereotypes tainted the way they were policed as they went about their daily routines.

Individuals living in areas with stronger noncooperation policies were less likely, on balance, to discuss a fear of deportation as a central preoccupation in their daily life. In light of the complex realities of immigration policy on the ground, it is unsurprising that the experiences of immigrant residents do not neatly track the stated policies of their state and cities. Organizers and lawyers were cognizant that subfederal protections from immigration enforcement were spotty and uneven across jurisdictions. In a June 10, 2016, interview, Willa, a lawyer with a Los Angeles–based public interest organization that also did a lot of work in the then-existing ICE detention center in Santa Ana, noted that TRUST Act implementation had been completely uneven, depending almost entirely on hyperlocal, and even individual, decisions. She told a story of a clear TRUST Act violation in a case involving someone who was apprehended in West Covina (a restrictionist-leaning locality in Los Angeles County) for a minor offense and who was reported to ICE contrary to TRUST Act restrictions. Many months after the passage of the TRUST Act, she still sensed a great deal of distrust between her clients and law enforcement (whether federal, state, or local) across the Southern California region.

Still, some of the findings in our interview data do track the general storyline of Los Angeles and Orange Counties as anti–enforcement cooperation and pro–enforcement cooperation, respectively. For example, Orange County residents that we interviewed were more likely than Los Angeles County residents to express concern that their encounters with local police would lead to their removal or that of a loved one. The contrast came through most sharply in conversations with several young adults who had experience living in both counties—people like Mireya, whose comments are captured at the beginning of this chapter. Mireya explicitly contrasted Orange County and Los Angeles County, generally concluding that she felt more concerned about her father's vulnerability to deportation when he was visiting her in Orange County than when he was in Los Angeles.

Similarly, a May 2015 interview with Imelda, a twenty-year-old Mexican national with DACA who, like Mireya, was attending college in Orange County, included the following exchange with Edelina Burciaga, one of our research assistants:

IMELDA: [Orange County is] different from LA. They have pulled my dad over [in LA] and they're like, "Oh, you'll get a ticket." But they've been lenient, I guess. Here [in Orange County], they're like, if you get pulled over and you don't have a license, automatically assume that you're going to be deported. I have been told that there are cases where the police officers actually have to do that process. So I'm just like, "Oh man, I wouldn't want my parents driving down here."

EDELINA: Have you talked to your parents about [this]?

IMELDA: My dad already knew that, or he was the one who told me that, and then I heard from several of the students who live in Orange County. Yeah, I don't know if it's true but my dad's like, "Yeah, that's what's going to happen if I get pulled over." I'm just like, "Dad, don't say that." But yeah.

The views of these college students coincided with the views of a number of Los Angeles County residents not enrolled in college, who, when asked if they worried about the possibility of being targeted for deportation while going about their daily routine, explicitly said that they did not. Some of these residents were not concerned about either local police or immigration enforcement officials. Graciela, a Mexican national in her thirties who was a hairdresser working while out of status, said that she had not had any negative encounters with local authorities, "nor," she continued in an August 2016, interview, "have I heard of family members who've had problems as far as being Latino, no, thank God, no." She describes passing through driver's license checkpoints without fear, because the authorities "are looking for . . . people who are, well, driving drunk."

Some Los Angeles residents' sense of security was undermined by the conduct of other residents, but not by concerns about immigration enforcement. For example, when Michaela, the fifty-two-year-old Mexican national and Los Angeles resident introduced in Chapter 1, was asked whether she felt safe going about her daily business, she replied, "No, there are places that I have to go through where drugs are used. For example, today. To get here early, I waited until it was 6.00 a.m., because I didn't want to be at the bus stop before 6:00 a.m., while it was still dark. That could be dangerous." Other middle-aged women, including Alondra, expressed concerns about crime and disorder, and Alondra cited lower crime rates as an important reason why she felt secure in her Woodland Hills neighborhood. In contrast, residents of Orange County tended to mention concerns about the risk of deportation if stopped by police, and ongoing immigration enforcement in their area, when asked what threatened their feelings of personal security.

Although some of the people we spoke with offered reflections of their own experiences that seemed to track the political divide between Orange County and Los Angeles County, much of what we learned in these conversations suggested a much more complicated picture. There were several reasons for such complications. First, within each of these jurisdictions, residents have to navigate a geographical patchwork of overlapping jurisdictions. This patchwork includes passing through and interacting with restrictionist localities, agencies, and individuals in Los Angeles, and with more immigrant-inclusive localities, agencies, and individuals in Orange County. Second, across jurisdictions, sheriff's departments tend to favor relatively robust immigration enforcement cooperation, and this attitude has a dampening effect on efforts to create immigration sanctuaries, even in relatively immigrant-friendly jurisdictions. Third, the focus on immigration-related sanctuary provisions in some ways misses the mark on what matters to a resident's sense of security and belonging. Many of the people we spoke to do not live in daily fear of removal—either because they do not think that it will happen to them (a statistically justifiable assumption), or because they are philosophical about their ability to cope with that disaster should it befall them. One surprising aspect of our conversations was the extent to which concerns about law enforcement focused not on fears of deportation, but on fears about being treated disrespectfully or being exposed to costly, low-level policing practices that many residents believe are focused upon immigrant communities. Fourth, and relatedly, other aspects of daily life are just as important to most residents as a jurisdiction's public stance on enforcement cooperation. When asked to describe how secure they felt in their neighborhoods, cities, and counties, many participants focused less on policing and more on factors like the availability of work for people without documents, the presence of a robust community of similar background to their own, and their sense of whether the people they interacted with in their communities welcomed or exhibited discriminatory attitudes toward them.

Immigrant residents develop complex and nuanced understandings of their vulnerability to policing and immigration enforcement based on their own experiences. Depending on their precise location, their own personal characteristics, and the government officials with whom they are interacting, they might feel safe from the threat of deportation even within more pro-enforcement jurisdictions, and they are also aware of the risks that face them in jurisdictions that bill themselves as sanctuaries. The residents of any city or town in Southern California are subject to multiple (and sometimes competing) enforcement policies and practices that overlap in the same physical space. The Orange County Board of Supervisors' restrictionist preferences govern in the same geographic space as the City of Santa Ana's sanctuary ordinance. Community college districts and state colleges and universities are public spaces that have their own immigration enforcement policies in place, which are often much more immigrant-protective than the policies of the surrounding cities and county. The LAPD has long maintained official policies of noncooperation around enforcement (although the policies have sometimes been breached). But people who live in Los Angeles must routinely pass through cities with more restrictionist policies and practices, and cities within Los Angeles County employ their own police forces with their own laws to administer and policies to follow.

In a July 2016, interview with Alondra and Carla—a mother and her college-aged daughter, both Peruvian nationals—the two discussed local variation within Los Angeles County as they perceived it:

> ALONDRA: We are living near here. It is a small apartment, but we are in a peaceful atmosphere. This zone of Woodland Hills is an area where not many immigrants live . . . at least, Hispanic ones. Because there are people from Vietnam and India. There are quite a few Jewish people in this area. But immigration, in the sense of conducting raids, doesn't come to this area. Nevertheless, the people who live in Van Nuys, or Reseda—
>
> CARLA: Or even in Canoga Park, where we lived before.

ALONDRA: —they live in constant fear, constant terror that one day they can be captured.

CARLA: Remember when you went shopping in Vallarta and they were there?

ALONDRA: I went shopping in Vallarta, which is a shop in Canoga Park. And the people in that shop were scared and said, "Don't go there because the *migra* is there. They are going down Sherman Way. Don't go there."

SUSAN: Wow.

ALONDRA: They live in constant fear.

CARLA: They don't have many white friends to help them. We do have a lot of white friends to help us.

For Alondra and Carla, whiter neighborhoods were less likely to be targeted for immigration enforcement, and therefore safer for them. Notably, this sentiment directly conflicted with views expressed by other people that we spoke to—people like Karina, who expressed greater comfort in the predominantly Latinx neighborhood of Cudahy where she grew up, than in the whiter and more affluent Orange County area where she now lives. But Alondra also made clear that she distinguished herself and her situation from many Mexican and Central American immigrants, whom she viewed as having distinct experiences from her own.

There were also places within Orange County where undocumented residents felt protected from immigration enforcement initiatives. A few students spoke of their campuses as spaces largely protected from immigration enforcement, and as a relatively safe haven in Orange County—something that is also consistent with formal campus policies. Lupita, a Mexican national with DACA whom we interviewed in August of 2016, worked as a bus driver on a college campus in Orange County. She frequently drove past police officers, and it sometimes caused her to tense up, but she combated that fear by telling herself, "I have DACA and I have my license and I'm driving okay." Yet, as Imelda and Mireya noted above, even when students felt safe on campus, they remained fearful when they or their relatives drove from LA County into Orange County.

Katrina, a college-aged Mexican national, also talked about avoiding the city of Costa Mesa (including its famed South Coast Plaza mall) for a long time after that city passed a bill to maximize enforcement cooperation with federal immigration agents. Indeed, several people mentioned Costa Mesa as a distinctly unwelcoming and potentially risky place to visit.

High-profile changes in federal immigration policy also shaped how immigrant residents felt, regardless of state and local policies where they lived. For example, notwithstanding Los Angeles County's immigrant-friendly reputation, well-publicized federal immigration enforcement efforts would trigger heightened concern among the county's residents. The Obama administration announced planned enforcement actions against recently arrived Central American migrants in the summer of 2016. Joaquin, a Guatemalan national and US college graduate, spoke in July 2016, about warning his Los Angeles–based family not to open the door for uniformed officers unless they had a warrant. He noted that his family generally tried to avoid talking or thinking about immigration enforcement because it was beyond their control, but at times, he used his knowledge of current events to warn his family about heightened risk. He said, "I was like, oh hey, I have to go home and I have to tell them about this because it's important for them to be aware of what's going on. You know, they were shocked. . . . I mean, it's difficult to, to talk to them about immigration because they, they really don't want to talk about it."

Importantly, concerns about immigration enforcement were interwoven with, and sometimes much less significant than, other worries of residents, including discriminatory policing, concerns about public safety, and demeaning treatment by employers and service providers. The possibility of removal was a source of stress, but people were not contemplating departing the US voluntarily, nor was fear of removal the defining concern of everyday life. As Joaquin's comments suggest, many immigrant residents did not focus excessively on risk of deportation—something that was a statistically improbable event—in navigating their daily lives.

County sheriff's departments played a significant role in shaping conditions for immigrant residents in both counties. Lawyers and organizers in Los Angeles County viewed the Los Angeles Sheriff's Department as much less immigrant-friendly than the LAPD, less likely than the LAPD to work with them to develop immigrant-protective policies, and more likely to turn residents over to ICE. When we asked Marge, an advocate who had worked for many years for a large immigrant-serving organization in Los Angeles about the attitude of local law enforcement toward immigrants, she responded, "Well, I think if you compare local law enforcement, meaning the LAPD with Arizona, we're definitely more friendly." Despite this dynamic, Marge was quick to point to the high number of deportations that originated in Los Angeles County, revealing a fundamental and important truth: lots of deportations took place in Los Angeles over the last decade thanks to the active role of Sheriff Arpaio's counterparts in Los Angeles—Sheriffs Lee Baca (1998–2014), Jim McDonnell (2014–2018), and Alex Villanueva (2018–2022). Their oversight of the massive Los Angeles jail system—the largest in the country—put them in control of a critical aspect of the deportation pipeline, funneling detainees into ICE custody or removal proceedings on a regular basis.

In Orange County, however, the concerns regarding ICE-sheriff collaborations are even greater. Sheriffs in both counties generally exercise jurisdiction over arrestees coming from a variety of cities because they run most of the jails. But in Orange County, the Sheriff also polices broad swaths of the southern part of the county by contract. And that part of the county is reputed to be the site of some of the most aggressive immigration enforcement efforts in the county. Katrina is a Mexican national who had recently graduated from college in Orange County and was living with her parents in Santa Ana, a city in the northeastern part of Orange County. In an August 2016 interview, Katrina shared that her parents did not live in fear of deportation, even though ICE had recently engaged in a series of enforcement actions in Central American neighborhoods in nearby Los Angeles. She explained: "My parents aren't really, you know, they're not worried. They don't live, you know, with like, oh, if they come knocking at our door, like things like that." But through her organizing work in south Orange County, Katrina heard many more firsthand stories of immigration enforcement than her parents. "[W]ith the organizing group, the ladies who live down in south Orange County, um, you know, we didn't realize like raids happen constantly over there." This increased her own concerns about her parents.

The OCSD also polices Orange County Transit (OCTA) by contract, giving it jurisdictions over buses regardless of whether they are in sanctuary cities or not.[78] Prior to A.B. 60, this created a particularly harsh dilemma for residents who could not access a driver's license, but also could not safely use public transit.

Doris Marie Provine and others have noted that nationwide, sheriffs tend to be more pro-immigration-enforcement cooperation than big city police chiefs.[79] Our conversations with residents in Southern California helped to highlight what this means for jurisdictions that undertake immigrant-protective measures. The broad policing powers of the sheriff in jurisdictions like Los Angeles, particularly the power that the LASD wields in its oversight of the largest jail system in the country, undercut some of the sanctuary protections of those jurisdictions.

Our interviews with area residents also taught us that focusing only on the extent to which local law enforcement cooperates in federal immigration enforcement efforts missed important dimensions of individuals' experiences and interactions with law enforcement agents. The fact that Los Angeles residents did not fear that police would collaborate with ICE does not mean that they did not worry about the police.[80] Alessandra, a Guatemalan national and DACA recipient, discussed this concern in her August 2016, interview. She said:

> [T]here's this motorcycle cop that literally would wait for my dad to get in his car and then pull him over because he already knew about my dad. And there's a lot of . . . areas which . . . they already know, so they keep pulling the same people over. Sometimes just for looks. This one time, my brother was with my dad and he had just got his license. The cop pulled him over, he goes, "You know why I pulled you over? Because the clothes you're wearing are really dirty," you know, because he works at the shop, and they [were in] my dad's old car. He [the officer]— at the time because of the way [my brother] looked—he [the officer] pulled [my brother] over because my dad and my brother had no nice suits, so my brother goes, "No, sir, I do have a license." And so my dad, he's had a bunch of issues with the cops in the run-up before he had his license, because they would literally wait for him. They know the little spots, you know, where they work

or where they—so when they leave, so the minute they get into a car, they have the right to pull them over and they're like, "You haven't got a license, we're going to give you a fine."

When she was asked whether this might be more likely to happen to men than women, Alessandra said she did not think that gender was the critical distinguishing factor, noting that LAPD officers had targeted her mom for this kind of stop:

> SUSAN: It's mainly your father, so it's like they're targeting men, maybe?
>
> ALESSANDRA: No, before I got my license, I wasn't really driving. I couldn't afford getting the car back when they took it. It was just too much money. So I was just taking public transportation because it was easier than getting my car taken away and paying that amount, because it's not really cheap. I know my mom did.
>
> SUSAN: Okay, so yes, it's not just gender?
>
> ALESSANDRA: No, she definitely got pulled over many times.

But others' experiences suggest a gendered dynamic to these encounters. Margarita, a Guatemalan national introduced in Chapter 3, expressed concerns about going to her pharmacy near downtown Los Angeles because police had set up license checkpoints, and she also recounted being asked for her license in an encounter with a police officer when she was picking up her son from school. "That day the police stopped me, and he asked me if I knew that I couldn't stop there. I said I was just picking up my son. He said, 'Do you or do you not have a license?' He didn't get out. He was in his car. And I just looked at him. I said, 'Are you going to investigate me?' [laughs] He said, 'You can't stop here. Move away quickly.' But, 'Do you or do you not have a license?' And I, [makes gasping sound, indicating fear or outrage]. I defended myself with my English. That made the difference. No one thinks that I don't have documents!"

While Margarita was able to put an end to a stop with her response in English, law enforcement encounters described by many of the men that we interviewed were not so easily concluded. Statistical data suggest that this may be part of a broader pattern.[81] In a December 2014 interview, Erasmo discussed the existence of license checkpoints in the city of Pasadena in Los Angeles County. He said:

> I had to pass through the checkpoint. The first thing the police officer asks for is your driver's license. They don't ask whether you're under the influence or driving fast. The first thing they ask for is your license. If you don't have a license, you get pulled over and they take away your car. This time they asked for the license. I didn't have one, so they asked me to get out of the car. My wife and my son's two friends were with me, and they asked us all to get out and they took away our car and in that moment, I asked the police officer if I could call someone to pick up the car, someone who had a license. The police officer was Asian, and he was generous. He gave me an opportunity. I called someone who had a license and they allowed me to keep the car. The only thing is I had to go to court to pay the fine for driving without a license. They allowed me to keep the car, but I had to pay a fine of $460 for not having a license.

Lucas, a Mexican national and Orange County resident in his fifties who lacked legal immigration status, described experiencing similar feelings in Orange County until the passage of A.B. 60. He noted that the driver's license he was able to access after the passage of A.B. 60 allowed him to buy cheaper auto insurance and facilitated numerous transactions, like renting an apartment. He also noted that possessing a license significantly decreased his fear when he saw a police officer behind him. "I've had a lot of cops behind my car looking up the plate number," he explained. "And sometimes they follow me for one or two miles, behind me, but then when they complete their search they go, and they leave me alone. However, before [A.B. 60], you had to crouch in fear thinking, 'Please don't let them stop me, don't let them stop me.' You see? I would plead with God that they not turn on those ugly lights. They are so beautiful, but they are so ugly."

Joaquin, a recent college graduate living in Orange County, talked about how A.B. 60 changed life for him, too. In a July 2016, interview, he recounted that he was "able to benefit from A.B. 60." He said:

> I got very lucky . . . because, um, I was commuting from, from Pomona to Irvine, um, my first year, and it was probably the most stressful situation because I had to be watching every side of me in the car, watching the back, to see if there were any cops. And when I'd see a cop, I would be like,

"Please just go away." So I would get home, and I would be so tense, you know, my shoulders. . . . And you know, what if the car gets taken away? I've already—I had already had that situation happen. And it wasn't pretty, um, because I deal with depression, too, so, when that happened, I got so depressed. I couldn't even go out. I just didn't even want to go out. . . . I think I am a little more at ease about driving knowing that I have a license and that I won't get the car taken away. . . . Of course we're still vulnerable to being, um, deported . . . so it's not a hundred percent. I think it's still fifty-fifty. But at least I know that cops are going to be nice—hopefully. And that won't happen, hopefully. So to some point, I do drive with a lot of, of freedom and ease and knowing that, um, I'm not going to pretty much get the car taken away.[82]

Given the varied approaches of local governments to enforcement cooperation, it is notable that people in both sanctuary jurisdictions and pro-cooperation jurisdictions regarded local police warily and recounted examples of harsh policing practices and racial profiling in their communities.

Anaheim, which has enacted an immigrant welcoming ordinance, was singled out by some Orange County residents as an area dangerous for immigrants to interact with police—not just because, or even primarily because, of the possibility of local enforcement cooperation with ICE. Anaheim's long and tainted racial past may help explain this. Indeed, in recent years, Anaheim has been the site of highly visible white supremacist organizing, including a Ku Klux Klan rally in February 2016 that left three people with stab wounds.[83] Although Anaheim billed itself as a "welcoming" city for immigrants, this did not translate into security for young men of color in their encounters with police.

César, introduced in Chapter 1, is a US citizen, the child of Mexican immigrants, and the director of a labor-focused nonprofit in Santa Ana. He explained the situation in this way:

[Starting in] the year of 2012 in the city of Anaheim, one young man of color was shot and killed by Anaheim PD [police department] every single month for that twenty-four-month period, okay. As soon as we got involved . . . to highlight, that the son of one of our members has been shot and killed, guess what? There was a little shift. All of a sudden, a police chief retired, there was a new police chief, there was some changes, although somewhat mediocre, guess what? Since then, I believe only—there's been four [officer-]involved, you know Anaheim PD fatalities. So has it improved? Meh, right, but at least my people aren't getting killed, right. So I'm not going to go out there and brag about how great the APD is, but at the same time less people have been shot and killed by them. [But] it's always in a pendulum for me, because the more we improve, at the same time there's—say we've got improvement in Anaheim PD, Santa Ana PD is becoming more horrible, right, and it's always a system that kind of shifts, you know.

Similarly, some respondents viewed Santa Ana, which enacted a sanctuary ordinance at the end of 2016, as having a police department hostile to Latinx immigrants and as a trouble spot for being racially profiled if Latinx. Specifically, the Santa Ana Police Department's anti-gang policing notably targets Latinx residents in ways that leave them feeling in danger of police harassment,[84] and that can in many cases place noncitizen residents on a path to removal.

César described his own encounter with Santa Ana police (briefly summarized in Chapter 1) as follows:

One day I was riding my bike and it was getting dark so me and my friend, my old roommate, were driving through Santiago Park on our bikes, and it's not sunset yet, but two cops stop us on horses because the park closes at dusk, okay. It wasn't night, it wasn't like we weren't wearing reflective clothing, you know we were all in like, I don't know, fucking green and stuff, and obviously we're all like huffing and puffing, and so they stop me and they're like, "Sit on the curb." I'm like "I'm not sitting on the curb." And they're like, "Well how do I know you're not going to run?" I'm like, "Officer, I can barely fucking ride my bike, I'm three hundred pounds, I ain't running nowhere. I'm going to stand here, here's my stuff, you go do your thing." I made them laugh, okay. But guess what? I never paid for that ticket because I went to the city council and yelled at them. Like, are you kidding me? Here we're talking about health and making people more healthy, he stopped me at six-o-fucking-one and now you're going to give me shit for this? Like, fuck you all. You're not going to do that to me, you know. Why? Because I was more of a prominent Santa Anero so of course they excused it, but like, policies like that? [S]ure, if it's dark and there's nice signage that says the park is closed, I get it. But, like, just because I'm riding my bike and the sun is going down, like, no. That's not fair, right. And again, those are my personal experiences, but again if you're wearing a Raider's jersey and you're young, younger than forty, and you're walking down the street the chances are you are going to get stopped. And unfortunately, that's across the nation, not just here, you know. And of course, that's not the type of community that I would like—I don't have kids, but raise my kids in. But as a person of color, my biggest fear in America is some man with a badge.

This experience of being stopped on a bicycle is one that is echoed by Latinx residents of Los Angeles as well. A study by the *Los Angeles Times* found significant racial disparities in bicycle stops by LASD deputies. Their review of forty-four thousand bicycle stops in the period from 2017 to 2021 found that deputies search 85 percent of bike riders they stop, even though they often have no reason to suspect illegal activity. Furthermore, seven of every ten stops involve Latinx cyclists, and bike riders in poorer communities with large nonwhite populations were stopped and searched far more often than those in more affluent, whiter parts of the county.[85]

Activists and organizers in Orange County expressed an additional concern: one of lack of police protection for organizing activities related to immigrant justice, even as those efforts came under increasing attack by opponents. At least one organizer thought Orange County was much worse in this regard than Los Angeles. Marilyn, a Los Angeles–based service provider at an API-serving organization, drew the contrast in an April 2018, interview when asked to describe how things had changed after the election of Donald Trump:

A lot of the work we're doing now is in Orange County and it's just . . . been . . . awful. It's really, really awful. You know, I actually grew up in Orange County and I thought it was such a boring place to be. So I thought I was gonna move to LA where there's stuff going on . . . but now all the stuff is in Orange County! You know people passing [anti-immigrant] resolutions—but to me it's just like people want to say, "I hate you! I hate you for not looking like me. I hate you, I don't want you to be here, we don't welcome you at all." I don't know what word to describe that feeling. Like if you're a resident of Los Alamitos, and now I think they're going to try to pass it in Fullerton. . . . I feel like people are looking at me in a different way than before. And I'm scared. I don't feel comfortable hanging out in Laguna Beach. Like Huntington [Beach], that area, I don't feel that safe. . . . [S]afety is like the biggest thing on my mind because you don't want people to get hurt . . . because we've seen the police not do anything.

Marilyn's comments about people "looking at [her] in a different way" point to another frequently expressed sentiment: when asked about their feelings of comfort and security, many people did not focus directly on policing activities. Instead, they defined their relative sense of security depending upon how welcome other people in their community made them feel, and how safe they felt. As previously noted, Mireya, a DACA recipient and Mexican national, worried about the possibility that her father—a dark-skinned Mexican national who spoke little English—would be profiled by the police. She did not express similar concerns for herself, in part, she said, because she was fair-skinned and college educated. But Mireya distinctly recalled feeling unwelcome in Costa Mesa—as noted earlier, viewed by many as a restrictionist city in Orange County—when she and her mother went out for brunch together. In a May 2015, interview, she told this story in this way:

> MIREYA: [W]henever I used to think about Orange County, I just thought it was a prettier place, and it was very calm and quiet, and that is all I thought about when I came to Orange County, and now it's not that way. It's kind of like, "Oh, will the police stop me because I am speaking in Spanish?"
>
> EDELINA: How have you come to this place where you think about OC that way? Can you describe to me . . .
>
> MIREYA: One of the sadder ones is that my mom came here for Mother's Day, because I kind of forced her to come. So she was here for two days and on Mother's Day, on the Sunday, we went out to eat. We went to a mall in Costa Mesa, and we went to a restaurant called Ruby's and . . . that manager really didn't want us there, um, he, we went in and the waitress was very nice and my mom would be talking and we were talking in Spanish and then the manager, called the waitress and then he told her to give us our check. [I]t was like three minutes in.

This feeling of being unwelcome was another recurring theme, and parts of Orange County received a good deal of criticism for being unwelcoming. As Marilyn's earlier comments suggest, this feeling of being unwelcome was sometimes compounded when people felt that police were unwilling to protect them.

Some people focused specifically on the difficulties they encountered gaining employment without formal authorization. Nidia noticed clear differences between various Orange County cities in this regard, noting in a June 2015, interview that "they're more strict around Irvine, like Costa Mesa even. I think Santa Ana is a good place, like Fountain Valley you could get away [without documents]."

Some residents reported that their own feelings of security were not dictated by external factors at all, but instead were the result of their idiosyncratic and internal ways of dealing with the threat of removal. For some, that meant retaining an attitude of comfort and acceptance toward the possibility of deportation. But this was easier to retain in a context of community solidarity.

In a June 2015, interview, Lupita, the DACAmented student bus driver introduced earlier, shared some of her experiences growing up in her hometown of Cudahy, a small city in South Los Angeles: "We would always see when people and families would get a knock on the door and deported and stuff. We were never really afraid of it. I don't know what it was, it was just like, 'If it happens it happens.' We're like, 'We have a house in Mexico, who cares?' [My parents were] like, 'Oh, we'll go back to our regular lives that we had back then.' I was like, 'Oh, okay, I guess.'" Lupita later explained that her family felt comfortable in the neighborhood because almost everyone there was Latinx and she and her family felt at home. Though Cudahy declared itself a sanctuary, Lupita suggested that she and her family did not derive their sense of security from that, and her family even joked that this was just a strategy to get undocumented people to move to one place, where they could be found and deported. Her family's comfort derived from the solidarity they experienced in their neighborhood and from their sense that they could rebuild a life in Mexico if they absolutely had to do so. The cynical humor they expressed was also a common coping mechanism deployed by other residents with whom we spoke.

For Patricio, a twenty-six-year-old Mexican national who was out of status, and who strongly subscribed to the power of positive thinking, it seemed important to feel a degree of control over the possibility of deportation. He believed that the likelihood that one would be investigated for immigration status violations during ordinary police encounters was determined by the attitude of the individual. He told one of us,

> PATRICIO: [S]ometimes I put myself right in front of the police hoping they will stop me, right? And they don't do anything to me? . . . [I]t's really, like I say, because of the confidence they see in you. It has so much to do with your attitude and confidence level. If the police see you are fearful, they say, 'This guy's into something,' and next thing you know they stop you.
>
> SUSAN: So if one drives confidently, the police aren't going to—
>
> PATRICIO: Yes, they know you have confidence, they see that you aren't afraid they are going to stop you . . . it has a lot to do with that. I've always wanted to go through a checkpoint, now that I have a license, I say, 'I'm going to go through a checkpoint,' but I've never found a checkpoint!"

Patricio's supreme sense that one could control outcomes through attitude—and the politically conservative ideas he espoused throughout his interview—were outliers. But it is important to note the wide variety of ways that people have of understanding and characterizing their situations.

As is evident throughout the interviews already highlighted, individual characteristics operate to increase or decrease the security of immigrant residents, regardless of the official policies of the jurisdiction. Vulnerability may be increased or decreased by factors beyond their control—whether they have deferred action status, whether they have criminal convictions, and the way their physical appearance and presentation might trigger a given officer's propensity to engage in racial profiling. Indeed, many people we spoke to reflected frankly and openly on the role that race played in shaping their daily lives and their interactions with officials. We encountered many people who felt that they were more likely to be pulled over in a traffic stop or otherwise questioned by police because they were Latinx, and those who were college-educated or who could "pass" as white (with lighter skin color and fluent English) felt that their darker-skinned and Spanish-dominant relatives were more vulnerable to these encounters, even though they, too, lacked formal legal status.

The experiences of many API residents were different—and most expressed less fear of being stopped and investigated by police based on racial profiling. Reese, the Orange County college student and Chinese national from Hong Kong with DACA, told one of us in an August 2016, interview, "because I'm Asian, I don't really get pulled over that often, as much as, like, my darker-skin friends. So I guess, driving is not really something that I feel uncomfortable with or, you know, driving. . . . I don't have to fear as much about getting pulled over or getting stopped by the police." For her, geography was less determinative of her feelings of security—she felt that her perceived racial identity protected her from unwarranted police stops and investigation. But she was quite clear that this was not true for her "darker-skin friends." Dean, a South Korean national in his twenties who grew up in Los Angeles's Koreatown and was attending college in Orange County, did worry that his father, who was a professional driver, could get pulled over and deported. But his fear seemed pegged to the fact that his father did not have a driver's license, and his fear lessened when his father was able to access a driver's license. Julia, a South Korean college student with DACA said in a June 2017, interview that she thought it was somewhat "easier" to be undocumented for API residents than for Latinx residents because "people don't expect you to be undocumented when you are Asian." And a Korean participant in a focus group that we conducted at an API-serving organization commented, "I guess even though we are all undocumented, Mexicans have more disadvantage sometimes. For example, if we get stopped by police, they're more likely to get detained than us."

But it is not the case that API immigrants were untouched by policing excesses. Sovannar and Fiona, two people working at an organization providing services to the API immigrant community in Los Angeles, noted that the federal government has conducted targeted sweeps in some cities to round up and deport removable Cambodians. The priorities are individuals with criminal records. Unfortunately, because of the failure of US policy to integrate children who came to the US as refugees from Cambodia, a significant number of young Cambodian refugees had encounters with the criminal legal system that continue to follow and haunt them.[86] Fiona recounts, "They're like, 'I already served my time. I've turned my life around. I own a house. I have a good job. I'm not even a gangster anymore. And I just got swept up, and now I'm stuck in Cambodia. I can never come back.' Some of [their crimes] very minor, very, very minor, and some of them, you know, bigger crimes, but I think the thing is, no one knew that this was going to happen because" the laws subjecting people to deportation for a wide range of offenses and conduct were retroactive.[87]

Data collected by the TRAC research service also showed that Vietnamese immigrants were overrepresented among those removed in Orange County in 2016 relative to their presence in the immigrant population. This overrepresentation might be explained by the focus of Orange County law enforcement agencies on purported gang activity in the Vietnamese community. These data suggest that for some API subgroups, contact with the criminal legal system—and consequently for the immigration enforcement system—was less easily avoided.

Conclusion

The views of Southern California residents suggest that the enactment of protective immigration policies may be a necessary but insufficient condition for inspiring community trust among immigrants. To the extent immigrants still feel targeted for unnecessary enforcement actions on the basis of race or are concerned that such targeting may happen to their friends and families, noncooperation policies are not panaceas for insecurity and distrust of the police. Furthermore, their underlying distrust is likely aggravated when the practices of individual officers fail to align with formal policies.

These findings have implications for research and policy design. Discussions of immigration enforcement efforts often assume that trust in immigrant communities is dependent largely on the formal degree of cooperation or noncooperation between local law enforcement and federal immigration enforcement efforts. A closer look at residents' own experiences suggests three problems with this assumption. The first is that many geographic locations are subject to multiple, overlapping governmental jurisdictions with different enforcement policies and prerogatives. The second is that the formal cooperation policy is often an imperfect proxy for the degree of actual enforcement cooperation in particular places, either because formal policy is subverted by informal workarounds or because the existence of overlapping yet distinct formal regimes means that some governmental actors will undercut the cooperation policies of other governmental actors in the same geographic space. A third problem with assuming a simple relationship between trust in police and immigration cooperation policies is that trust between the police and residents—including individuals who are, in fact, undocumented—is based on an interplay of factors that relate in complex ways to immigration status. Trust may be lacking because these residents fear that interactions with law enforcement will lead to deportation. But immigrant residents also have ambivalent and even oppositional views toward police when they believe that their perceived immigration status and racial identity will subject them to unfair police treatment that has nothing to do with the goal of deportation.

SIX

Performing Citizenship

A MEMBER OF OUR research team met Margarita, who we first introduced in Chapter 3, at a community presentation on executive action in Los Angeles in November of 2014, two days after President Obama announced DAPA and the expansion of DACA. Three weeks later, during an interview, Margarita told us that she was eager to apply for deferred action. Margarita originally came to the United States from Guatemala in 1995, after she lost her job and had no money to pay for medical care for her daughter, who was seriously ill. In the United States, Margarita quickly found work as a nanny and then began working in elder care. After having two more children in the United States—a son and a daughter—Margarita quit working to care for them. She experienced multiple challenges, including a serious medical issue that generated considerable medical debt, as well as the pain of being separated from her daughter in Guatemala. Margarita couldn't bring her daughter to the United States legally, nor could she travel there to visit without risking being able to return. Margarita saw deferred action as an imperfect form of relief: "How long it is going to help one? I think, 'It will only be valid for two years.' After, there will be another president, and he can decide to eliminate it." Yet, she still hoped to benefit, at least temporarily: "This executive action, for me, this is the logic that it has: the hope of being able to say that I can at least breathe more easily for a while, while my son reaches the right age [to petition for me at the age of twenty-one]. He will be turning fourteen." With executive relief, Margarita hoped to continue her studies and to accept a job offer from her local school district, where she had volunteered for seven years. Margarita explained that the school district was unaware of her immigration status. "But always, I have had to invent an answer [in declining their paid job offers] .... Only [I say], 'No, it's because I have to take my children here and there!'"

Margarita's experiences exemplify the complex ways that interviewees were situated in relation to popular discourses regarding immigration. On the one hand, Margarita was proud that others—such as personnel at her son's school—did not perceive her as undocumented. This comment reflects Margarita's awareness that those who appear to be Latinx are often profiled as undocumented.[1] Demonstrating pride in defying this stereotype, Margarita recounted another instance (detailed in Chapter 5) when she successfully defended herself to an officer who, based on her physical appearance, accused her of not having a license. She "defended [her]self with English."[2]

Margarita also relayed that at her church, others sought her out for advice and assistance: "There I seem to everyone like a citizen due to my way of acting. People are always coming to me, desperate, asking me whether it is worth it to stay in the country, whether they should open a business, or whether they should just leave." On the other hand, despite her ability to appear to be a citizen, Margarita experienced the challenges of living in the United States without legal status, including lack of access to medical insurance, racial profiling by the police, separation from family in Guatemala, lack of work authorization, and fear that she or her husband would be deported. She found the injunction against DAPA and DACA+ particularly galling. During a follow-up interview in March 2015, she told us:

> We lived through suffering for so many years, and then we had a hope. And now it is gone. It is very traumatic. When we learned about executive relief, we were able to begin to plan. I am completing my high school equivalency now and I was planning to continue studying. Now, it is not clear what to do. In my case, for example, I had plans! With a *permiso* [a work permit, which can also serve as an ID], I would be able to study, to go back to school. First, I would complete a short course in something, and then I would enroll in a longer program of study. Now, however, it is difficult to plan. One doesn't know what is going to happen.

In a highly criminalized context, in which the only large-scale form of relief that could be offered was prosecutorial discretion, an enforcement strategy, the narratives and social interactions of would-be deferred action applicants such as Margarita took on the character of performances, akin to what anthropologist Angela García describes as "legal passing," that is, "attempts to mask 'illegality.'"[3] Such performances were a way to "speak back" to the state, staking claims to belonging while also mitigating the impacts of illegalization and criminalization. Documents, such as work permits, are key to performances, as we see in the above quote from Margarita. The specter of citizenship haunted performances, in that interviewees viewed citizenship as a resolution to their problems, something that could be envisioned but was beyond reach, and as a promise that had, for many nonwhite residents, been hollowed out by racism. Margarita's repeated insistence that others perceived her as a citizen conveys her sense that her legal status as undocumented and potentially subject to deportation did not reflect her moral worth or social value. Indeed, she told us, "When the country realizes that we are good for the country, that the work that we do is valuable, then they will give us papers. We should show that it is worthwhile for the country for us to be here."

Margarita's comments demonstrate the pervasive and often insidious nature of the "bad immigrant/good immigrant," "felon/family" dichotomy that underlies intensified immigration enforcement and limits regularization opportunities.[4] Interviewees' narratives of deservingness and accounts of their own lives engaged with but also sought to transform this dichotomy. Margarita seemingly saw herself as a quasi-citizen, both undocumented *and* deserving. In her alternative vision of society, as she related, she would be able to plan, study, and "breathe easily." While interviewees espoused multiple perspectives and certainly did not all agree, many argued that in a more just world, citizenship would be both less necessary and more meaningful. It would be less necessary in that rights and services would be more widely available, regardless of legal status, and it would be more meaningful in that it would reflect and confer social belonging on all citizens.[5]

Margarita and others could engage and seek to transform the limited scripts that defined their lives, in part, because these scripts are not static:

legal status is malleable due to the erosion of citizenship's protective quality, the expansiveness of executive authority, and the resulting fluidity of immigration law and policy.[6] Just as the enforcement practices that produce immigrant subjectivities vary by location, as we saw in Chapter 5, the practices that determine belonging varied over the 2012–2022 period covered by our book. In 2012, when DACA was created, US authorities had sought to divide the undocumented population between those who were high priorities for deportation and those with equities deserving recognition for humanitarian reasons. This "sorting" between high- and low-priority immigrants emerged first in the Morton memos (which built on similar, earlier prosecutorial discretion memos), then DACA. But neither approach proved effective in fully preventing the deportation of long-term residents with strong equities.[7] By 2017, when we were concluding our data collection and beginning to write this manuscript, Donald Trump had assumed the presidency and circumstances dramatically changed. Among interviewees, even US citizens expressed concern about racial profiling, discrimination, and denaturalization. In Chapter 4, we captured the reaction of César, a labor and immigrant rights advocate whom we interviewed two days after the 2016 election. He described how the election results reduced both noncitizens' and citizens' sense of security, noting how the spectrum of fear expanded from undocumented residents under Obama to everyone including citizens under Trump. "The conversation ceased to be on this side [of the spectrum] and now it's all the way over here." César's comments highlight the limited or spectral nature of the protections that citizenship provides when confronted with aggressive gendered and racialized enforcement.

While authorities' political imagination focused on expanding enforcement, the constituents and advocates whom we interviewed for this project envisioned alternative worlds in which society would recognize the economic and human value of noncitizens' lives, as Margarita hoped. Through discursive and embodied performances of citizenship, immigrants and their allies became shapeshifters, in the terms described by anthropologist Aimee Cox, who analyzed how the narratives, relationships, and actions of young Black women and girls in a Detroit homeless shelter redefined the institutional practices within which they were embedded.[8]

In other words, instead of merely altering one's own actions and narratives in order to conform to existing definitions, performing citizenship enacts alternative institutional forms, attempting to bring about a more desired future. Shapeshifting is directed not only inward, at performers, but also outward, at institutions themselves. Cox writes, "Shapeshifting is an act, a theory, and, in this sense, a form of praxis that . . . reveals our collective vulnerabilities. . . . *Shapeshifting* most often means shifting the terms through which educational, training, and social service institutions attempt to shape young Black women into manageable and respectable members of society whose social citizenship is always questionable and never guaranteed, even as these same institutions ostensibly encourage social belonging."[9] In the case of immigrants and their allies, shapeshifting through discursive and embodied performances redefines institutions and narratives, such as the dichotomy between "families" and "felons," that produce illegalization. Such shapeshifting both engages and critiques notions of respectability underlying the DREAMer narrative.[10]

Examining the shapeshifting practices and discourses of would-be deferred action applicants reveals the spectral nature of DAPA and DACA+. As Margarita told us when the injunction suspended her plans, "All of my hopes died." A phantom is what remains after death, leaving Margarita and other potential DAPA and DACA+ applicants haunted by what might have been. Banished from the limited regularization opportunity that deferred action would have provided while also facing deportation, criminalization, and economic deprivation (indeed, some interviewees had experienced periods of homelessness), interviewees sought a reckoning. Many described mental health impacts, physical effects, and social deprivation that cumulatively result in considerable harm. Yet, interviewees also exhibited resilience through activism, persistence, and the development of new individual and collective strategies. In demanding a reckoning, interviewees critiqued not only the injunction that suspended DAPA and DACA+ but also the insufficiency of the "deal" that President Obama had offered. By resisting political manipulation, defining belonging in more local terms, and developing forms of activism and political consciousness that expanded and transcended boundaries, interviewees reenvisioned not only citizenship but the nation itself.

Legal Criteria

The Morton memos, which delineated criteria for determining who should be a low priority for deportation, and deferred action programs, which likewise offered limited protections to those with compelling equities, are grounded in the notion that immigration policy is a moral system in which "deserving" immigrants can be distinguished from those who are "undeserving." In contrast, Tomás, an undocumented construction worker interviewed by a member of our research team in 2015, conveys the flawed and dehumanizing nature of the dichotomy that underlies such distinctions. As an undocumented immigrant who was ineligible for relief, Tomás was treated as undeserving, akin to the "felons" in President Obama's contention that deportation should prioritize "felons, not families." Tomás, who was subject to exploitative labor practices and wage theft, had experienced extreme deprivations, including life-threatening hunger and thirst while traveling to the US. Tomás did have family, but most of his immediate family members were in Mexico and so were not seen as grounds for granting relief. On the contrary, due to his immigration status, Tomás was unable to travel there to see his parents when they were dying. Tomás equated these physical and emotional hardships with being treated like an animal, instead of being accorded the basic respect and comforts that ought to accompany being human. Tomás's experiences demonstrate how the criminalization and racialization inherent in immigration law undermine the criteria that comprise legal definitions of deservingness. Treating immigration as a national security and crime control matter renders minor infractions, evidentiary discrepancies, and even living and working in the United States without authorization, as Tomás did, grounds for criminalization and illegalization. Likewise, racialization compounds the arbitrariness and unfairness of the enforcement system, generating the sorts of mistreatment that Tomás experienced. Systems that are discriminatory, dehumanizing, and arbitrary cannot be moral. As Tomás insisted: "We are treated like animals. But we are not animals. We are people."

During interviews that we conducted for this study and at public presentations on immigration law that we attended during fieldwork, advocates outlined how one could qualify for deferred action through DACA, DAPA, and DACA+ and described other avenues through which individuals could acquire temporary or permanent legal status. From advocates' points of view, deferred action and these other opportunities were connected, in that applicants who consulted with service providers regarding deferred action might discover that they were eligible for another, more robust remedy. Those with family ties in the United States could possibly qualify for visas through relatives. Crime victims who collaborated with the police in an investigation might be eligible for U visas. Domestic violence survivors who were married to their abusers could potentially self-petition under the Violence Against Women Act. Employees in certain professions might be able to qualify through their employers.

For deferred action programs, applicants would have to demonstrate continuous presence in the United States since specific dates; either educational attainment or parentage of a US citizen or lawful permanent resident child; a clean criminal record; and satisfaction of the age requirements. At a public talk in 2015, shortly after the district court judge enjoined DAPA and DACA+, an advocate reviewed the sort of evidence of continuous presence that applicants would need, if the injunction were lifted:

> You have to have a document for every three or four months since the first of January of 2010. Each document has to have three things: your name, the date, and the place. Remember, when you are reviewing your documents: name, date, and place. These are some examples: receipts, bank statements, if you have a bank account it is very good to submit that because it has all the things that you have bought with the date and place. Visits to the doctor, if you are a mother or father and you have taken your children to the doctor and you had to sign something, that can be evidence. . . . So your license, if you have had traffic tickets, those can work because they have your name, and the date, and the place where you got the ticket. And as I say, it's a document every 3 to 4 months.

As this quote demonstrates, individuals must document compliance with the supposedly value-neutral "presence" requirement according to evidentiary rules that favor those with greater financial security (a bank account, bank statements, receipts), who have heteronormative family structures (marriage and children), and who perform "responsible" behaviors, such as taking children to doctor appointments. Such documentation requirements ignore the conditions that prevent some from working, opening bank accounts, or accessing healthcare.[11]

The standards that individuals had to meet to qualify for deferred action or other immigration remedies suggested that, if individuals could exemplify these standards in their daily lives, they potentially would be deemed deserving for status, or at least low priorities for deportation. Some advocates explicitly encouraged such behavior. At a document preparation workshop that one organization held in 2016, shortly before the Supreme Court decision in *United States v. Texas*, an attorney advised attendees to live their lives in ways that would produce the documentation that they needed, such as medical or school attendance records. Likewise, in 2017, after the Trump administration attempted to rescind DACA, speakers on a "Life After DACA" panel urged participants to actively build records that would enable them to defend themselves if they faced deportation. To do so, panelists suggested, participants should volunteer, get good grades, become involved in community organizations, and donate money to charitable causes. Some who sought status internalized this sort of message. During a 2015 interview, Nidia, a DACA recipient, related,

> My dad has always told us, like, hey, we are here illegally so don't do anything that someday you'll regret and if someday we get to fix papers, you will not have that opportunity. So I think that was always in our minds of not being a bad kid, just do what you have to do but don't get in trouble because someday, if you want to get papers, you will not get papers.

In essence, advocates and immigrant community members noted, those who hoped to acquire status had to be more "citizen-like" than actual citizens, a sort of "supercitizen immigrant."[12] To paraphrase one speaker at the Life After DACA event, "You need to be doing more things than your citizen-neighbor is doing."

Deferred action programs and the priority system outlined in the Morton memos implied that a moral calculation undergirded decisions about deportation priorities, yet the criminalization of immigration law and policy undermined the very criteria used in such assessments. Criminal convictions and problematic encounters with immigration officials played oversized roles in determinations of eligibility for immigration relief. Service providers routinely advised those with any prior law enforcement encounters to request their court files to determine whether they had records of an arrest, conviction, or police reports. At a 2014 conference on immigration representation, speakers warned participating attorneys that their clients could be in a gang database and therefore be deemed security risks, even if they had never participated in gangs.[13] At public presentations on immigration law, speakers spent considerable time reviewing the ways that criminal convictions, or even failure to pay taxes, could adversely impact individuals' cases. At a 2015 community presentation on deferred action, an attorney explained:

> We are going to review the criminal convictions that disqualify one for DACA. Any person who has the following criminal convictions is not eligible for deferred action. So any felony, three minor crimes, three misdemeanors. . . . For DAPA, for the parents it is a little different, they have put more crimes. The most important one that I want to mention is any crime related to gangs after the age of sixteen years. . . . If, for example, the police have stopped you in the street saying that you are part of a gang, they can refer you to deportation even though you do not have any criminal conviction.[14]

As this advice makes plain, police officers' racialized perceptions of gang membership, even in the absence of criminal conduct, could cut off access to deferred action status and heighten the threat of removal.

Attendees who had not filed tax returns were advised to develop a payment plan because, as one attorney stated, "If you have not been doing your taxes, they can deny your application." Authorities now sometimes prosecute individuals who have worked with false social security numbers—a practice common among those who lack work authorization, and one that authorities used to more or less tolerate—for fraud or identity theft.[15] At a document preparation workshop, an attorney warned participants not to use a false social security number when completing immigration forms, as doing so could put applicants at risk. Paradoxically, even though demonstrating citizenship-like qualities was potentially beneficial, actually claiming to *be* a citizen was not. An attorney warned audience members that if a noncitizen claims to be a US citizen in order to obtain an immigration benefit, that person may be denied future immigration relief, and risks deportation.

Individuals' immigration histories could also pose challenges. Those who had failed to attend previous immigration court hearings could have been ordered deported in absentia, and therefore, unbeknownst to them, have pending deportation orders that could be immediately executed if they came into contact with immigration officials. Individuals who returned to the United States after agreeing to leave voluntarily or being deported were likely ineligible for remedies. Tragically, those who returned to their home countries—for instance, to visit a sick relative—after unknowingly receiving in absentia deportation orders could be removed in the future without a hearing. In such instances, the government considers in absentia removal orders to be "self-executing," even if the recipients were unaware of the existence of these orders at the time they temporarily left the US. Individuals who subsequently returned to the US could be guilty of reentering the United States following deportation, and therefore not only could be prosecuted and deported but also subject to a bar on regularizing their status. To check for such issues, service providers routinely called the immigration court hotline with their clients' alien numbers to learn about their immigration histories and advised clients who had contact with immigration authorities to request their immigration records through the Freedom of Information Act (FOIA) process.

These issues played out in the experience of Michaela, a Mexican seamstress in her fifties who was first introduced in Chapter 1. Michaela had entered the United States multiple times, always with a passport and visa, and then she had stayed in the country continuously since the late 1990s. In 1993, she had gone to a law office recommended by her employer and submitted what she thought was an application for a work permit. Immigration authorities called her to what she described as a hearing, where she learned that the office had submitted an asylum application on her behalf, without her knowledge or understanding. She withdrew her application, and an immigration official told her that she would receive a new appointment with immigration officials. But she moved and never received an appointment notice. When Michaela entered her "alien registration number" or A-number into a government hotline, she heard that: "In 1998, the judge entered an administrative decision in the court located at [address]." Michaela had been ordered deported. Michaela discussed the possibility of reopening her case with an attorney—she has an adult son who is a US citizen and could file a visa petition for her. But recall that Michaela has been in jail. Michaela says she had been charged with a felony due to a work dispute, though she neither had a hearing nor received a sentence. She has been told by a courthouse employee that her criminal record is clean, but she has also been denied public housing based on her "criminal history," so she is very confused about what might be in her immigration and criminal records.

An attorney at a community-based organization advised Michaela to complete a Livescan fingerprint transaction—through which fingerprints are submitted to government agencies—to learn what, if anything, was in her criminal file. Until she knows what is in her file, she cannot move forward with an application to regularize her status. That attorney noted that to file a family-based visa petition while having an outstanding deportation order would "be saying, 'Here I am.' They can deport you right away. It has happened."

Michaela's experiences demonstrate how the criminalization of immigration law undercuts the criteria that determine merit. Michaela had a US citizen son, approximately two decades of residence in the United States, and a history of being employed. Yet, her previous effort to regularize her status likely resulted in a deportation order, and a single work-related dispute had generated an ambiguous criminal record. Her lack of work authorization also meant that she had to work under someone else's name. Assessments of merit that focus on individual behavior ignore the circumstances—shoddy and even predatory legal counsel, exploitative working conditions, poverty, and exclusionary employment laws—that haunt Michaela's paper record. Many of the barriers she now faces to regularizing her status exist not because she has a particularly high level of moral culpability, but because the condition of being undocumented channeled her actions and their consequences in particular ways.

An individual's race and gender can exacerbate this criminalization. As we discussed in Chapter 5, numerous interviewees reported being stopped by the police based on their Hispanic or Latinx appearance. Alondra, the Peruvian computer programmer, explained:

> If you have an old car, the police will stop you and ask for documents. If you are Hispanic, the police will stop you. . . . Because before [California extended driver's licenses to the undocumented], an immigrant who was driving and was stopped due to a broken headlight, the police could stop them and impound the car. The police got a lot of money from the cars of immigrants.

Samuel described how such police stops could result in arrests and possibly deportation: "You get stopped by the cops and they have immigration [officials] at the time when you are, you know, at the jails, they can get deported at that time, like right away, like, when you don't know your rights, it's easier for them to deport you." The over-policing of communities of color and racial profiling of Latinx and Black drivers resulted in higher rates of traffic stops, arrests, and criminal convictions among members of these groups. Interviewees discussed the discriminatory facets of police interactions.[16] Fátima's car was sideswiped by a driver she described as an "American." The driver offered her two hundred dollars in compensation, much less than the cost of the damage to her vehicle. Fátima refused this offer and, unable to reach an agreement, she and the other driver called the police. When they arrived, they took the other driver's side, advising Fátima to either accept the two hundred dollars or have her car impounded due to driving without a license. Fátima was furious. She reported that she told the police, "Because you see the color of my skin and that I don't speak English, you think that I am *mediocre* [second-class/insignificant]? I'm not *mediocre*. I am not doing anything wrong by asking for [the other driver's] insurance information." Fátima opted to have her car towed rather than accept the two hundred dollars that she considered an affront to her dignity.

In addition to such overt mistreatment, racialization also influenced perceptions of belonging. At a 2016 conference sponsored by an API-serving organization, a speaker noted that others regarded him as perpetually foreign: "I tell them [my students] what my last name is [name omitted] and they say, 'What kind of name is that? Oh, well you don't sound

Japanese.' Well, I've had that several times and I ask, 'What does that mean, why are you saying that?' To get this person to think about what they just asked. 'What's your last name? Smith? What kind of a name is that?'" The perception of being an outsider, regardless of length or residence or history in the United States, was widespread. Oscar, a restaurant worker originally from Mexico (whom we introduced in Chapter 3) complained in his 2016 interview, "We need to get people to think about Latinos differently. These stories need to get out so we can help people. People assume Latinos are foreigners just because of the color of our skin."

Racialized perceptions of foreignness intensified following Trump's election. While volunteering at an Orange Country community organization in November 2016, a member of our research team spoke with Ester, a recently naturalized US citizen. She said that dating back from the time of her migration from Mexico to the US in 1974, she had never felt so unsafe, uneasy, and lacking in security as she did after the election of Donald Trump. She was disappointed by the outcome in the first election in which she was able to vote, after years spent organizing other people to vote. But more importantly, she felt afraid. She had witnessed elections transpire as part of a union, as a teacher, but for the first time since her arrival in 1974, the election outcome made her feel fear because she fit within the stereotypes of demonized immigrants. She explained that she was a "worthy citizen" who had never broken any laws, never been a financial burden on the state, and had always been productive. She nevertheless felt that the new administration would target her because of her last name and skin color. Dismayed by the gap between her self-perception and her sense of how others saw her, she described herself as feeling "in limbo right now." Of course, racialization also influences *how* "citizenship" can be performed, depending on age, gender, national origin, appearance, race, ethnicity, and social class. Undocumented Black immigrants often felt invisible within immigrant rights advocacy circles, even as they also felt highly visible to police and immigration enforcement bureaucracies.

Awareness of the limited criteria used to assess merit, coupled with experiences of criminalization and racialization, led interviewees to develop their own understandings of deservingness. Taken collectively, these understandings sought to shapeshift the institutions in which interviewees were situated.

Definitions of Deservingness

During an interview conducted by a member of our research team in 2014, Willa, an attorney at an immigrant-serving organization, described the optimistic attitude that she encountered among her clients: "If there is justice, I should qualify," But of justice, she notes, "sometimes, there is not." This quote identifies a tension between *justice* as an abstract concept and the notion that *one should qualify*, that is, that the particularities of individuals' lives should be encompassed within that notion of justice. In the above quote, this tension is coupled with a critique of the legal system: sometimes there is *not* justice. And yet, as Willa implied, there could be justice, so there is some reason for hope.

Interviewees' visions of a more just immigration system derived from their own experiences, whether of immigrating to this country or of advocating for legal rights. Taken collectively, the visions they articulated during interviews provide insight into alternative institutions, and therefore constitute a form of shapeshifting that deserves to be taken seriously both as theorizations and aspirational interventions. While interviewees' perspectives and experiences differed, we identified three key interventions. First, *expansive inclusion*: a critique of the current immigration system for excluding individuals who, interviewees argued, were deserving based on their contributions to US society. This critique suggested that categorical allocations of legal status would need to be significantly expanded in order to be meaningful rather than arbitrary. Second, *racial justice*: a denunciation of discrimination based on race, ethnicity, national origin, or income. Such denunciations suggest that immigration processes based on white privilege and economic advantage should be dismantled. Third, *rights for all*: an abolitionist, open-border perspective that recognized everyone as deserving of rights, regardless of criminal history, time in the country, or particular contributions. This perspective transcended boundaries between citizens and noncitizens, contending that the extension of citizenship to some additional members is insufficient to address the inequities they faced, given that race, gender, and socioeconomic status also limit social inclusion. The visions that we heard articulated during interviews also circulated within activist circles and among immigrant community members. Interviewees' discussions of justice thus pointed to how social institutions could be transformed.

Interviewees who advocated *expanding inclusion* tended to be associated with more established nonprofits. They contended that state efforts to control borders and determine who merits legal status were legitimate, but they argued that the criteria should be meaningful rather than arbitrary, reflecting moral worth and national interest. Those who advocated expanding inclusion generally favored the existence of some limits, arguing that those who had committed crimes, abused receipt of public benefits, or failed to secure employment did not deserve to remain in the United States. Such boundary-setting propagates to some degree exclusionary rhetoric and practices that are widespread in the United States—for example, the demonized figure of the criminal and the welfare recipient are at the heart of anti-Black racism; assessing moral worth on the basis of individual financial success is key to neoliberal governance; privileging children or marriage as grounds for inclusion can reproduce heteronormative notions of family; stressing Americanization or assimilation also amplifies a nationalist discourse that privileges whiteness; and stressing work ethics without providing access to workers' compensation or healthcare is ableist.[17] At the same time, this vision is transformative in that it critiques the existing US immigration system for being overly exclusionary, counterproductive, and unfair. In its place, advocates of this vision propose expanding formal membership to many long-term unauthorized residents who already participate in social, political, and economic institutions and are therefore "de facto" members.[18] Notions of expansive inclusion thus are grounded in interviewees' day-to-day experiences of belonging and enforcement.

The inclusionary criteria that interviewees articulated during interviews reflect but simultaneously expand notions of merit that are part of US law and policy. Many cited a version of the American Dream narrative,[19] arguing that they had come to the United States in search of a better life, they had set down roots through work, family ties, and long-term residence, and they had come to identify with the United States. For example, during a 2016 interview, Oscar, the restaurant worker, told us: "The United States is a country of dreams." He explained that he began as a cook and had worked his way up to assistant manager of a restaurant. A friend advised Oscar that, whatever job he takes, he should be the best one that he can be. So if he were a bus boy, he would be the best bus boy; if he were a cook, he would be the best cook; if he were an assistant manager, he would be the best assistant manager. "In this country," he concluded, "those who can do so, are able to move forward." When asked if he wanted to become a US citizen someday, Oscar replied, "Yes! I've lived here for fifteen years, and I have seen my children grow up here. I love this country!"

Interviewees singled out paying taxes as a transaction that conferred both moral worth and a quasi-legal status. Imelda, an undocumented college student, told us how she explained her legal status to her roommate: "She was like, 'So you live here illegally?' I'm like, 'Yeah but my parents pay taxes, not really illegally.' I'm like, 'I just don't have citizenship.'" To Imelda, her parents' tax payments converted her into a quasi-legal resident who simply lacked citizenship. Graciela, the hairstylist who was undocumented and likely ineligible for deferred action (and was introduced in Chapter 3), argued that participating in the US economy as workers, taxpayers, and consumers made her and others members of US society. Graciela explained, "We are citizens who are here. We don't do any wrong, right? We are people who work. We contribute by shopping here. They charge taxes on that so the economy will flourish, but unfortunately I wasn't within that package [DAPA or DACA+]." References to work, paying taxes, and shopping seemed to invoke social contract notions of citizenship,[20] according to which residents who contributed to society had fulfilled their end of an implicit contract, such that the US government should then fulfill its obligation to grant them recognition.

Interviewees deployed these concepts to defend themselves against accusations of illegality. Alfaro, the owner a catering business introduced in Chapter 1, felt that he was unfairly punished by US laws that required individuals who had not been formally admitted to the country and sought relief through family petitions to go to the consulate in their country of origin for visa processing, thus triggering a ten-year bar on reentering the United States.[21] Alfaro recounted:

I am married to a US citizen, my family depends on me, I have a daughter, I pay my taxes, I am a decent person, a hard worker, I don't have crimes in the United States. That is, I am a responsible person, moral. But I can't get status. So for that reason it is a little bit of disagreement with the laws in my case, for that reason. Because for example, if I were a criminal, of course, obviously, I have no right to anything. But in my case, it isn't like that, but for nothing more than the simple fact that they punished me for ten years, I can't get status. For a punishment for nothing more than on the border they told me, "You are punished for crossing the border."

In this quote, Alfaro appeals to some of the same criteria of moral worth mentioned by Oscar (family ties, hard work) and Imelda (paying taxes) while also distinguishing "crossing the border" (officially known as "entry without inspection," a misdemeanor offense) from "crimes in the United States." Alfaro depicts himself as law-abiding and productive, contending that a civilly imposed "punishment" of a ten-year bar on reentry is undeserved. Significantly, Alfaro states that real criminals "have no right to anything." While he does not specify who these criminals might be, this reference to criminals as rightless, at least in an immigration context, echoes the broader criminalization of racialized others.[22] Furthermore, the association of moral worth with being "a responsible person," participates in the respectability politics associated with anti-Blackness.[23]

Interviewees who espoused expansive inclusion sometimes identified subgroups, such as students, farmworkers, or highly skilled workers, that they felt should be placed ahead of others in gaining status. For some, this contention reflected their sense of who was the most deserving. In a focus group that we conducted with parents affiliated with a Korean community organization, Eunice argued, "Our children have been growing up in the US with its culture embedded in them. They know nothing about the Korean culture. So even if we get kicked out of this country, we (the parents) can live in Korea but the children cannot. They are not familiar with the Korean language, and they lack the cultural knowledge. I question if my children can live their lives in Korea. I mean, they've attended school in the United States since preschool. They're Americans." From Eunice's perspective, prioritizing youth was a practical matter: these children, she felt, fit in in the United States but might not be able to cope with moving to Korea.

For other interviewees, prioritizing certain groups was strategic. Samuel, a youth organizer, expressed ambivalence, saying that on the one hand, it is important to fight for comprehensive policies that support everyone, but on the other hand, obtaining some relief for a subset of people is still valuable:

> You have to start peeling the onion from wherever you can. . . . I have mixed opinions. Sometimes I think that people can fight for everybody, but at the same time, I know . . . not everybody is going to qualify. . . . That's why [Obama] passed DACA first because they say it's not our fault, you know. But by saying that, it's another way of shifting the whole thing on the parents. . . . But it was a good tactic to pass DACA, to do something, you know, at the end of the day something is better than nothing.

Expansive inclusion, therefore, can be a strategic process of getting partial status for some and continuing to advocate for others.

Significantly, those who advocated expansive inclusion often identified groups that they considered undeserving. Such boundaries were evident in Alfaro's contention that criminals deserved nothing. Other interviewees echoed such exclusions explicitly or implicitly. Beatriz, the homemaker from Peru introduced in Chapter 3, commented, "When there's a law, one has to behave, study," implying that those who did not behave or study might be unworthy of status. Margarita, whose story opened this chapter, distinguished those who are in the United States to contribute and develop from those who might be seeking government benefits:

> Many organizations and the government or the people or the United States think that the majority of the undocumented are here because we want documentation to be able to get benefits from the government. And I want to mention that it is not the case. There may be some, maybe many. But there are so many others who are only hoping for an opportunity to develop themselves in this country and to be a good pillar [of society] to help the economy, their own family, to have two or three employees, but yes. And to serve the community.

Patricia, a house cleaner from Guatemala, went further, characterizing "people who in reality sometimes live solely off government handouts" as "parasites of this place. . . . They don't work . . . but they are easily given the opportunity of being here, people who want to destroy the country as well." Patricia's comment invoked the specter of a lazy and destructive welfare recipient.

Interviewees who advocated expansive inclusion seemed to find it particularly galling that they were held to higher standards than US citizens. Tomás, a painter and construction worker, claimed that Latinx workers occupied the bottom rung of a racialized labor hierarchy:[24] "We do the jobs that the *güeros* [whites] are not going to do. We do it. . . . We take care of children. All the agricultural workers that are in the fields. *Hispanos* do the work to grow the vegetables and fruits. Manual labor—the *hispanos*. When was the last time you saw a *gabacho* [white person] picking the fruit to bring to the market? No. It's us." Likewise, Nidia, a college student and waitress, complained, "Sometimes I see that, like, kids that are not doing good and they are from here, like, on drugs and are in gangs, it's like, and they have everything to work here, too, you know, and they don't take care, they don't want to have something for their lives." Tomás and Nidia critiqued the racialized divisions of labor in society and bemoaned the fact that US citizens of all races, who had opportunities denied to the illegalized workers, might nonetheless use drugs or join gangs. Such comments highlight the injustices that immigrant workers face, but also depict criminalized sectors of US society as not caring or making bad choices. Expansive inclusion broadens but does not eliminate boundaries, and it can reinscribe certain kinds of criminalizing rhetoric.

Rather than (or in addition to) advocating expansive inclusion, many interviewees adopted a *racial justice* perspective by critiquing discrimination based on race, ethnicity, income, gender, and family status. Through such critiques, interviewees sought to dismantle white privilege and economic advantage and instead create a more racially just system. Yet, while critical of the discrimination that they had experienced, some interviewees reproduced anti-Black racism in subtle ways by invoking discourses that condemned criminality (ignoring the ways that the criminal legal system has historically been deployed to police Black people) and espousing respectability politics (whereby the injuries of structural racism inflicted on Black people, Indigenous people, and other racialized communities—such as unemployment, poverty, and exclusion from education systems and positions of power—are treated as individual failings). At the same time, some interviewees, particularly youth activists who adopted racial justice perspectives, explicitly challenged anti-Black racism by seeking to connect the immigrant rights movement to Black Lives Matter. The differences in these approaches reveal how racial politics, which became increasingly polarized over the course of our study, infused claims-making and notions of merit in strikingly diverse ways.[25]

Accounts of discrimination abounded in our interviews. We have already detailed many instances of racial profiling at the hands of police, so here, we focus on the ways that interviewees critiqued labor exploitation and the racial slurs that they experienced. Oscar, the restaurant worker, became emotional as he described being repeatedly passed over for promotions. Oscar related, "Where I work, the people who are in the kitchen earn twelve dollars or fifteen dollars an hour. And the chefs make so much more! Like fifty dollars an hour. But I can't become a chef because of my immigration status. It is a barrier." Similarly, Oralia, whom we met at an immigrant-serving organization in Los Angeles, told us of humiliating and inappropriate comments about her language skills:

> Where I worked [as a janitor] in the school, there was a supervisor. He told me, "[Oralia] you should be grateful to be working here during the day." "Why?" I said. He said, "Because those that don't speak English work at night." "In that case am I working with my tongue? Am I cleaning with my tongue? No, I work with my hands, not with the manner in which I am speaking." So I felt bad, he belittled me, because he told me that.

Interviewees criticized employers who failed to pay them, exposed them to dangerous working conditions, did not provide healthcare or pay if they were injured on the job, underpaid them in comparison to peers who had work authorization, and threatened to have them deported. In addition to such material deprivations, disturbing personal humiliations were common experiences. Marisol, a house cleaner, told us of receiving her first paycheck from an employer who told her, "Wow! Your hands worked so quickly to swipe up the check, but not to clean the blinds thoroughly," as though she did not deserve the pay that she had earned.

Interviewees were also critical of racist comments directed at them, frequently by strangers. Perla, who was a front office worker at a healthcare agency, described one such experience: "There [are] a lot of racist people in this country too, we are sub[jected] to that. I had an encounter with a lady, and I was with my husband and my son at Cheesecake Factory, I went to the bathroom and she was just knocking [on] the door really hard and I said, well, you know, 'Give me a minute, I'll be right out.' When I got out, she's like, she told me, 'You immigrants, you shouldn't be here.'" Similarly, Esperanza, a housewife, was harassed in public. She related, "We have gone to the mall and have been waiting in line, and Americans mistreated us and say, 'What are these people doing in here?' We were in a store nearby and I told my husband, 'Did you hear what she said?' I get nervous right away and more scared." As Esperanza's comments indicate, such harassment takes an emotional toll. Esperanza encountered even more hostility when she traveled to New Orleans to participate in a protest related to the *United States v. Texas* case: "When we passed through Texas, we went to eat at a restaurant. There was so much racism even where we sat down to eat, an entire group next to us grabbed their plates and moved away from us. There was so much racism. Even in New Orleans, they nearly threw their plates at us once we ordered [our food]." Accounts of discrimination based on race, ethnicity, language skills, employment status, and gender abound in our interviews. By calling out such experiences and naming some of them as racism, interviewees critiqued the system that generated such hostility.

Direct experiences of blatant racism redefined whiteness for many interviewees, who expressed outrage and fear over the ways that the political and economic system seemed biased against them. Alondra, who had a background in computer science, told us that when white plumbers came to her home to make repairs after the election of Donald Trump, she worried "that they will say, 'You are an immigrant and you are here and you have a car, you dress well, and I am fixing your toilet.' . . . If . . . one of them would hit a Hispanic person, and the Hispanic person has no documents, we can't do anything." During a focus group interview with affiliates of an API immigrant–serving organization, a participant expressed a similar view: "Those who go against immigration and are racists is because they have little to no education, low income, working-class white people." Another interviewee felt that upper income families in the private school that her daughter attended were "nice" but "they will never be my friends and will not want to be my friends. Because they are people with money. And they, I think, do not want to be a friend of someone, of an immigrant." There are, of course, many immigrants with money. But her comments capture the perceived racial dynamics of her life, where "people with money" stand in contrast to Latinx immigrants, unwilling to befriend them.

Alfaro, the Southern California business owner first introduced in Chapter 1, thought that the Republican party itself was racist. During a 2015 interview, he shared his analysis: "Now that the House of Representatives and the Senate are completely Republican, they are going to battle Obama [in] the last months that remain of his presidency. . . . And it is clear, it is obvious, that it is due to racism. Even though they disguise it, they try to say that it isn't that, that it isn't racism, that it is the true way of seeing things. But that is a lie. Clearly, it is racism." Bertriz, who participated in an interview along with her daughter, a DACA recipient, attributed Republican opposition to DAPA to the desire to control low-wage workers by preventing them from pursuing better jobs. Bertriz explained, "All those people for whom DAPA is providing an opportunity, they'll start doing another type of job. More elevated. And who will perform the ones in the bottom? And the Republican needs to control the one in the bottom. So there are some of us that, perhaps we have a moderately superior education, not super university, but we're here and we want an opportunity to jump to the next step." These perspectives linked whiteness not only to potential violence but also to economic and political domination.

Interviewees were differentially positioned in regard to these racial dynamics. As we have noted, some API interviewees felt that authorities were less likely to racially profile them because their communities were not illegalized in the same ways as the Latinx community. Julia, who was originally from South Korea, felt less at risk. She explained, "I don't feel like threatened or like, oh, like they are going to deport me. . . . I feel like, if anything, there's probably all like so many, Koreans who live in K-Town and it was just like, kinda like, normal or not normal, but then like, you know, like you could, there's a lot of people who could, like, relate to me. . . . I guess Koreans might have it, like, a little easier than Hispanics." She speculated that the media "don't . . . even think, like, there such thing as, like, Korean immigrants." Yet, API interviewees also experienced racism, both in overt acts of discrimination and the quieter discrimination that takes the form of treating people as if they are invisible. A participant in a focus group that we conducted with an API immigrant–serving organization commented, "If you try going to Texas, not Dallas or Houston, but especially Waco, the non-white people [who] went there say that when Texans are looking at Asians, it's like as if they were looking at monkeys at a zoo." Such anti-Asian sentiment increased during the COVID-19 pandemic, which former President Trump persistently referred to as the "China virus."[26]

Each person's degree of vulnerability to racism was also influenced by how and whether others racially profiled them. Catalina, who was originally from Mexico, felt that her student status, light skin, and lack of accent protected her: "I get away with a lot because of the color of my skin and because I don't have an accent. So they don't really question me that far." When an immigration agent questioned Catalina and a friend with darker skin, the agent spoke to her briefly in English but questioned her friend at length, in Spanish. Similarly, as we discussed previously, Mireya, a college student and DACA recipient who was originally from Mexico, felt that her English skills, driver's license, and light skin protected her from being profiled, but that her father, who did not speak English and often drove when he was tired, was more vulnerable.

As we noted above, despite interviewees' critiques of racial injustice, in some instances, their own discourse fell into or failed to challenge anti-Black and other forms of racism. One participant in our focus group with affiliates of an API organization highlighted what she characterized as the racism of people in Korea: "Koreans are nice if you have a white face. They might be nice to a Black person, but to the laborers from Southeast Asia, especially Bangladesh, Pakistan, Indonesia, Koreans don't even treat them as human beings. Of course, not everyone is like that. [But] Koreans need to self-reflect . . . ." Another interviewee, who was from South America, suggested that her own middle-class community in the San Fernando Valley was tranquil, in part because there were fewer Latinx residents: "Here you don't find many immigrants. It is not a *barrio* of immigrants. There are few Latinos. The Latinos are in the restaurants, cooking. It is a calm *barrio.*" Some interviewees who had entered the United States on tourist or work visas were critical of "those who crossed the border" without authorization and whom they considered less educated. Oralia made it a point to mention the race of a bus driver who she felt had discriminated against her and her son:

> When my kid was little, I would get on the buses and he couldn't speak, he would just yell. They threw me off the bus two times. One time they made me get off the bus in San Fernando. Since I couldn't speak English, I felt frustrated. I couldn't find the ways by which to explain to the driver, she was Black. I told her, "You are not going to kick me off, because he's a little kid and he can't speak." No, she started yelling at me and a friend told me, "Let's get off."

Such inter- and intragroup tensions highlight the complexity of racialization and the challenges of pursuing racial justice against a backdrop of deeply embedded and socially reinforced racial assumptions.[27]

In contrast to seeking more expansive inclusion and consistent with a racial justice perspective, some advocated dismantling boundaries by granting *rights to all*. The "rights for all" perspectives generally took one of two forms. First, some argued that rights should be conferred on the basis of *humanity* rather than legal status, national affiliation, or behavior. These individuals conceptualized rights as universal and critiqued US immigration policies as dehumanizing. Recall Tomás's insistence that "we are not animals." Second, others—particularly students who participated in activist circles—adopted more abolitionist, open-border perspectives, critiquing the DREAMer narrative for abandoning those who did not fit "high achiever" categories, and advocating alliances with Black Lives Matter and other movements that challenged racism, regardless of its target. This quest for solidarity across social causes highlights the limitations of positing citizenship as the end goal for immigrant rights advocates. Citizenship alone would not eliminate injustice unless coupled with racial justice, an end to gender discrimination and homophobia, and, some argued, fundamental challenges to capitalism.[28]

The contention that rights should be granted on the basis of humanity, rather than serve the goal of national sovereignty, was sprinkled sparsely throughout our interviews. For example, during a 2014 interview, Pascuala, an advocate who worked for a nonprofit organization that sought to expand healthcare benefits to all, regardless of immigration status, stressed that healthcare should be considered a human right. Pascuala commented, "It's very difficult in the immigrant community to get people to demand a service or a public program that they don't feel they ought to have because they're still fighting for the basic, fundamental need, which could be status." Similarly, an advocate who worked for a Los Angeles–based immigrant rights organization critiqued policies that denied opportunities to noncitizens, arguing, "human rights are [the] right to education, right to work, right to have salary, right to health. That's a human right, not a constitutional right. Any government in the world should guarantee this for you, and this is being denied to people." A few interviewees did not mention human rights but did recommend that status be granted to everyone. When we asked Fátima, whom we met at a driver's license forum, who deserved to be included in any future grant of status, she answered simply, "The immigrants."

Some youth activists adopted a more absolute abolitionist stand, in solidarity and alliance with abolitionists involved the struggle against anti-Black racism and mass incarceration.[29] At a 2016 conference sponsored by an API organization, a speaker critiqued the "model minority" myth, admitting:

> I think we grew up with this idea that we are trying to aspire to whiteness. I talk to my Black friends and they say that this stuff you see has been happening for two hundred years, it's just that now people have camera phones. Now that we know about it, we can't ignore it. We can't just stand in solidarity but actually speak out. We cannot make progress, none of us, until the Black Lives Matter movement is successful.

Mateo, who was affiliated with a faith-based social justice organization in Orange County, argued that it was time for activists to move away from privileging stories of high achievers. He remarked, "I think the talk has been had of us, people like me, the cream of the crop, the AP honors students, but we are not talking about my parents, we are not talking about the people . . . who are building or getting the crops, the people who are out in the fields, the workers who are in the supermarkets cutting the meat. We are not thinking really about them." Likewise, Reese, who worked with an immigrant youth organization, thought that activists should "move away from the DREAM Act narrative. And instead, um, talk a lot more about undocumented workers, undocumented parents, LGBTQ immigrants, um, even like undocumented Black immigrants because nobody ever, ever talks about them, and they do exist." Drawing on the prison abolition movement,

Reese developed not only the appeal to universal humanity that we mentioned above, but also an abolitionist perspective on immigration law enforcement, as she explained in this interview excerpt:

> REESE: I really want to see . . . relief for all immigrants in their communities, obviously, like, no deportations, like, just stop, and then also just abolishing detention facilities. That seems a little excessive, but it can be done, you know, because the prison industry is making a lot of money, but . . . it's only because more communities are being criminalized. It's actually possible that we don't need prisons or detention facilities, and we find another alternative.
>
> INTERVIEWER: Right. What kind of alternative?
>
> REESE: A sort of justice and, you know, actually implement rehabilitation programs for "criminals" to, you know, be integrated back into society. So instead of, you know, separating families, actually provide a pathway for them to become . . . part of America, and . . . provide them a pathway to citizenship, but that shouldn't be the end goal. . . . I mean, this isn't just for immigrants, you know. It's for, like, all communities of color, that everybody has, like, fair access to education, housing, employment.
>
> INTERVIEWER: Okay. So a pathway to citizenship . . . is insufficient because it wouldn't address the challenges that are associated with racial discrimination.
>
> REESE: Mm-hm.
>
> INTERVIEWER: Okay. That makes sense. So it sounds like what you're saying is a policy would need to be about more than immigration.
>
> REESE: Yeah. For . . . social equity, yeah.

For Reese, both policing and immigration enforcement were grounded in racial discrimination, a problem that comprehensive immigration reform alone could not solve. While Reese supported a pathway to citizens for undocumented immigrants, she stressed that citizenship was not "the end goal," because without jobs, housing, or education, social equity would be out of reach. Importantly, those like Reese sought rights for all dismantled boundaries, not only between "deserving" and "undeserving" immigrants, but also between citizens and noncitizens, while also seeking greater protections and inclusions for all people.

Limits to Performing Citizenship

No matter how hard they strived to expand inclusion, or advocate for racial justice, or insist on rights for all, some interviewees encountered insurmountable barriers. A central barrier was that regardless of their behavior, they were haunted by ineligibility for relief, criminal convictions, or old deportation orders, any of which could prevent them from getting status. Interviewees were in a hyperlegalized environment,[30] in that they were confronted with illegalization and criminalization on an ongoing basis and were also abandoned by law, as even limited opportunities such as deferred action could be suddenly enjoined or rescinded. The emotional impact of these barriers was profound. Recall Margarita's somewhat bitter comment about how she experienced the DAPA injunction: "All of my hopes died." Indeed, living with uncertainty and a sense of betrayal led some interviewees into what Stephanie, a Korean interviewee and realtor, referred to as "a dark time." Interviewees described trauma, depression, fear, hopelessness, and pain. These emotional states were exacerbated by the precarious material conditions that we analyzed in earlier chapters: lack of work authorization, dangerous working conditions, ineligibility for worker's compensation, restrictions on travel, and painful separations from family members. Such emotional and material deprivations took a toll over time and constituted a form of "slow violence"[31] whose impacts are severe but also protracted, making them almost invisible. Moreover, individuals encountered limitations in performing citizenship due to the fact that, as some interviewees observed, citizenship alone was insufficient to resolve inequities, given that African Americans and other US citizens of color suffer the impacts of systemic racism.

Performing citizenship enacted futures that interviewees sought to bring about, but also was insufficient to secure these futures. Interviewees were haunted by the past and impeded by records that were often spectral in nature. As we discussed above, in an immigration context, allegations of criminality leave an almost indelible "mark" on individuals' records.

In addition to formal convictions, other more informal records—such as being entered in a gang database, being arrested, or even being the subject of a police report—could pose obstacles. Recall the case of Michaela, who never received a criminal conviction, but who feared that a police report about her involvement in a workplace dispute would result in any applications being denied.

Those who did have certain criminal convictions were statutorily ineligible for most immigration remedies. Old deportation orders or ambiguous immigration histories posed additional challenges. Even when individuals did not have histories of contact with the criminal legal system or immigration enforcement system, they might still face a lack of potential remedies. In 2017, a member of our research team accompanied an attorney who was conducting immigration consultations at the Salvadoran embassy in Los Angeles. Tellingly, the attorney remarked that some of the people who had consulted with her had been in the United States since before she was born but were still unable to regularize their status.

The ongoing stress of living in the United States without status or with only temporary status was challenging for many interviewees. Recall Oscar's distress over his inability to advance in the workplace, due to lack of work authorization. Lupita, introduced in Chapter 5 as the DACA recipient who drove a bus on her college campus while also working as an administrative assistant, described the worry she experienced when her work permit and driver's license were set to expire at around the same time:

> It was already January and it [the work permit] expired in February 22. I was like, "I'm not getting it [in the mail]. What's going on?" Then they started sending me a card from the DMV, like "Oh, it seems like your license is going to expire." I only had it for two years, but it was like right there. It expired when my DACA expired. I had to go and get a renewal for my driver's license. Then from work they're like, "It seems that your work permit is going to expire. If you don't bring us a new one, we can't continue your hiring process." I was like, "Oh my God." I was really worried, but then it got there around February.

Some interviewees were so distraught over their immigration status that they actually began to wish they were crime victims so that they would qualify for a U visa. Julieta, whose story was introduced in Chapter 3, once commented, "There are times when, in my moments of desperation, I say, please God, send someone to hit me on the face. Let me be a victim of robbery or something."

Such experiences cause long-term harm. At a community navigator training, one attendee who hoped to apply for DAPA commented to a member of our research team that she was "experiencing strong emotions" and the sense that "everything is up in the air." The uncertainty of legal opportunities that are "up in the air" takes a toll. A participant in a focus group held at a Korean-serving organization told us that she had made two plans for the future. If the DREAM Act passed and her child was able to obtain a green card, she would stay in the United States for the time being, but if it did not pass, then they would return to Korea. Interviewees were conscious of the insecurity of their status in the United States. Imelda related that ICE had visited her father's workplace and that he had been forced to write his name down, leading his family to fear that he would be deported. Imelda said, "That was really scary. . . . I never knew that my life could change like, so quick." Luckily, he was not apprehended. Nonetheless, both this incident and the possibility of removal continued to haunt this family.

For some, this legal violence[32] led to depression. A student who spoke at an Undocumented Student Forum at his university campus shared that he was "personally struggling with depression, like this place [campus] is a bubble that I can't get out of." Other interviewees described being traumatized by witnessing ICE apprehend relatives, border-crossing experiences, or learning that they were undocumented. Parents sometimes worried that such trauma was passed on to their children intergenerationally. Recall Coni, whose husband had been deported to Guatemala, and related in Chapter 5 how her children had "seen how they've [police have] taken my cars away from me. How they've left us on the streets. And I've cried in front of them. And so that affects them as well." The sense of betrayal by politicians who had promised to fight for immigration reform exacerbated the effects of these traumatic experiences. Interviewees used terms such as being "crushed," "disappointed," and "disillusioned" to describe their reactions to the DAPA injunction.

Such mental health impacts in some cases also took a physical toll, often revealing patterns of gendered inequality. Fátima, who sought help from the police only to be told that they were going to impound her car, suffered from dizziness, which she linked to the way that officials gave her the runaround. Alondra worried that she would have no recourse if she were victimized by plumbers coming to work in her home. Lupita's aunt was kidnapped and possibly sexually abused when she attempted to cross the US-Mexico border, a trip she had previously made without incident. The severity of these costs is also clear in a story that Oralia related regarding the terrible pain of not being able to be with her father on his deathbed:

> It was like he was waiting for me. A woman told me, "Talk to your dad, you will see, maybe it will make him better. Put the phone next to his ear, tell the doctor to give you permission." Okay, the doctor said, five minutes. That was when I talked to him and he said, "*Ya.*" ["Now."][33] That's when everybody started screaming, and I said, "What happened?" And they said, my father died.

When Oralia shared this story during an interview, she began crying uncontrollably, leading the interviewer to break down as well.

Interviewees also suffered workplace injuries but were unable to obtain medical care, disability pay, or unemployment from their employers. The physical, mental, and material impacts of immigration law are interconnected. Some interviewees resorted to metaphors to explain the harm that they experienced. Lucas, whom we met at an immigrant-serving organization in Los Angeles, told us that it was "as if I had a chain tied to me from behind, I can't take off," Samuel explained the feeling more prosaically "I think we are trapped. . . . The immigration system is so inflexible you cannot [travel back and forth] anymore. It used to be like, you come and you leave. You leave to your country. You go back to your country. Now, it's really hard."

While many interviewees hoped that if they could someday obtain citizenship, then their circumstances would improve dramatically, a few, such as Reese, questioned whether citizenship should be the end goal of immigrant rights activism at all. At a 2016 UC-wide Undocumented Student Summit attended by Elizabeth Hanna Rubio, a member of our research team, a speaker who was a member of a Black immigrant project on a UC campus expressed this perspective, quoted from Elizabeth's notes regarding this event:

She [the speaker] explained her transition to academia: "It was frustrating to have to explain my identity to everyone as an undocumented Black woman. Now, trying to fit into this space of academia is very difficult for me." The main point of her speech was to say that "citizenship is not the end goal" for a lot of people. We have been indoctrinated with the idea that citizenship means our humanization, "I feel with those in my community who have fallen under that spell." Assimilation is not liberation. Freedom is autonomy. She then said she wanted the audience to participate, almost as if shattering a perceived ethnographic gaze, she said "I hate feeling observed. I hate Black people feeling observed."

Similarly, Sally, an interviewee who worked with an immigrant rights organization, told us, "In a lot of ways we identify with the African American, like, movement for, like, you know, like, what is social justice. What is— what does it mean to be a citizen when people are still getting profiled?" These speakers' references to racialized surveillance and discrimination highlight the significant limits of equating social justice with citizenship.

Transformative Visions

As the Executive Director of one immigrant-serving organization told us, "You can't use a temporary solution to fix a permanent problem." This quote draws attention to the limitations of efforts to resolve the inequities that long-term undocumented residents experience through temporary programs such as deferred action. Indeed, the accounts that we have presented here not only address the circumstances of individual interviewees but also present transformative visions for a more just social order. These visions were complex and multifaceted, as the people with whom we spoke while we carried out our research cannot be pigeonholed or placed in a single ideological box. Moreover, interviewees' understandings evolved over time, as undocumented youth organizing provoked a rethinking of the DREAMer narrative in favor of insisting that undocumented youth were unapologetic and unafraid.[34] Furthermore, the rise of the Black Lives Matter movement led to increased consciousness of racial justice.[35]

Interviewees often centered formal citizenship in their visions of a more just social order. With citizenship, many argued, they would no longer have to experience what Imelda eloquently described: "I feel like my future is always like on a thin, like, line. Like any minute, it's going to change, and like, either bad or good, uncertain." Significantly, many people we spoke with stressed the ways that their participation in local communities had given them both a sense of belonging and some formal recognition, *regardless* of federal policy. Activists spoke to us, for example, of their efforts to extend healthcare and other public benefits to individuals who were excluded from federal programs, to persuade cities to issue municipal IDs, and to establish state laws (such as California's driver's license bill or the TRUST Act) that mitigated exclusionary impacts of federal policies. Interviewees spoke expansively of what they thought they could accomplish if the barrier of legal status was removed from their lives. They described the businesses they would establish, the jobs they would pursue, the education they would obtain, the trips they would take, the visits they would make with relatives in the countries of origin, and, generally speaking, the plans they would be able to make. But they also worked to create better worlds in the absence of legal status.

When we asked Lupita what she would do if there were to be an immigration reform, she immediately replied, "Like, hallelujah." This powerful, celebratory term indicates what was at stake for many who focused on formal citizenship. Interviewees emphasized the practical benefits that would flow from legal status, including the ability to have a social security number with which to work legally, apply for loans, and petition for family members, as well as the psychological relief that they anticipated if they no longer had to worry about deportation. Some interviewees emphasized that they would like to vote. Alfaro, for instance, told us that citizenship was "indispensable. Because that is the power that you have so that your vote can count, so that when something seems not right and something is causing difficulties to your community or your family, then with your vote, you can make the difference so that changes are made. And the only ones that can vote are, well, American citizens." Tellingly, though, voting, which to many political theorists is the hallmark of citizenship,[36] was not at the top of interviewees' minds, given the more fundamental benefits, such as work authorization, that legal status would confer.

In addition to articulating the transformations that could stem from formal citizenship, interviewees envisioned that political mobilization regardless of participants' formal citizenship, was a way of bringing about a more just world. While interviewees who attended marches, participated in actions, spoke publicly, or reached out to political leaders did so in order to accomplish social change, they also experienced such actions as opportunities to refuse to let legal status prevent political engagement. Beatriz, who participated actively in community meetings sponsored by a Los Angeles immigrant-serving organization, explained, "I feel valued. I feel I'm contributing a grain of my time. I'm not solely lost in my own world." By acting as constituents who had the right to shape public policy, interviewees claimed political voice.

Relatedly, immigrants articulated a vision of a social world in which they would not be manipulated by politicians. Fátima, whom we met at a community organization's driver's license forum, told us that, following the injunction, she had become fed up with what she experienced as manipulation on the part of politicians, who held out promises that they never fulfilled. She explained, "It was that way with the DREAM Act, they gave out the permits but they [recipients] still couldn't go to Mexico, so they only give you things halfway. Because they know how to manipulate us just as they please. Yes, they manipulate us according to their whims. Do you know what puppets are? They know how they are going to move us." Fátima said that she had determined that she would no longer allow herself to be treated like a puppet: "I'm no longer going to be like before, *al pendiente* [on alert], stressed out, thinking, 'Let's hear what they have to say or what they aren't saying.' No more." Fátima's vision, which also served as a form of self-protection, entailed refusing mentally and emotionally to allow legal status, reform schemes, or temporary programs to shape her life. She would refocus her attention on other priorities.[37] Performing citizenship could thus entail disinvesting in narratives of being *pendiente*, and instead committing to alternative versions of social belonging, versions that were still under construction.

As individuals advocate for expansive inclusion, racial justice, and rights for all, they enact these transformative visions, both discursively and in practice. In so doing, they simultaneously "shapeshift" social and political institutions. While such shapeshifting has limitations, as we saw in the previous section, these reimaginings hold the keys to social relationships that could transcend divisions brought into being through national borders. As we have seen, citizenship is not static. Rather, forms of social belonging and political inclusion can be manipulated, not only by government officials but also by those outside of citizenship, whether through their social activism or through persistence in insisting that they and their communities matter. Illegalization, criminalization, and racialization undermine the notions of "merit" embedded in the legal criteria for programs like DAPA and increase the difficulties associated with regularization of status. Phantom programs such as DAPA and DACA+ haunt, reminding immigrants and advocates of what could have been, of politicians' failed promises, and of the possibility of seeking broader forms of inclusion, forms that could be permanent rather than temporary in nature, and that would reconfigure the institutions that harm through exclusion.

Conclusion

THE PRECEDING CHAPTERS REVEAL the volatility and unpredictability of immigration policies in the period from 2012 through 2022. Immigrant residents confronted a wave of official promises in this period, many of which proved illusory. Governmental actors in the federal executive branch, and at the state and local level, tried to fill the policy void created by congressional stasis, to circumvent obstacles created by an activist federal judiciary. Yet, the majority of long-term immigrants lacking permanent legal status continued—and continue to this day—to live in conditions of precarity. Conversations with immigrant residents and the service providers and organizers who work alongside them in Los Angeles and Orange Counties revealed how phantom programs entrenched and exacerbated the precarity of migrant communities and how they reflected and reified broader processes of racialization. These discussions also shed light on the ways that individuals and organizations engaged in legal shapeshifting to accommodate, challenge, and, at times, reconfigure the official policies that sought to define and contain them.

The Harms of Phantom Programs

For many migrants and advocates, and indeed for some government officials, the only legal reform that is equipped to meaningfully alleviate the harms generated by the presence of more than ten million people living without authorization is a large-scale legalization program that provides a pathway to citizenship for all or almost all currently unauthorized residents in the US. Within the current immigration system, only citizenship can provide some baseline of security for migrants: the freedom to move across borders, meaningful protection against expulsion, and opportunities to access work in the formal economy.[1] Even if they had gone into effect, DAPA and DACA+ never could have eliminated the fears of daily life for its beneficiaries, not to mention those excluded. Many potential beneficiaries expressed both a disbelief that the program would deliver on its promise and a longing for something more lasting.

Conversations with the beneficiaries of the DACA program—the model for DAPA and DACA+—underscore the significant shortcomings of deferred action. Dean, the DACA recipient from South Korea, mentioned in Chapters 3 and 5, came to the US with his parents, and sister in 2001, just a few months before the 9/11 terrorist attacks. They came to visit his aunt but then decided to stay, hoping to try their luck in the United States instead of returning to Korea where the economy was still reeling from a financial crisis that took hold in the late 1990s. They settled in Los Angeles's Koreatown, where Dean's father began working as a chauffeur, a precarious job for someone lacking both work papers and, at the time, a driver's license. Dean described his life as living every day with the fear that "they were gonna get a call from ICE saying that 'Oh your parents are under custody and they're gonna be deported.'" Undoubtedly, DACA tamped down some of the fear for Dean in his encounters with police. But the impartial and incomplete nature of DACA meant that the fears associated with the modern immigration system continued in the lives of the family members of DACA beneficiaries. The DAPA and DACA+ announcements made clear that executive relief would not alleviate these fears because people like Dean's father were never included in the bargain. Dean's fears also speak to many of the other ways that temporary protections like DACA leave even the lucky recipients on the edge of precarious legal situations. Dean's father drove a car without a driver's license, rendering him vulnerable to police stops and immigration detention; other family members remained stuck with precarious jobs in the informal economy or trapped in the United States and unable to travel across borders for fear of being denied reentry.

Highlighting the phantom elements of deferred action programs—both DACA, which, as of August 2023, continues to exist, albeit in a limited and tenuous form, and DAPA and DACA+, which were enjoined by federal courts before ever taking effect— also illustrates how executive relief helped to normalize and formalize the notion that immigration law, a core civil and administrative regulatory project, is largely governed by criminal laws, actors, and rationales. Indeed, much legal and political discourse now proceeds as if the only way that immigration law can work is with the help of police and prosecutors who enforce the law on a terrain defined by principles of deservingness and moral innocence. There is an intimate and mutually constitutive relationship between deferred action and the draconian immigration enforcement policies that have captured headlines over the last decade.

When deferred action programs went into effect, they helped beneficiaries mitigate some of the harms that flow from lacking citizenship and legal immigration status in the US. The obvious benefit of DACA, for example, is the opportunity to find work in the formal economy—a benefit that green card holders and citizens already enjoy. These are the benefits that individuals eligible for DAPA and DACA+ were denied when those programs failed to take hold. But there are other benefits that lawful permanent residents and US citizens enjoy that DACA beneficiaries, let alone the immigrants excluded from those programs and denied access to comparable programs like DAPA and DACA+, still do not possess. A common thread among many of the migrants we interviewed was a desire to connect with family and friends in other countries, a desire that is tied up with the broader quest for freedom of movement across borders. Even with DACA, immigrant residents had to turn to programs like advance parole, which provided migrants with temporary official authorization to leave the United States and to reenter under a limited set of conditions. Like Chae Chan Ping of the foundational, late nineteenth century *Chinese Exclusion Case*,[2] who had resided in the US for a decade before travelling to China, these long-term US residents learn that their permission to reenter the US is easily revocable and unconstrained by the due process protections of the US constitution. For individuals who lack even the thin protections of deferred action, the ability to travel is even more circumscribed; advance parole generally is not available for those who lack the right to be present in the first instance. Recent figures suggest that 47 percent of unauthorized migrants have resided in the United States for fifteen years or longer. Sixty percent have resided for at least ten years.[3] For these individuals, long-term separation from family members outside of the United States is a haunting reality only partially alleviated by deferred action programs.

The data and findings in this book complicate the uplifting narrative that often surrounds DACA and that pervaded media coverage about the announcement of DAPA and DACA+. These beneficial programs were rolled out during an era intensely committed to exclusionary practices. As a result, the fight that constituents and advocates waged to secure DACA, DAPA, and DACA+ generated human costs in the form of constant frustration and uncertainty, as well as costs in time and money spent gathering materials and altering behavior in preparation for programs that sometimes never came into being, and for which some individuals may never have been eligible. By the time President Obama's announcement of the terms of the DAPA "deal" was projected onto a huge, inflatable screen in Los Angeles, DACA recipients well understood the cost of such a deal. The boos and the jeers that rained down that November evening in 2014, as an audience listened to President Obama's proposal for DAPA and DACA+, reflected understandable frustration and anger. DACA recipients had already been asked to perform their supercitizenship to gain a thin form of immigration protection. Now they were being told that many of their parents would not be part of that "deal." And for many long-term residents who thought that they were holding up their end of the bargain and might benefit from executive relief, the announcement was a slap in the face. The Obama administration's proposed program denied relief to the parents of DACA recipients and allocated benefits on the basis of "deservingness" as measured by one's ability to avoid contact with criminal legal systems that operated in ways that often seemed arbitrary and marked by substantial racial discrepancies. Those listening to Obama's announcement immediately perceived that this purportedly pragmatic approach to immigration enforcement would normalize their suffering and invisibility. On the November 2014 evening of the DAPA announcement, migrants and their supporters in Southern California and all across the country heard the president lay out the terms of the deal, and some celebrated, but many were left wondering whether they and their loved ones had been seen at all.

Racialization in a Criminalized Landscape

The voices and experiences of the people in this book both deepen and broaden our understanding of processes of racialization, offering some comparative perspectives that elucidate how immigration policies help define what it means to be part of Latinx and API communities in the US. Rather than focusing only on how Latinx or API migrants of various statuses might define their lives *against* the backdrop of whiteness or citizenship (or both), the voices and experiences captured in this book demonstrate the complicated ways that migrants define their lives within and against an array of migrant experiences.

This comparative frame reveals how race operates in the context of immigration enforcement. First, among those we interviewed, participants who identified as Latinx were more likely than residents who identified as API to discuss the negative impact that local police played in their everyday lives. Chapter 1 opened with a vignette about Erasmo, a Mexican migrant who recounted how a police stop led to a fast-tracked removal from the United States. He resented the frequent contact with and questioning by the police that happened to him even in the absence of any misconduct on his part, and he objected to the way that these low-level interactions constrained his ability to move freely within his community. Erasmo's story sheds light on the mechanisms that racialize migrants: extensive federal immigration enforcement—and related status vulnerabilities created by lack of access to employment authorization, driver's licenses, and the like—that interact with local policing practices in ways that reinforce a sense of second-class status and exclusion.

Fátima also provided insight into how racialization can undercut formal legal protections. When we interviewed her, Fátima shared that she had recently gotten her driver's license and said that "[life] had gotten a little bit better because now I have a license. That is a good thing." At the same time, simply possessing a license didn't stop police from pulling her over. Indeed, she recounted a story in which a police officer stopped her, and at that time, she felt as if the officer "was hoping that [she] wouldn't have a license." Fátima explained the power of the license in her life: "Now I can drive more tranquilly, more at ease. The police no longer have the luxury of taking away my car." While Fátima evinced relief and gratitude at having a license to move freely in her community, she continued to express frustration at the inconvenience of having to continually prove that she possessed the right to have a car and to use it. State laws like California A.B. 60 driver's licensing law can help include migrants in the daily practices and connections that maintain their community ties, but both Erasmo and Fátima know that this is not enough to end racialized harassment.

Latinx residents with whom we spoke also expressed other feelings of alienation. We often asked people whether and how much they identified with being "American." Samuel, the aspiring accountant, described feeling like he was being treated "not even as a second-class citizen." He also described the feeling of not having rights, which, in his mind, made his own experiences worse than what he understood to be the situation of Black Americans: "I think Blacks and how they are treated in some parts, treated like second-class citizens, but they still have rights. We don't have those rights." Samuel's comment does not take account of the many instances in which Black US citizens are *not* treated as people who have rights, second-class or otherwise. Among other things, Black residents are targeted more often, and more intrusively and violently, by the police than other racial groups.[4] Samuel's comment also fails to acknowledge the reality of Black migrants, who experience both the exclusionary effects of immigration law and the harsh, discriminatory edge of anti-Black racism. Yet, the experiences of Erasmo, Fátima, and Samuel all demonstrate that Latinx racial identity shapes and is shaped by Black racialization in complicated ways. Latinx individuals who do not identify as Black recount their own experiences of being targeted as a result of racialized policing practices. They then make different (and sometimes situational) choices about whether to counteract these experiences by seeking stronger cross-racial alliances or by making greater efforts to distance themselves from communities experiencing the worst discrimination. In our interviews, which took place before the large racial justice uprisings of 2020 triggered by the brutal police killing of George Floyd, many young, grassroots Latinx organizers were expressing their strong view that racial solidarity was the best and only way to combat discrimination and violence. That solidarity took visible form in the marches and protests of the summer of 2020.

In contrast with Latinx residents, who felt hypervisible to certain forms of policing, invisibility is a theme that emerged often in our interviews with API residents in Southern California. This sometimes took the form of official neglect or of private violence. Joonseo, introduced in Chapter 3, described his high school years as a time filled with bullying at the hands of his Latinx and Black classmates. He explained, "They had preconceived notions that Asians are rich. That Asians are here to take away jobs and create a business to hire Latinos and they don't pay them well, which is part of the truth, you know?" Interestingly, Joonseo saw some truth in and empathy for his classmates' resentment, particularly given the discrimination that they also faced, but during our interview with him, he kept hitting on this idea that he was not being seen, not by his classmates or by high school teachers. And when he was seen, it was sometimes with a criminalizing gaze. "[M]y teacher saw me because I wasn't able to speak any English, not even A, B, C, D. . . . I was always sleepy, and my eyes kind of like were sleepy, so they thought I was doing [drugs]. I never done drugs before, I never smoke. But they assume."

Ironically, API migrants—members of the fastest-growing group of immigrants to the US—often reported feeling invisible within the immigrant justice community as well. Although a great deal of immigrants' rights advocacy was intended to benefit *all* migrants, particularly low-income and vulnerable migrant communities, regardless of racial or ethnic identity, several unauthorized API migrants reported a feeling of being left out of the conversation. This reality seemed to generate significant ambivalence among the API migrants we interviewed.

At times, invisibility operates as an acknowledged benefit for API residents, albeit one with other costs. The focus on Latinx experiences within immigration discourse and activism provided API migrants an opportunity to "pass" as authorized or documented because they did not fit popular conceptions of the unauthorized migrant experience. Moreover, it was fairly typical for the Latinx interviewees in this book to speak of harassment by and fear of police, and the broader immigration enforcement apparatus they represented. Many of the API residents we interviewed seemed to agree that immigration enforcement bears down differently on Latinx communities. Some suggested that this political reality conferred a kind of benefit to API residents.

But this kind of benefit has drawbacks. Bryce, a Thai American DACA recipient, grew up in the Central Valley region of California where he knew few if any other API residents, but lived in a community with a significant Latinx population. Although he embraces his undocumented identity, when asked to reflect on whether he perceives any barriers for undocumented API migrants to participating in political activity, he suggests that inertia works against mobilization efforts: "I feel like with a lot of API folks, it comes with the luxury of not aligning with that stereotype of what the undocumented immigrant looks like so . . . you can go under the radar . . . and just get by. Also, it's definitely a lot more stigmatized in our families, well, at least for my family . . . it's taboo, you can't talk about it." Bryce's comments confirm his perception that Latinx migrants bear a significant burden of being racialized as particular kinds of outsiders. He perceives this reality as conferring a kind of benefit to API migrants passing within this racial arrangement, but his comments also suggest that he perceives there to be less of a stigma in communities, particularly the Latinx community, surrounding discussions of immigration status. Though his views are far from universal, Bryce's perception is a noteworthy view that is shared by others.

The interviews gathered in this book also speak to the challenges of serving and advocating with and on behalf of API migrants, a group that reflects a diverse set of migration histories. A common idea expressed by API migrants, especially those in advocate positions, was that it is difficult to mobilize a community that is comprised of heterogeneous nationalities, ethnicities, and subgroups with distinct migration traditions and histories. Time and again, API-focused advocacy organizations mentioned the difficulty of serving the entire API community given its language and cultural diversity. This reality was sometimes contrasted with the Latinx experience, based on the facile assumption that Latinx immigrants were entirely Spanish speaking. (As we made clear in Chapter 4, this assumption is also problematic.). Serving a diverse community required organizations to spend more time, money, and resources in order to connect with migrants across significant subgroup distinctions.

Several government officials stated that they understood themselves as working within an informal partnership with those at the advocacy and constituent levels, and moreover that they *relied* on organizing and cohesive messaging, especially on the parts of advocates, to advance change within the administration. A distinct feature of shapeshifting in the legal services and law practice context involved the renegotiation of social meaning across different institutions comprised of different actors—constituents, advocates, and government officials—and aligned according to legal hierarchies. When we interviewed Serena, she had already been working as a lawyer for more than ten years. The child of Korean immigrants, Serena had spent her time since graduation working in the nonprofit sector or in government. After accumulating significant experience serving API migrants, she eventually obtained a government position, moving between multiple departments. When we asked Serena about the challenges of reaching out to API-serving organizations, she explained that "there were times when I would reach out to the Asian American groups and say 'You guys need to show up. I need you to like stomp your feet, like, you know, be a bigger voice.' Like when I go to the White House, they want to know what the community groups are saying. So that was both a privilege, but sometimes I found it frustrating." During the same interview, Serena pressed the point that API advocates did not always take full advantage of opportunities to meet with government officials. Describing a meeting in Southern California with API stakeholders, Serena recounted with some exasperation: "Sometimes . . . groups were too polite. I would go ahead and take advantage of the opportunity and say, 'You all are being like way too nice. . . . I want your voice to be as big and loud and clear as possible, so you know, put it in writing! Don't just complain, but also say what you want. Give us recommendations and send it to us, send it to the White House, to departments, send it to your senator.'"

Serena's comments fit within a popular narrative that could be read as veering toward a stereotype, namely that APIs tend to be too meek or polite and would rather avoid upsetting the status quo. But when putting Serena's comments alongside the experiences of advocates in API-serving organizations all over Southern California, a slightly different picture emerges: one in which advocates must contend with limited resources and navigate a competitive funding terrain saddled with conditions (a reality confronting all advocates), but in addition, must make these resources stretch even further given the internal community divisions tied to distinct languages, cultures, and migration histories. Serena makes passing reference to the limited bandwidth of advocates, but these limitations may impact the API advocacy world in ways deeper than commonly recognized.

There are other factors that push community members away from being louder and more visible. Being seen and heard by public officials can also invite unwanted attention in the form of intrusive, racialized policing or repressive local policy responses. As we discussed in Chapter 4, one organizer, a Latinx-identifying man organizer who worked for a prominent community-based organization in Los Angeles, cited "Asians" as a good "example" for Latinx migrants to follow to avoid conflict with the police. In so doing, he reiterated a version of the model-minority myth, of course. But his comments also reflect the broader dynamic of state-induced violence— be it under the cover of federal immigration or local police power—that focuses on and normalizes violence against Black and Latinx migrants. His comments inadvertently highlight how negative police relations are fueled, in part, by the very kinds of vocal and oppositional community organizing that he leads and encourages. Given the possibility and advantages of remaining quiet, the efforts of API organizers opting for activism, visibility, and racial solidarity in both immigration and policing reform efforts over the past decade are all the more notable.

Overlooking the racial and linguistic diversity of immigrants from Latin American and API countries can perpetuate the invisibility and marginalization of Afro-Latinx, Black, and mixed-race migrants. In Chapter 6, Tomás criticized the racialized hierarchy of the US labor market, complaining that Latinx workers fill out the bottom of the workforce. His critique could be extended and refined. Many migrants from Mexico and Central America identify as indigenous, which compounds their isolation in the United States. As non-English and non–Spanish language speakers, indigenous migrants miss out on both the broadly available resources available to native-born Americans and the community resources that are geared toward Spanish-speaking migrants. Existing studies suggest that indigenous migrants are more likely to be assigned the least desirable jobs in worksites like agricultural settings, even relative to other non-indigenous Latinx migrants. Attending to intragroup distinctions like these provides texture and descriptive clarity to the contours of the marginalization process.[5]

Despite differences and diversity between and among racial groups, a common thread that emerges across immigrant groups is the way that US policing practices play a role in racial identity. A broad and deep vein of scholarship in Critical Race Theory already explores many aspects of this issue.[6] For example, legal scholar (and immigrant from the United Kingdom) Devon Carbado has theorized the role of policing in the "racial naturalization" process for Black people in the US. Carbado argued that he "became a black American long before [he] acquired American citizenship" through repeated and dangerous episodes of police harassment in the United States. According to Carbado, "De facto racial naturalization occurs when race is implicitly being used to establish, solidify, or sediment race-based American identities. Police interactions often perform this function."[7] In other words, while federal immigration and citizenship laws laid out the prerequisites for acquiring legal citizenship, constitutional criminal procedure and the broad discretion it confers upon police set the terms for functional citizenship—a key aspect of racial identity formation.[8]

The harms documented in our book extend Carbado's analysis, showing how the broader immigration enforcement system also contributes to the "racial naturalization" process. First, the tight nexus of policing and immigration enforcement has a significant effect on the lives of Black migrant. Kevin Johnson mapped the problem in his analysis of the Supreme Court case of *Moncrieffe v. Holder*. Adrian Moncrieffe, a Black Jamaican who had been a lawful permanent resident since age three, was nearly deported and barred for life based upon charges stemming from a problematic arrest by Georgia police for possession of a small amount of marijuana. Expounding on the significance of this case, Johnson observes that "Moncrieffe's story exemplifies how a racially disparate criminal justice system exacerbates racially disparate removals."[9] The criminal and immigration systems function as parts of a broader set of social systems in which anti-Blackness informs multiple steps in the official processes of containment, control, and removal.

Second, the racial logics of immigration enforcement—premised on long histories of excluding API and Latinx immigrants from whiteness—have infused ordinary policing practices as well. Residents in certain immigrant communities feel that they are policed differently as a consequence of perceived immigration status. Though the merger of criminal and immigration enforcement bureaucracies has exacerbated the scale of the problem, the problem was not caused by this merger. There is a long history of state and local law enforcement playing an integral part in excluding API[10] and Latinx[11] immigrants and their descendants from integration and full citizenship in the US. Ordinary street policing has always involved the policing various kinds of racial borders, and this continues to be the case, albeit in newer and more formal ways. The historical record thus demonstrates the futility of ongoing efforts on the part of some immigrant-serving organizations, and immigrants themselves, to protect themselves by distinguishing themselves from, and defining themselves against, the Black communities that consistently have been on the receiving end of the harshest law enforcement practices. Many people we spoke with recognized that the way forward was to exist and organize in solidarity with, rather than against, other marginalized communities.

Legal Shapeshifting

In Chapter 4, we discussed advocates and organizers, and the ways they engaged in legal shapeshifting, using differences in self-perceptions and external perceptions to remake broader understandings of immigrant communities and the laws that governed them. As we noted in that chapter, Professor Aimee Cox describes shapeshifting, in part, as the "renegotiation of the contract of citizenship."[12] In Cox's account of shapeshifting, law operates in the background. Because we focus on moments of legal inflection in communities where outsider status is generated in important ways by law, the law figures into our analysis more prominently, and we chart the ways that individuals and organizations engage in legal shapeshifting.

The precarity and injustice described in our book can be traced largely (though not exclusively) to shortcomings in the law. Many of the advocates and government workers whom we interviewed were lawyers or had aspirations to work as or with lawyers (law school applicants, law students, graduate students, organizers, etc.). They used legal shapeshifting strategies within and against the contested constraints of law and legal norms. Laws set the parameters for migrant identities, but the experiences of the people we interviewed reveal how legal shapeshifting activities challenged the notions of what those identities mean socially and politically. Many of the organizers and activists interviewed for this book repeatedly called attention to the arbitrariness of the distinctions used by law and legal actors. Existing laws distribute benefits and mete out punishment on the basis of distinctions grounded in presence, entry, and criminal records, all of which are categories created by law. These categories can be changed, and there is sometimes legal discretion to disregard them. Yet, legal actors and institutions often suffer from a lack of imagination when confronted with these categories.

In contrast, many of the people that we spoke with were easily able to imagine a world in which these legal categories were far less significant. Sometimes, they were able to help work to make those possibilities into legal realities. California law, for instance, has been changed in critical ways, thanks to legal shapeshifting. The law governing driver's licenses provides one example. We wrote about Bryce in previous chapters. Bryce's experience as an undocumented Thai American was certainly precarious, but was also shaped in positive ways by his parents' access to driver's licenses.[13] By successfully pushing for expanded access to California driver's licenses for undocumented residents, organizers shifted the shape of the law in ways that allowed migrants like Bryce to move in ways previously foreclosed to those in the status category of "undocumented."

A similar transformation occurred in the realm of higher education, beginning well before the period of our study, but continuing throughout. In Chapter 3, we recounted Joonseo's story of challenging an Orange County college's effort to deny him in-state tuition benefits. Well before he brought a legal challenge against that college, Joonseo had applied to a California state school. He planned to attend right after high school, in an attempt to pursue the conventional and normatively idealized educational track of a high-achieving student. He was accepted, but he could not attend. He lacked a social security number, and the school charged him the fees designated for international students, which he could not pay. "So I passed on that, and then I thought 'Okay, college was not my thing anyway.'" When advocacy efforts yielded a change of state law, however, Joonseo was designated an in-state resident, qualifying for much lower tuition. He then fought for that tuition at his college, engaging in his own legal advocacy to make that change in the law concrete. His experience demonstrates not only that the categories into which people are sorted can change with a change in law, but also that those same people are instrumental in effectuating and enforcing those law changes.

The people whom we interviewed worked alongside others to fundamentally transform assumptions about who merits legal inclusion, not only as a matter of local and state law, but also at the federal level. Many different parts of the book feature the voices of immigrant constituents and advocates pushing the federal government to go beyond the tightly circumscribed and narrow story of the DREAMers. Government officials portrayed DREAMers as the normative ideal and the moral baseline for determining the outer boundaries of what was politically possible in Congress. But the interviews recounted in this book illustrate the ways that advocates and constituents pushed lawmakers and officials to reimagine how a much broader set of immigrants might benefit under the law. Many advocates were not satisfied with the DACA narrative that rewarded high-achieving migrants who were presented as blameless, and they worked to revise this narrative. Like the "Dream 9,"—the nine politically active DACA recipients who crossed the border into Mexico (thereby technically eliminating their DACA eligibility), and then attempted to reenter at the US-Mexico border as an act of political defiance—the advocacy efforts of many organizers and activists in Southern California in the 2012–2022 period broadened popular understandings of who should benefit from immigration relief.[14]

At the time of this book's publication, the fate of DACA remains undetermined as the legal challenge to the program continues to make its way to the Supreme Court. Nevertheless, deferred action and other forms of temporary executive relief continue to exist, and these programs now extend well beyond the original DREAMers. Under the Biden administration, the DHS is granting deferred action benefits to migrants who are working in businesses under investigation for labor and employment violations. Importantly, the DHS's announcement of this policy does not mention DACA or DREAMers at all. Instead, Secretary of Homeland Security Mayorkas describes this policy as an effort to "effectively protect the American labor market, the conditions of the American worksite, and the dignity of the workers who power our economy."[15] This shift in policy unmistakably expands the possible range of identities and experiences that might be shaped by and protected under deferred action. In addition to benefiting high-achieving college graduates and certain others, this approach enables deferred action to reach people working within exploitation-ridden industries.

At the same time, there are limits to this form of legal shapeshifting. As temporary programs expand to cover new populations, they do so in ways less rights protective than the more robust forms of status that they replace or supplement. For example, the Biden administration has extended temporary relief through parole to migrants from Venezuela, Cuba, Nicaragua, and Haiti. The process is open to people who might have difficulty claiming asylum in the existing system. But it also creates new limits on protection. Unlike asylum, the protections extended to these groups require individuals to identify sponsors in the US, and allow them to remain only temporarily.

Even when legal shapeshifting apparently falls short, however—when laws remain frozen in the face of movement activism, or when law reform fails to meet the urgent needs of the moment—it may still shift the norms that undergird the legal order. Within the federal government, officials who helped develop and roll out the expanded deferred action programs recognized opportunities for maneuvering within the gaps of the immigration code. But after the announcement of DAPA and DACA+, some within the government had clearly become convinced that their agency should have been more ambitious. A member of our team spoke with Charles, a senior immigration official who served in the second term of the Obama administration. Charles was a seasoned immigration lawyer, one who had spent a career cycling between law practice, teaching, and government service. He disagreed with the Office of Legal Counsel's decision to extend deferred action protection to the unauthorized migrant parents of US citizens and lawful permanent residents but not to the parents of DACA recipients. Charles explained: "To me it's like a very artificial way, or a limited way, of thinking about the immigration statute.... I thought, they're trying to read too much into the statute and saying this is a hard line you couldn't do. You know that there's something so special about the parent-child relationship that's different than anything else." The legal shapeshifting of immigrant activists that once made DACA relief popular later helped make the justice claims of their family members more visible and meaningful. This did not change the DAPA and DACA+ policy, but it has highlighted questions about the exclusionary logic undergirding these programs, and immigration law more broadly.

The original political vision for DACA as a stepping stone toward mass legalization never came to pass. Rather than leading to mass legalization, the policies and practices described in this volume have marked an era of mass illegalization. Ironically, as our discussion of related litigation makes clear, conservative activism and litigation around DAPA and DACA+ have played an important role in hardening the contours of immigration law and diffusing organizing energy. In so many ways, these programs continue to haunt not just those who hoped to qualify, but all of us. They have shaped and limited political imagination and the reality of our borders.

Nevertheless, many of the immigrants who were denied the benefits of deferred action, let alone more permanent forms of relief, have managed to forge pathways to inclusion and participation, against the odds, and sometimes with the assistance of the governmental entities that formally will not cognize their presence. In the conversations captured in this book, DACA and the other, thwarted deferred action programs elicited a range of responses, from audible relief to vocal disappointment. There are no unmitigated success stories here. At the same time, the life stories that we have tried to capture in this book confirm that the stability, mobility, and security that so many seek are still the subject of powerful contestation and claim making. And the struggle continues.

NOTES

Introduction

1. See, for example, Marie Gottschalk, "Razing the Carceral State," *Social Justice* 42, no. 2 (2015): 31-51.

2. Gerald L. Neuman, "The Lost Century of American Immigration Law (1776–1875)," *Columbia Law Review* 93, no. 8 (December 1993): 1833–1901.

3. Kerry Abrams, "Polygamy, Prostitution, and the Federalization of Immigration Law," *Columbia Law Review* 105, no. 3 (April 2005): 641–716.

4. Kelly Lytle Hernández, *City of Inmates: Conquest, Rebellion, and the Rise of Human Caging in Los Angeles, 1771–1965* (Chapel Hill, NC: University of North Carolina Press, 2017).

5. Kitty Calavita, *U.S. Immigration Law and the Control of Labor: 1820–1924* (London: Academic Press, 1984); Rachel E. Rosenbloom, "Policing Sex, Policing Immigrants: What Crimmigration's Past Can Tell Us About Its Present and Its Future," *California Law Review* 104, no. 1 (February 2016): 149–199.

6. Francisco E. Balderrama and Raymond Rodríguez, *Decade of Betrayal: Mexican Repatriation in the 1930s* (Albuquerque: University of New Mexico Press, 1995); Juan Ramón García, *Operation Wetback: The Mass Deportation of Mexican Undocumented Workers in 1954* (Westport, CT: Greenwood Press, 1980).

7. Mae M. Ngai, *Impossible Subjects: Illegal Aliens and the Making of Modern America* (Princeton, NJ: Princeton University Press, 2004); Natalia Molina, *How Race Is Made in America: Immigration, Citizenship, and the Historical Power of Racial Scripts* (Berkeley, CA: University of California Press, 2014); Kelly Lytle Hernández, *Migra!: A History of the U.S. Border Patrol* (Berkeley, CA: University of California Press, 2010).

8. Elizabeth Hinton, *From the War on Poverty to the War on Crime: The Making of Mass Incarceration in America* (Cambridge, MA: Harvard University Press, 2016).

9. Nancy Morawetz, "Understanding the Impact of the 1996 Deportation Laws and the Limited Scope of Proposed Reforms," *Harvard Law Review* 113, no. 8 (June 2000): 1936–1962.

10. Jennifer M. Chacón, "Unsecured Borders: Immigration Restrictions, Crime Control and National Security," *Connecticut Law Review* 39, no. 5 (July 2007): 1827–1891; Daniel Kanstroom, "Deportation, Social Control, and Punishment: Some Thoughts about Why Hard Laws Make Bad Cases," *Harvard Law Review* 113, no. 8 (June 2000): 1890–1935; Teresa A. Miller, "Citizenship and Severity: Recent Immigration Reforms and the New Penology," *Georgetown Immigration Law Journal* 17, no. 4 (Summer 2003): 611–666; Juliet Stumpf, "The Crimmigration Crisis: Immigrants, Crime, and Sovereign Power," *American University Law Review* 56, no. 2 (December 2006): 367–419.

11. Yolanda Vázquez, "Constructing Crimmigration: Latino Subordination in a 'Post-Racial' World," *Ohio State Law Journal* 76, no. 3 (2015): 599–657; César Cuauhtémoc García Hernández, "Creating Crimmigration," *Brigham Young University Law Review* 2013, no. 6 (February 2014): 1457–1515; Jonathan Simon, *Governing Through Crime: How the War on Crime Transformed American Democracy and Created a Culture of Fear* (Oxford: Oxford University Press, 2007).

12. See e.g., Jennifer M. Chacón, "Overcriminalizing Immigration," *Journal of Criminal Law and Criminology* 102, no. 3 (Summer 2012): 613–652.

13. See *Arizona v. United States*, 567 U.S. 387 (2012).

14. Jennifer M. Chacón, "A Diversion of Attention? Immigration Courts and the Adjudication of Fourth and Fifth Amendment Rights," *Duke Law Review* 59, no. 8 (May 2010): 1563–1633.

15. Mat Coleman and Austin Kocher, "Rethinking the 'Gold Standard' of Racial Profiling: §287(g), Secure Communities and Racially Discrepant Police Power," *American Behavioral Scientist* 63, no. 9 (August 2019): 1185–1220, https://doi.org/10.1177/0002764219835275; Aarti Kohli, Peter L. Markowitz, and Lisa Chavez, *Secure Communities by the Numbers: An Analysis of Demographics and Due Process* (Berkeley, CA: Chief Justice Earl Warren Institute on Law and Social Policy, October 2011).

16. Adam B. Cox & Cristina M. Rodríguez, The President and Immigration Law (Oxford: Oxford University Press, 2020).

17. Government statistics show that approvals for total initial applications through 2017—when new applications were frozen—numbered 798,980. "Number of Form I-821D, Consideration of Deferred Action for Childhood Arrivals by Fiscal Year, Quarter, Intake, Biometrics and Case Status Fiscal Year 2012–2017

(September 30)," US Citizenship and Immigration Services, September 30, 2017, https://www.uscis.gov/sites/default/files/USCIS/Resources/Reports%20 and%20Studies/Immigration%20Forms%20Data/All%20Form%20Types/ DACA/daca_performancedata_fy2017_qtr4.pdf. Although many recipients have routinely renewed their application, over time, the number of DACA designees declined either because individuals lost eligibility, gained access to other, more permanent immigration relief, or left the country. By late 2019, only about 650,000 individuals were DACA designees. "Deferred Action for Childhood Arrival (DACA) Data Tools," Data Hub, Migration Policy Institute, accessed February 17, 2023, https://www.migrationpolicy.org/programs/data-hub/deferred-action -childhood-arrivals-daca-profiles.

18. President Barack Obama, "Remarks by the President in Address to the Nation on Immigration," November 20, 2014, https://obamawhitehouse.archives .gov/the-press-office/2014/11/20/remarks-president-address-nation-immigra-tion; Memorandum from Jeh Charles Johnson, Secretary of Homeland Security, to León Rodríguez, Director of US Citizenship and Immigration Services, et al., "Exercising Prosecutorial Discretion with Respect to Individuals Who Came to the United States as Children and with Respect to Certain Individuals Who Are the Parents of U.S. Citizens or Permanent Residents," November 20, 2014, https://www.dhs.gov/sites/default/files/publications/14_1120_memo_deferred _action_2.pdf.

19. In February 2015, the Migration Policy Institute estimated that about 3.7 million unauthorized immigrants in the United States were potentially eligible for DAPA. Migration Policy Institute, "MPI Releases Detailed Data Profiles of Unauthorized Immigrants and Estimates of Deferred Action Populations for Top U.S. Counties," January 15, 2015, https://www.migrationpolicy.org/news/mpi-re leases-detailed-county-profiles-unauthorized-immigrants-and-estimates-de ferred-action. At that time, there were about 11 million unauthorized immigrant residents, nearly a million of whom were DACA eligible.

20. Complaint for Declaratory and Injunctive Relief at ¶¶ 3, 21, 62, *Texas v. United States*, 2015 WL 648579 (S.D. Tex. Dec. 3, 2014) (No. B-14–254), ECF No. 1; see Alicia A. Caldwell, "Judge on Immigration Case Had Criticized US Policy," Associated Press, December 9, 2014, 9:56 AM, http://perma.cc/AV4K-DNWZ.

21. *United States v. Texas*, 579 U.S. 547 (2016).

22. Tal Kopan, "Trump Administration Reverses DAPA in 'House Cleaning,'" *CNN*, June 16, 2017, https://www.cnn.com/2017/06/16/politics/dhs-scraps-dapa -keeps-daca-deferred-action/index.html

23. Memorandum from Elaine C. Duke, Acting Secretary of Homeland Secu-rity, to James W. McCament, Acting Director of US Citizenship and Immigration Services, et al., "Rescission of Deferred Action for Childhood Arrivals (DACA),"

September 5, 2017, https://www.dhs.gov/news/2017/09/05/memorandum-rescis
sion-daca.

24. Jennifer M. Chacón, "Immigration and the Bully Pulpit," *Harvard Law Review Forum* 130, no. 7 (May 2017): 243–268, https://harvardlawreview.org/wp-content/uploads/2017/05/vol130_Chacon.pdf.

25. Muzaffar Chishti and Jessica Bolter, "Biden at the One-Year Mark: A Greater Change in Direction on Immigration Than Is Recognized," *Migration Information Source*, January 19, 2022, https://www.migrationpolicy.org/article/biden-one-year-mark.

26. Chishti and Bolter, "Biden at the One-Year Mark."

27. Hiroshi Motomura, "Immigration Law After a Century of Plenary Power: Phantom Constitutional Norms and Statutory Interpretation," *Yale Law Journal* 100, no. 3 (December 1990): 545–613. Motomura, in turn, credits Alex Aleinikoff for coining the term.

28. Motomura, "Immigration Law After a Century of Plenary Power," 549.

29. Ana Muñiz, "Gang Phantasmagoria: How Racialized Gang Allegations Haunt Immigration Legal Work," *Critical Criminology* 30 (2022): 159–175.

30. Shoba Sivaprasad Wadhia, "The Role of Prosecutorial Discretion in Immigration Law," *Connecticut Public Interest Law Journal* 9, no. 2 (Spring 2010): 243–299.

31. Nicholas P. De Genova, "Migrant 'Illegality' and Deportability in Everyday Life," *Annual Review of Anthropology* 31, no. 1 (2002): 419–447; Jonathan Xavier Inda, *Targeting Immigrants: Government, Technology, and Ethics* (Malden, MA ; Oxford : Blackwell Pub, 2006); Catherine Dauvergne, *Making People Illegal: What Globalization Means for Migration and Law* (Cambridge: Cambridge University Press, 2008).

32. Michael Kearney, "From the Invisible Hand to Visible Feet: Anthropological Studies of Migration and Development," *Annual Review of Anthropology* 15, no. 1 (1986): 331–361.

33. Alejandro Portes and Rubén G. Rumbaut, *Immigrant America: A Portrait* (Oakland: University of California Press, 2006).

34. William J. Carrington and Enrica Detragiache, "How Extensive Is the Brain Drain?" *Finance and Development* 36, no. 2 (June 1999): 46–49.

35. Robert L. Bach and Lisa A. Schraml, "Migration, Crisis and Theoretical Conflict," *International Migration Review* 16, no. 2 (Summer 1982): 320–341.

36. Saskia Sassen, "America's Immigration 'Problem,'" *World Policy Journal* 6, no. 4 (Fall 1989): 811–832.

37. Dauvergne, *Making People Illegal.*

38. Nicholas De Genova and Nathalie Mae Peutz, eds., *The Deportation Regime: Sovereignty, Space, and the Freedom of Movement* (Durham, NC: Duke University Press, 2010).

39. Alison Mountz, "The Enforcement Archipelago: Detention, Haunting, and Asylum on Islands," *Political Geography* 30 (March 2011) 118-128. Mountz reveals how states rely on islands to control migration as part of "a broader enforcement archipelago of detention." Borders also can be externalized well beyond a nation's physical territory through the use of technological innovations. For an illustration, see Austin Kocher, "Glitches in the Digitization of Asylum: How CBP One Turns Migrants' Smartphones into Mobile Borders," *Societies* 13 (July 2023):149-164.

40. Gilberto Rosas, "The Thickening Borderlands: Diffused Exceptionality and 'Immigrant' Social Struggles during the 'War on Terror,'" *Cultural Dynamics* 18, no. 3 (November 2006): 335–349.

41. Joanna Dreby, "The Burden of Deportation on Children in Mexican Immigrant Families," *Journal of Marriage and Family* 74, no. 4 (August 2012): 829–845.

42. Cecilia Menjívar, "Liminal Legality: Salvadoran and Guatemalan Immigrants' Lives in the United States," *American Journal of Sociology* 111, no. 4 (January 2006): 999–1037.

43. De Genova, "Migrant 'Illegality' and Deportability in Everyday Life."

44. Robert S. Chang and Keith Aoki, "Centering the Immigrant in the Inter/National Imagination," *California Law Review* 85, no. 5 (October 1997): 1395–1447; Mary Romero, "Crossing the Immigration and Race Border: A Critical Race Theory Approach to Immigration Studies," *Contemporary Justice Review* 11, no. 1 (March 2008): 23–37; Kevin R. Johnson, "Race, the Immigration Laws, and Domestic Race Relations: A 'Magic Mirror' into the Heart of Darkness," *Indiana Law Journal* 73, no. 4 (Fall 1998): 1111–1159.

45. E. Tendayi Achiume, "Empire, Borders, and Refugee Responsibility Sharing," *California Law Review* 110, no. 3 (June 2022): 1011, 1020, 1035–36; E. Tendayi Achiume, "Migration as Decolonization," *Stanford Law Review* 71, no. 6 (June 2019): 1509–1574; Radhika Mongia, *Indian Migration and Empire: A Colonial Genealogy of the Modern State* (Durham, NC: Duke University Press, 2018).

46. Geoff Ward, "The Slow Violence of State Organized Race Crime," *Theoretical Criminology* 19, no. 3 (August 2015): 299–314.

47. Mari J. Matsuda, "Looking to the Bottom: Critical Legal Studies and Reparations," *Harvard Civil Rights-Civil Liberties Law Review* 22 (1987): 323-399.

48. See "The Southern California Deferred Action (DACA, DACA+, DAPA) Project," UCI Law Scholarly Commons, University of California Irvine, accessed February 17, 2023, https://scholarship.law.uci.edu/deferred-action-daca-dapa/.

49. Aurora Chang, "Undocumented to Hyperdocumented: A Jornada of Protection, Papers, and PhD Status," *Harvard Educational Review* 81, no. 3 (September 2011): 508–521; Juan Thomas Ordóñez, "Documents and Shifting Labor Environments Among Undocumented Migrant Workers in Northern California," *Anthropology of Work Review* 37, no. 1 (July 2016): 24–33.

50. Kara Cebulko, "Documented, Undocumented, and Liminally Legal: Legal Status during the Transition to Adulthood for 1.5-Generation Brazilian Immigrants," *The Sociological Quarterly* 55, no. 1 (Winter 2014): 143–167.

51. Leo R. Chavez, *The Latino Threat: Constructing Immigrants, Citizens, and the Nation* (Stanford, CA: Stanford University Press, 2013).

52. The question of whether to use the term "Hispanic" or "Latino" is unsettled in law and society. See, e.g., *Village of Freeport v. Barrella*, 814 F.3d 594, 603–604n21 (2d Cir. 2016), in which Judge Cabranes observes that "[t]he choice between 'Hispanic' and 'Latino' occasionally provokes anxiety" and opts throughout the opinion to "use 'Hispanic,'" because, in his view, it is the term "which Hispanics themselves are more likely to choose (to the extent that they wish to adopt a pan-ethnic identity at all)," and it "sidesteps the need for awkward neologisms, such as 'Latin@' or 'Latinx,' in the name of 'gender-neutral' language." Preferences between the terms are likely influenced by geography. Judge Cabranes made his choice to use "Hispanic" as a judge living in the Northeast and adjudicating a case in that geographic context. But preferences differ on the West Coast. As Judge Cabranes noted, the *Los Angeles Times* has preferred "Latino" to "Hispanic" in most contexts since at least 2011. See "Usage: 'Latino' Preferred Over 'Hispanic,'" *Los Angeles Times*, July 28, 2011, https://latimesblogs.latimes.com/readers/2011/07/latino-preferred-over-hispanic-in-most-cases.html. Spanish-speaking interviewees of Latin American descent whose responses provide some of the underlying article also tended to refer to themselves and their coethnics as "Latino" or, to a much lesser extent, "Hispano" when they were referring to this diverse national origin group. Given the geographic and social context of our study, it seems reasonable to give preference to the term "Latino" over "Hispanic."

53. The next question is whether to use the term "Latino" or the newer term "Latinx." The latter term is not without its critics. See Concepción de León, "Another Hot Take on the Term 'Latinx,'" *New York Times*, November 21, 2018, https://www.nytimes.com/2018/11/21/style/latinx-queer-gender- nonconforming.html. León notes that the term is widely used on college campuses and appears in the Merriam-Webster dictionary, but still draws criticism for being an awkward anglicization of a Spanish term that is not widely familiar or popular. While we acknowledge the many reasonable criticisms of the term, we adopt its use here. In doing so, we embrace the reasoning of Ed Morales, that the "X"—which is not Spanish—marks a "new hybrid idea" that "imagin[es] a future of more inclusion for people that don't conform to the various kinds of rigid identities that exist in the United States." Ed Morales, *Latinx: The New Force in American Politics and Culture* (Brooklyn, NY: Verso Books, 2018). We also share the sense expressed by Dr. Lourdes Torres that, in moving beyond gender binaries, the terms can be more "inclusive of . . . identities that have had less visibility." de León, "Another Hot

Take." In short, we use the term "Latinx" to reflect an understanding of an imagined community that is cognizant of its indigenous and not just colonial roots, and that is inclusive of the broad spectrum of gender identities held by those within the community.

54. Michelle Mark, "Trump Just Referred to One of His Most Infamous Campaign Comments: Calling Mexicans 'Rapists,'" *Business Insider*, April 5, 2018, https://www.businessinsider.com/trump-mexicans-rapists-remark-reference-2018-4.

55. Ibram X. Kendi, "The Day *Shithole* Entered the Presidential Lexicon," *The Atlantic*, January 13, 2019, https://www.theatlantic.com/politics/archive/2019/01/shithole-countries/580054/.

56. Julie Hirschfeld Davis and Niraj Chokshi, "Trump Defends 'Animals' Remark, Saying It Referred to MS-13 Gang Members," *New York Times*, May 17, 2018, https://www.nytimes.com/2018/05/17/us/trump-animals-ms-13-gangs.html.

57. Annika Kim Constantino, "Border Patrol Agents Who Posted Racist, Sexist Content in Facebook Groups Remain on the Job, House Panel Finds," *CNBC*, October 25, 2021, https://www.cnbc.com/2021/10/25/border-patrol-agents-who-posted-racist-sexist-content-remain-on-the-job.html; A.C. Thompson, "After a Year of Investigation, the Border Patrol Has Little to Say about Agents' Misogynistic and Racist Facebook Group," *ProPublica*, August 5, 2020, https://www.propublica.org/article/after-a-year-of-investigation-the-border-patrol-has-little-to-say-about-agents-misogynistic-and-racist-facebook-group; Greta de Jong, "Ron DeSantis and Greg Abbott Pull from Segregationists' Playbook with Their Anti-Immigration Stunts," *The Conversation*, September 20, 2022, https://theconversation.com/ron-desantis-and-greg-abbott-pull-from-segregationists-playbook-with-their-anti-immigration-stunts-190896.

Chapter 1

1. Matter of Roldan, 22 I&N Dec. 512 (1999), vacated in part sub nom. In *Lujan-Armendariz v. INS*, 222 F.3d 728 (9th Cir. 2000), the Board held that no effect would be given in immigration proceedings to any state action that purports to expunge, dismiss, cancel, vacate, discharge, or otherwise remove a guilty plea or other record of guilt or conviction by operation of a state rehabilitative procedure. The same is not true of a criminal conviction that is vacated due to procedural error, and the California legislature has, in recent years, enacted legislation that allows individuals to bring post-conviction procedural challenges to their criminal convictions where they were prejudiced by counsel's failure to properly advise them of the immigration consequences of their pleas. Cal. Penal Code § 1473.7; People v. Vivar, 11 Cal.5th 510 (Cal. 2021).

2. Tanya Golash-Boza, "Racialized and Gendered Mass Deportation and the Crisis of Capitalism," *Journal of World-Systems Research* 22, no. 1 (2016): 38–44.

3. César Cuauhtémoc García Hernández, "Creating Crimmigration," *Brigham Young University Law Review* 2013, no. 6 (February 2014): 1457–1515.

4. García Hernández, "Creating Crimmigration." See also Yolanda Vázquez, "Constructing Crimmigration: Latino Subordination in a 'Post-Racial' World," *Ohio State Law Journal* 76, no. 3 (2015): 599–657; Amada Armenta, "Racializing Crimmigration: Structural Racism, Colorblindness, and the Institutional Production of Immigrant Criminality," *Sociology of Race and Ethnicity* 3, no. 1 (January 2017): 82–95.

5. Black immigrants are disproportionately represented among lawful permanent residents removed. Tanya Golash-Boza, "Racialized and Gendered Mass Deportation and the Crisis of Capitalism."

6. Shoba Sivaprasad Wadhia, "National Security, Immigration and the Muslim Bans," *Washington and Lee Law Review* 75, no. 3 (2018): 1475–1506.

7. Randy Capps, Muzaffar Chishti, Julia Gelatt, Jessica Bolter, and Ariel G. Ruiz Soto, *Revving Up the Deportation Machinery: Enforcement and Pushback under Trump* (Washington, DC: Migration Policy Institute, 2018). The report notes that the Obama administration had prioritized the removal of individuals with criminal convictions – particularly in the later part of the second Obama term. It also reveals that, though the Trump administration took a more scattershot approach to enforcement (declining to set explicit priorities), individuals transferred from local law enforcement continued to comprise the bulk of deportations in the Trump era. And President Biden has attempted to restore an enforcement priority system that gives substantial weight to an individual's contact with the criminal legal system, though state legislators have challenged the President's power to set *any* priorities, and that question remains pending in court. Amy Howe, "In U.S. v. Texas, Broad Questions over Immigration Enforcement and States' Ability to Challenge Federal Policies," *SCOTUSblog*, November 28, 2022, 3:43 PM, https://www.scotusblog.com/2022/11/in-u-s-v-texas-broad-questions-over-immigration-enforcement-and-states-ability-to-challenge-federal-policies/.

8. Capps et al., *Revving up the Deportation Machinery.*

9. See also Christina M. Getrich, *Border Brokers: Children of Mexican Immigrants Navigating U.S. Society, Laws, and Politics* (Tucson, AZ: University of Arizona Press, 2019).

10. See, e.g., Dara Lind, "The Campaign Promise That's Still Haunting Obama," *Vox*, June 9, 2014, https://www.vox.com/2014/6/9/5793870/the-promise-haunting-obama-immigration-reform-promesa.

11. Adam B. Cox and Thomas J. Miles, "Policing Immigration," *University of Chicago Law Review* 80, no. 1 (2013): 87–136.

12. Hernández, *Migra!*; Jennifer M. Chacón, "Immigration and Race," in *Oxford Handbook of Race and Law in the United States*, ed. Khiara Bridges, Devon Carbado, and Emily Houh (Oxford: Oxford University Press, 2022); Bill Ong Hing, *Defining America through Immigration Policy* (Philadelphia: Temple University Press, 2004); Kevin R. Johnson, "Race, the Immigration Laws, and Domestic Race Relations: A 'Magic Mirror' into the Heart of Darkness," *Indiana Law Journal* 73, no. 4 (Fall 1998): 1111–1159, https://www.repository.law.indiana.edu/cgi/viewcontent.cgi?article=1959&context=ilj.

13. See, e.g., Dale Russakoff and Deborah Sontag, "For Cops Who Want to Help ICE Crack Down on Illegal Immigration, Pennsylvania Is a Free-for-All," *Pro Publica*, April 12, 2018, https://www.propublica.org/article/pennsylvania-immigration-ice-crackdown-cops-free-for-all.

14. Capps et al., *Revving up the Deportation Machinery*.

15. "Criminal Apprehension Program," US Immigration and Customs Enforcement, last modified March 21, 2022, https://www.ice.gov/identify-and-arrest/criminal-apprehension-program.

16. American Immigration Council, *The Cost of Immigration Enforcement and Border Security* (Washington, DC: January 2021), https://www.americanimmigrationcouncil.org/research/the-cost-of-immigration-enforcement-and-border-security.

17. "Budget Trend Data: Immigration and Naturalization Service," US Department of Justice Archives, US Department of Justice, accessed February 20, 2023, https://www.justice.gov/archive/jmd/1975_2002/2002/html/page104-108.htm.

18. American Immigration Council, *The Cost of Immigration Enforcement*.

19. Rachel E. Rosenbloom, "Policing Sex, Policing Immigrants: What Crimmigration's Past Can Tell Us About Its Present and Its Future," *California Law Review* 104, no. 1 (February 2016): 149–199.

20. 8 U.S.C. § 1387(g).

21. 8 U.S.C. § 1387(g).

22. Department of Homeland Security Office of Inspector General, *The Performance of 287(g) Agreements* (Washington, DC: March 2010), 2, https://www.oig.dhs.gov/sites/default/files/assets/Mgmt/OIG_10-63_Mar10.pdf.

23. Randy Capps, Marc C. Rosenblum, Cristina Rodríguez, and Muzaffar Chishti, *Delegation and Divergence: A Study of 287(g) State and Local Immigration Enforcement* (Washington, DC: Migration Policy Institute, 2011), https://www.migrationpolicy.org/pubs/287g-divergence.pdf.

24. "Secure Communities Program Presentations," US Immigration and Customs Enforcement, accessed February 20, 2023, 4, https://www.ice.gov/doclib/foia/secure_communities/securecommunitiespresentations.pdf.

25. "Secure Communities Program Presentations," 4.

26. Jennifer M. Chacón, "Immigration and the Bully Pulpit," *Harvard Law Review Forum* 130, no. 7 (May 2017): 243–268, https://harvardlawreview.org/wp-content/uploads/2017/05/vol130_Chacon.pdf.

27. Jennifer M. Chacón, "Immigration and the Bully Pulpit."

28. See, e.g., Barack Obama, "The President's Role in Advancing Criminal Justice Reform," *Harvard Law Review* 130, no. 3 (January 2017): 815 ("[W]e cannot deny the legacy of racism that continues to drive inequality in how the justice system is experienced by so many Americans."), https://harvardlawreview.org/wp-content/uploads/2017/01/811-866-Online-Rev-vf.pdf.

29. Violent Crime Control and Law Enforcement Act of 1994, Pub. L. 103–322, 108 Stat. 1796.

30. Illegal Immigration Reform and Immigrant Responsibility Act, Pub. L. No. 104–208, 110 Stat. 3009, 543–724.

31. *See, e.g.,* Kevin R. Johnson, "The Antiterrorism Act, the Immigration Reform Act, and Ideological Regulation in the Immigration Laws: Important Lessons for Citizens and Noncitizens," *St. Mary's Law Journal* 28, no. 4 (1996): 838–843; Daniel Kanstroom, "Deportation, Social Control, and Punishment: Some Thoughts about Why Hard Laws Make Bad Cases," *Harvard Law Review* 113, no. 8 (June 2000): 1890–1935, (explaining and criticizing the 1996 expansion of deportability and excludability); Nancy Morawetz, "Understanding the Impact of the 1996 Deportation Laws and the Limited Scope of Proposed Reforms," *Harvard Law Review* 113, no. 8 (June 2000): 1936–1962.

32. Doris Meissner et al., *Immigration Enforcement in the United States: The Rise of a Formidable Machinery* (Washington, DC: Migration Policy Institute, 2013), 11, https://www.migrationpolicy.org/sites/default/files/publications/enforcement pillars.pdf.

33. Meissner et al., *Immigration Enforcement*, 92.

34. Meissner et al., *Immigration Enforcement*, 92.

35. Meissner et al., *Immigration Enforcement*, 92.

36. "Criminal Immigration Prosecutions Down 14% in 2017," Transactional Records Access Clearinghouse, Syracuse University, December 6, 2017, https://trac.syr.edu/tracreports/crim/494/.

37. Hannah Lewis and Louise Waite, "Asylum, Immigration Restrictions and Exploitation: Hyper-precarity as a Lens for Understanding and Tackling Forced Labour," *Anti-Trafficking Review*, no. 5 (2015): 49–67, https://www.antitraffickin greview.org/index.php/atrjournal/article/view/83/138.

38. Magnus Lofstrom et al., *Racial Disparities in Traffic Stops* (Public Policy Institute of California, October 2022), https://www.ppic.org/publication/racial-dis parities-in-traffic-stops/; Ben Poston, Cindy Chang, "LAPD searches blacks and Latinos more," *Los Angeles Times*, Oct. 8, 2019.

39. See also Amada Armenta, *Protect, Serve, and Deport: The Rise of Policing as Immigration Enforcement* (Oakland, CA: University of California Press, 2017) (observing the same phenomenon in Nashville, Tennessee, where police frequently cited Latinx residents for their lack of official documentation—including driver's licenses).

40. State of California Department of Motor Vehicles, "DMV Surpasses 1 Million Driver Licenses under AB 60," April 4, 2018, https://www.dmv.ca.gov/portal/news-and-media/dmv-surpasses-1-million-driver-licenses-under-ab-60/.

41. Laura E. Enriquez, Daisy Vazquez Vera, and S. Karthick Ramakrishnan, "Driver's Licenses for All? Racialized Illegality and the Implementation of Progressive Immigration Policy in California," *Law & Policy* 41, no. 1 (January 2019): 34–58, https://doi.org/10.1111/lapo.12121 (finding that because Latinx populations are racialized as "illegal aliens," other groups, and particularly API immigrants, had greater difficulty than Latinx immigrants in accessing California's driver's license benefits because outreach efforts were geared primarily toward Latinx immigrants).

42. Armenta, *Protect, Serve, and Deport.*

43. US Department of Justice Civil Rights Division, *Investigation of the Ferguson Police Department* (2015), 4, http://www.justice.gov/sites/default/files/opa/press-releases/attachments/2015/03/04/ferguson_police_department_report.pdf [hereinafter *Ferguson Report*] ("[Ferguson municipal] court practices exacerbate the harm of Ferguson's unconstitutional police practices. They impose a particular hardship upon Ferguson's most vulnerable residents, especially upon those living in or near poverty. Minor offenses can generate crippling debts, result in jail time because of an inability to pay, and result in the loss of a driver's license, employment, or housing.") The report also provided detailed examples of police officers giving citations for conduct that was not, in fact, in violation of any law. *Ferguson Report*, 22. Racial animus has been an important driving force in this unconstitutional conduct. *Ferguson Report*, 4. For a discussion of the constitutional problems with these sorts of fines and fees, see, e.g., Beth A. Colgan, "The Excessive Fines Clause: Challenging the Modern Debtors' Prison," *UCLA Law Review* 65, no. 2 (2018): 2–77. For a discussion of the ways that these systems of fines and fees can ultimately result in incarceration, see, e.g., Alexandra Natapoff, *Punishment without Crime: How Our Massive Misdemeanor System Traps the Innocent and Makes America More Unequal* (New York: Basic Books, 2018).

44. See, e.g., American Civil Liberties Union, *In for a Penny: the Rise of America's New Debtors' Prisons* (New York: October 2010), https://www.aclu.org/report/penny-rise-americas-new-debtors-prisons.

45. Memorandum from Elaine C. Duke, Acting Secretary of Homeland Security, to James W. McCament, Acting Director of US Citizenship and Immigration Services, et al., "Memorandum on Rescission of Deferred Action for Childhood

Arrivals (DACA)," September 5, 2017, https://www.dhs.gov/news/2017/09/05/memorandum-rescission-daca.

46. *Vidal v. Nielsen*, 279 F. Supp. 3d 401 (E.D.N.Y. 2018) (granting motion for preliminary injunction requiring US Citizenship and Immigration Services to accept DACA applications from people who have had DACA previously); *Regents of the Univ. of Calif. v. Dep't of Homeland Sec.* (lead case), 279 F. Supp. 3d 1011 (N.D. Cal. 2018) (granting the preliminary injunction requiring the federal government to accept applications for renewal of DACA); *CASA de Maryland, Inc. v. Trump*, 284 F. Supp. 3d 758 (D. Md. 2018) (granting summary judgment to the plaintiffs on their information-sharing estoppel claim, prohibiting the government from using or sharing information provided through the DACA application process for enforcement or deportation purposes); *NAACP v. Trump*, 298 F. Supp. 3d 209 (D.D.C. 2018) (granting summary judgment to the plaintiffs on grounds that the DACA termination was arbitrary and capricious, but staying for 90 days its order requiring the continued acceptance of first-time applicants in order to give the government time to issue a new memo or better explain why it ended DACA).

47. Ernesto Hernández-López, "LA Taco Truck Wars: How Law Cooks Food Culture Contests," *University of Miami Inter-American Law Review,* 43, No. 1 (2011): 243-268.

48. Sarah Horton, "Identity Loan: The Moral Economy of Migrant Document Exchange in California's Central Valley," *American Ethnologist* 42, no. 1 (2015): 55–67, https://doi.org/10.1111/amet.12115.

49. 18 U. S. C. §1028A(a)(1); Flores-Figueroa v. United States, 556 U. S. 646 (2009).

50. See, for example, Kan. Stat. Ann. §21–6107(a)(1). The Kansas identity-theft statute criminalizes the "using" of any "personal identifying information" belonging to another person with the intent to "[d]efraud that person, or anyone else, in order to receive any benefit." Kansas v. Garcia, 589 U.S. ___ (2020).

51. In fact, in some instances, government officials have aggressively pursued plea agreements in order to secure convictions and removals on aggravated identity theft grounds. See Cassie L. Peterson, "An Iowa Immigration Raid Leads to Unprecedented Criminal Consequences: Why Ice Should Rethink the Postville Model," 95 *Iowa L. Rev.* 323, 337 (2009).

52. These are terms used to describe white people. A *güero* refers to someone who is fair-skinned. *Gabacho* is a term that is commonly used by Mexicans to describe white people. It has a pejorative edge. Gustavo Arellano, "As a Mexican: Is it OK for a Gabacho to Use the Word 'Gabacho'?," *Coachella Valley Independent*, May 4, 2016, https://www.cvindependent.com/index.php/en-US/opinion/ask-a-mexican/item/3046-ask-a-mexican-is-it-ok-for-a-gabacho-to-use-the-word-gabacho.

53. This experience of being stopped while biking was replicated for thousands of Latinos in Southern California. A *Los Angeles Times* study in 2021 revealed that of the 44,000 bike stops made by the Los Angeles County Sheriff's Department in the years from 2017 to 2022, "7 of every 10 stops involve Latino cyclists, and bike riders in poorer communities with large nonwhite populations are stopped and searched far more often than those in more affluent, whiter parts of the county," and that illegal items were found in just 8% of those stops. Alene Tchekmedyian, Ben Poston, and Julia Barajas, "L.A. Sheriff's Deputies Use Minor Stops to Search Bicyclists, with Latinos Hit Hardest," *Los Angeles Times*, November 4, 2021.

54. In *United States v. Brignoni-Ponce*, for example, the US Supreme Court approved the use of "Mexican identity" as a legitimate factor among other factors for justifying an investigative stop, even though the individual who had been stopped on the basis of "Mexican identity" in that case was actually Puerto Rican and a US citizen. 422 U.S. 873 (1975). See also Mae M. Ngai, *Impossible Subjects: Illegal Aliens and the Making of Modern America* (Princeton, NJ: Princeton University Press, 2014) (analyzing the historical developments that have led to the social construction of Mexicans as the archetypal "illegal alien"); Kevin R. Johnson, "Racial Profiling in the War on Drugs Meets the Immigration Removal Process: The Case of *Moncrieffe v. Holder*," *University of Michigan Journal of Law Reform* 48, no. 4 (2015): 980–81, https://repository.law.umich.edu/cgi/viewcontent.cgi?article=1140&context=mjlr (analyzing of the problematic judicial greenlighting of the use of "Mexican appearance" in immigration enforcement); Laura E. Enriquez, "Border-Hopping Mexicans, Law-Abiding Asians, and Racialized Illegality: Analyzing Undocumented College Students' Experiences through a Relational Lens," in *Relational Formations of Race: Theory, Method, and Practice*, ed. Natalia Molina, Daniel Martinez HoSang, and Ramón A. Gutiérrez (Oakland: University of California Press, 2019) (analyzing differences in the experiences of API and Latinx undocumented students).

55. Krsna Avila, Belinda Escobosa Helzer, and Annie Lai, *The State of Orange County: An Analysis of Orange County's Policies on Immigration and a Blueprint for an Immigrant Inclusive Future* (Immigrant Legal Resource Center, Resilience Orange County, and UC Irvine School of Law Immigrant Rights Clinic, January 2019), 11, https://resilienceoc.org/wp-content/uploads/2019/01/State-of-OC-Report.pdf.

56. See, e.g., Enriquez, "Border-Hopping Mexicans."

57. Magnus Lofstrom et al., *Racial Disparities in Traffic Stops* (Public Policy Institute of California, October 2022), https://www.ppic.org/publication/racial-disparities-in-traffic-stops/ (relying on 2019 data and showing that Black residents in California are overrepresented in the population stopped for traffic violations and in the population subject to more intrusive police conduct during those stops). See also Carlos Granda and Grace Manthey, "Data Analysis Shows Racial Disparity in

Police Stops in Recent Years by Los Angeles Law Enforcement," *ABC7*, September 8, 2020, https://abc7.com/lapd-lasd-racial-disparities-police-stops/6414103/ (finding the same overrepresentation in Los Angeles County); Dustin Gardiner and Susie Neilson, "'Are the Police Capable of Changing?': Data on Racial Profiling in California Shows the Problem is Only Getting Worse," *San Francisco Chronicle*, July 14, 2022.

58. Juliana Morgan-Trostle and Kexin Zheng, *The State of Black Immigrants* (Black Alliance for Just Immigration and NYU School of Law Immigrant Rights Clinic, January 2022), https://baji.org/wp-content/uploads/2020/03/sobi-fullre port-jan22.pdf); Golash-Boza, "Racialized and Gendered Mass Deportation"; Johnson, "Racial Profiling."

59. DACA recipients who marry citizens generally become eligible for a family-based visa. For unauthorized residents who entered the country without official inspection, however, adjusting immigration status requires leaving the country, and a 10-year bar on reentry applies to anyone seeking to enter the country who has a year or more of unauthorized presence in the US, even if the individual is otherwise eligible for an entry visa. But some DACA recipients were able to obtain advance permission to leave and reenter the country with a waiver of the 10 year bar. After their official reentry, they could adjust their status without needing to leave the country—or contend with the entry bar—again. For a discussion of the impact of the 10-year bar and other immigration restrictions on families, see Jane Lilly Lopez, *Unauthorized Love: Mixed-Citizenship Couples Negotiating Intimacy, Immigration, and the State* (Stanford: Stanford University Press, 2022).

60. *Texas v. United States*, Civil Action No. 1:18-cv-00068 (S.D. Tex. July 16, 2021).

61. Eisha Jain, "Arrests as Regulation," *Stanford Law Review* 67, no. 4 (April 2015): 809–867, http://www.stanfordlawreview.org/wp-content/uploads/sites/3/2015/04/67_Stan_L_Rev_809_Jain.pdf.

62. See, for example, Drew Harwell & Erin Cox, "ICE has run facial-recognition searches on millions of Maryland drivers," Washington Post, Feb. 26, 2020, https://www.washingtonpost.com/technology/2020/02/26/ice-has-run-facial-recognition-searches-millions-maryland-drivers/.

63. Margaret B. Kwoka, "First-Person FOIA," *Yale Law Journal* 127, no. 8 (June 2018): 2204–2585, https://www.yalelawjournal.org/article/first-person-foia (discussing the lack of discovery rules governing immigration proceedings, which has forced many migrants to use FOIA as a way to get crucial documents in the hands of the government.)

64. The Supreme Court recently addressed this issue in *Pereira v. Sessions*, 138 S. Ct. 2105 (2018), in which the Court ruled that the government must comply with the immigration statute's requirement that a Notice to Appear contain the time

and date of the noncitizen's hearing. Thousands of immigrants received deficient notices in the years leading up to that decision, and even after *Pereira*, the remedies for defective notices are not always sufficient to address the problems generated by the insufficient notice.

65. *Pereira*, 138 S. Ct. 2105 (2018); see also Ana Muñiz, *Borderland Circuitry: Immigration Surveillance in the United States and Beyond* (Oakland, CA: University of California Press, 2022).

66. Jennifer Lee Koh, "Removal in the Shadows of Immigration Court," *Southern California Law Review* 90, no. 2 (January 2017): 181-236, https://southerncali forialawreview.com/wp-content/uploads/2017/01/90_181.pdf (describing in absentia removal orders); Margot Mendelson, Shayna Strom, and Michael Wishnie, *Collateral Damage: An Examination of ICE's Fugitive Operations Program* (Washington, DC: Migration Policy Institute, 2009), https://www.migrationpolicy.org/sites/default/files/publications/NFOP_Feb09.pdf (discussing and critiquing the targeting by Fugitive Operations Teams of, inter alia, individuals who have received in absentia removal orders).

67. See *Niz-Chavez v. Garland*, 141 S. Ct. 1474 (2021) (holding that the immigration statute required Notices to Appear to specify the time and date of an immigration hearing, and that notices lacking such information were procedurally deficient).

68. See, e.g., *Platero-Rosales v. Garland*, 55 F.4th 974 (5th Cir. 2022) (declining to find procedural deficiencies when the immigrant was not served in a language that she understood).

69. United States. v. Texas, 599 U.S. ____ (2023).

70. Nicolas is referring to an enforcement program in which ICE "cross-checks" criminal convictions against immigration records to choose targets of enforcement actions. As critics have noted, this does not necessarily mean that the targets of enforcement are dangerous, or even that they have records of serious past criminal conduct.

Chapter 2

1. See Jens Manuel Krogstad, "Americans Split on Deportations as Latinos Press Obama on Issue," *Pew Research Center*, March 11, 2014, https://www.pewre search.org/fact-tank/2014/03/11/americans-split-on-deportations-as-latinos -press-obama-on-issue/.

2. On August 30, 2022, the Biden administration promulgated a rule that incorporated the substance of the original 2012 DACA memorandum. The policy relies extensively on the concept of discretion in justifying the rule, noting that "deferred action under DACA would be granted only if USCIS determines in its sole discretion that the requestor meets the threshold criteria and otherwise

merits a favorable exercise of discretion." See *Deferred Action for Childhood Arrivals*, 87 Federal Register 53152, 53156 (Aug. 30, 2022), at https://www.govinfo.gov/content/pkg/FR-2022-08-30/pdf/2022-18401.pdf. As a general matter, discretionary agency actions are subject to only minimal review especially where Congress has clearly indicated an intent to give agencies discretionary authority. This is especially the case where an agency exercises its discretion not to pursue an action altogether. See *United States. v. Texas*, 599 U.S. ___ (2023); *Heckler v. Chaney*, 470 U.S. 821 (1985).

3. Saskia Sassen, "America's Immigration 'Problem,'" *World Policy Journal* 6, no. 4 (Fall 1989): 811–832

4. *Testimony of Secretary Napolitano before the Senate Committee on the Judiciary, "Oversight of the Department of Homeland Security,"* 111th Cong. (2009) (statement of Janet Napolitano, secretary of the US Department of Homeland Security), https://www.dhs.gov/news/2009/05/07/secretary-napolitanos-testimony-oversight-department-homeland-security [https://perma.cc/U56F-QMR5] ("In identifying individuals for removal, DHS will prioritize those who pose the most obvious threats to public safety.").

5. "Revised Memorandum of Understanding between the Departments of Homeland Security and Labor Concerning Enforcement Activities at Worksites," March 31, 2011, https://www.dol.gov/sites/dolgov/files/ofccp/regs/compliance/directives/files/DHSICE-DOLMOU-Final3-31-2011ESQA508c.pdf. Memorandum from John Morton, Assistant Secretary of US Immigration and Customs Enforcement, to Peter S. Vincent (Principal Legal Advisor) and James Chaparro (Executive Associate Director, Enforcement and Removal Operations), "Guidance Regarding the Handling of Removal Proceedings of Aliens with Pending or Approved Applications or Petitions," August 20, 2010, https://www.ice.gov/doclib/detention-reform/pdf/aliens-pending-applications.pdf. [hereinafter August 2010 Morton Memo.]

6. August 2010 Morton Memo.

7. August 2010 Morton Memo.

8. The director of the Executive Office for Immigration Review, which is the agency housing all immigration judges, is empowered by regulation to "direct that the adjudication of certain cases be deferred." See 8 C.F.R. § 1003.0(b)(1)(ii). See also David L. Neal, "Administrative Closure," November 22, 2021, https://www.justice.gov/eoir/book/file/1450351/download.

9. Memorandum from John Morton, Director of US Immigration and Customs Enforcement, to All ICE Employees, "Civil Immigration Enforcement: Priorities for the Apprehension, Detention, and Removal of Aliens," March 2, 2011, https://www.ice.gov/doclib/news/releases/2011/110302washingtondc.pdf.

10. Memorandum from John Morton, Director of US Immigration and Customs Enforcement, to All ICE Employees, "Civil Immigration Enforcement:

Priorities for the Apprehension, Detention, and Removal of Aliens," March 2, 2011, https://www.ice.gov/doclib/news/releases/2011/110302washingtondc.pdf.

11. Memorandum from John Morton, Director of US Immigration and Customs Enforcement, to All Field Officer Directors, All Special Agents in Charge, All Chief Counsel, "Exercising Prosecutorial Discretion Consistent with the Civil Immigration Enforcement Priorities of the Agency for the Apprehension, Detention, and Removal of Aliens," June 17, 2011, https://www.ice.gov/doclib/secure-com munities/pdf/prosecutorial-discretion-memo.pdf

12. Memorandum from John Morton, Director of US Immigration and Customs Enforcement, to All Field Officer Directors, All Special Agents in Charge, All Chief Counsel, "Exercising Prosecutorial Discretion Consistent with the Civil Immigration Enforcement Priorities of the Agency for the Apprehension, Detention, and Removal of Aliens," June 17, 2011, https://www.ice.gov/doclib/se cure-communities/pdf/prosecutorial-discretion-memo.pdf; Memorandum from John Morton, Director of US Immigration and Customs Enforcement, to All Field Officer Directors, All Special Agents in Charge, All Chief Counsel, "Prosecutorial Discretion: Certain Victims, Witnesses, and Plaintiffs," June 17, 2011, https://www .ice.gov/doclib/foia/prosecutorial-discretion/certain-victims-witnesses-plaintiffs .pdf; Memorandum from John Morton, Director of US Immigration and Customs Enforcement, to All ICE Employees, "Civil Immigration Enforcement: Priorities for the Apprehension, Detention, and Removal of Aliens," March 2, 2011, https:// www.ice.gov/doclib/news/releases/2011/110302washingtondc.pdf; Memorandum from John Morton, Assistant Secretary of US Immigration and Customs Enforcement, to Peter S. Vincent (Principal Legal Advisor) and James Chaparro (Executive Associate Director, Enforcement and Removal Operations), "Guidance Regarding the Handling of Removal Proceedings of Aliens with Pending or Approved Applications or Petitions," August 20, 2010, https://www.ice.gov/doclib/ detention-reform/pdf/aliens-pending-applications.pdf.

13. See Rufus E. Miles, Jr., "The Origin and Meaning of Miles' Law," *Public Administration Review* 38, no. 5 (September/October 1978): 399–403. See also Ming H. Chen, "Where You Stand Depends on Where You Sit: Bureaucratic Politics in Federal Workplace Agencies Serving Undocumented Workers," *Berkeley Journal of Employment and Labor Law* 33, no. 2 (2012): 227–298.

14. "Office of the Principal Legal Advisor (OPLA)," US Immigration and Customs Enforcement, accessed March 15, 2019, http://www.ice.gov/opla#wcm-sur vey-target-id [http://perma.cc/B9P3-SYP6]. OPLA employs 1,100 lawyers and 350 support personnel. It is divided into several "Offices of Chief Counsel," which are scattered throughout the United States.

15. Nicholas Kulish, Caitlin Dickerson, and Ron Nixon, "Immigration Agents Discover New Freedom to Deport Under Trump," *New York Times*, February 25,

2017, https://www.nytimes.com/2017/02/25/us/ice-immigrant-deportations-trump.html.

16. Secretary Napolitano was using the term "Dreamers" to refer to young immigrant residents who would have qualified for relief under various proposed bills known as the DREAM Act (the Development, Relief, and Education for Alien Minors Act), which has been introduced by legislators in various forms over the course of many years, beginning in 2001. These individuals are sometimes called "Dreamers" or "DREAMers," with reference to those failed legislative proposals. As we explore further below, many intended beneficiaries of this legislation now eschew the "Dreamer" label insofar as it suggests that they deserve some type of legal relief while other members of their families and communities do not.

17. See Gerry Hadden, "ICE Out of Control: Time to Rein in Rogue Agency and Pass Immigration Reform," *Huffington Post*, May 30, 2010, https://www.huffingtonpost.com/frank-sharry/ice-out-of-control-time-t_b_519201.html [https://perma.cc/B9CB-TH2L].

18. See Susan Carroll, "Report: Feds Downplayed ICE Case Dismissals," *Houston Chronicle*, June 27, 2011. The documents obtained through this FOIA request are available at US Department of Homeland Security, *2011 ICE Report/FOIA Request*, https://www.scribd.com/document/58810530/2011-ICE-Report-FOIA-request [https://perma.cc/84NU-Q9TR].

19. See US Department of Homeland Security, *2011 ICE Report/FOIA Request*.

20. Memorandum from John Morton, Director of US Immigration and Customs Enforcement, to All Field Office Directors, All Special Agents in Charge, All Chief Counsel, "Exercising Prosecutorial Discretion Consistent with the Civil Immigration Enforcement Priorities of the Agency for the Apprehension, Detention, and Removal of Aliens," June 17, 2011, https://www.ice.gov/doclib/secure-communities/pdf/prosecutorial-discretion-memo.pdf; Memorandum from John Morton, Director of US Immigration and Customs Enforcement, to All ICE Employees, "Civil Immigration Enforcement: Priorities for the Apprehension, Detention, and Removal of Aliens," March 2, 2011, https://www.ice.gov/doclib/news/releases/2011/110302washingtondc.pdf.

21. *Working Agenda: Field Legal Operations Management Planning Session,* August 2–3, 2010, 5–6, https://www.scribd.com/document/58810530/2011-ICE-Report-FOIA-request [https://perma.cc/84NU-Q9TR].

22. See Email from Gary L. Goldman to Riah Ramlogan, "Houston," August 6, 2010, 5:36 PM, 7, https://www.scribd.com/document/58810530/2011-ICE-Report-FOIA-request [https://perma.cc/84NU-Q9TR].

23. Memorandum from Gary Goldman, Chief Counsel, Houston Office of the Chief Counsel, US Immigration and Customs Enforcement, to All Attorneys, Houston Office of the Chief Counsel, August 16, 2010, 17–18, https://www

.scribd.com/document/58810530/2011-ICE-Report-FOIA-request [https://perma
.cc/84NU-Q9TR]. Goldman further observed: "It broadly encompasses NTA
review, court litigation, not opposing relief, joining in a Joint Motion, not appealing an adverse decision, etc. Further opportunities arise at the appellate level with
the extraordinary amount of work reaching the Board of Immigration Appeals
and the Circuit Court of Appeals. We also seek efficiencies in the removal process
through continuing dialogue with ERO, HSI, CIS, CBP, and EOIR, through improved written advocacy, remands, etc."

24. Memorandum from Gary Goldman, 17–18. This memo was ultimately rescinded and replaced by one issued by central leadership, but it still confirms that
the message sent by political leaders like Edgar and Frank regarding the need to use
prosecutorial discretion was one that was received by lawyers in at least one field
office. See Memorandum from John Morton, Assistant Secretary of US Immigration and Customs Enforcement, to Peter S. Vincent, Principal Legal Advisor, and
James Chaparro, Executive Associate Director of Enforcement and Removal Operations, "Guidance Regarding the Handling of Removal Proceedings of Aliens with
Pending or Approved Applications or Petitions," August 20, 2010, https://www.ice
.gov/doclib/detention-reform/pdf/aliens-pending-applications.pdf [https://perma
.cc/Y5JS-59RZ]; see also email from Gary L. Goldman to Richard W. Bennett et
al., "Guidance on Aliens with Pending Applications," August 24, 2010, 2:04 PM,
28, https://www.scribd.com/document/58810530/2011-ICE-Report-FOIA-request
[https://perma.cc/84NU-Q9TR].

25. Matter of Lopez-Barrios, 20 I&N Dec. 203, 204 (BIA 1990) (stating that
administrative closure "allows the removal of cases from the immigration judge's
calendar in certain circumstances" but "does not result in a final order").

26. Administratively closed cases from this period were reopened by DHS
during the Trump administration. Hamed Aleaziz, "The Trump Administration Is Seeking to Restart Thousands of Closed Deportation Cases," *BuzzFeed
News*, August 15, 2018, https://www.buzzfeednews.com/article/hamedalea
ziz/trump-deportations-immigration-ice-dhs-courts [https://perma.cc/Y7G4
-U425].

27. Email from Arthur E. Adams on behalf of Mike P. Davis, Acting Director,
Office of the Principal Legal Advisor, to Raphael Choi et al., "OCC FY11 Tracking of Motions to Dismiss," November 3, 2010, 4:33 PM, 51–52, https://www
.scribd.com/document/58810530/2011-ICE-Report-FOIA-request [https://perma
.cc/84NU-Q9TR]. This email was released pursuant to a FOIA request by the
Houston Chronicle. See infra note 128 and accompanying text.

28. See, e.g., Ken Dilanian, "Tough Enforcement Against Illegal Immigrants
Is Decried," *Los Angeles Times*, April 21, 2010, http://articles.latimes.com/2010/
apr/21/nation/la-na-obama-immigration-20100422 [https://perma.cc/P8GF

-7WMV] (quoting Deepak Bhargava, Executive Director of the Center for Community Change: "The president never said he was going [to] end immigration enforcement, but he sent a clear signal that he would redirect it to a focus on people with criminal records who are a threat to the country. That hasn't happened.").

29. Memorandum from John Morton, Assistant Secretary of US Immigration and Customs Enforcement, to All ICE Employees, "Civil Immigration Enforcement: Priorities for the Apprehension, Detention, and Removal of Aliens," June 30, 2010, 2, https://www.ice.gov/doclib/news/releases/2010/civil-enforcement-prior ities.pdf.

30. See Josh Bowers, "Legal Guilt, Normative Innocence, and the Equitable Decision Not to Prosecute," *Columbia Law Review* 110, no. 7 (November 2010): 1655, 1657.

31. Memorandum from Janet Napolitano, Secretary of Homeland Security, to David V. Aguilar (Acting Commissioner), Alejandro Mayorkas (Director), and John Morton (Director), "Exercising Prosecutorial Discretion with Respect to Individuals Who Came to the United States as Children," June 15, 2012, https://www .dhs.gov/sites/default/files/publications/s1-exercising-prosecutorial-discretion -individuals-who-came-to-us-as-children.pdf.

32. See Bowers, "Legal Guilt," 1656–57.

33. See *Wayte v. United States*, 470 U.S. 598, 607 (1985); Kate Stith, "The Arc of the Pendulum: Judges, Prosecutors, and the Exercise of Discretion," *Yale Law Journal* 117, no. 7 (May 2008): 1422–23, https://www.yalelawjournal.org/pdf/ 691_2w13sx9h.pdf.

34. Bowers, "Legal Guilt," 1701.

35. Bowers, "Legal Guilt," 1701.

36. See Daniel C. Richman, "Prosecutors and Their Agents, Agents and Their Prosecutors," *Columbia Law Review* 103, no. 4 (May 2003): 749–832, https://schol arship.law.columbia.edu/cgi/viewcontent.cgi?article=3494&context=faculty _scholarship.

37. See Paul Butler, *Let's Get Free: A Hip-Hop Theory of Justice* (New York: The New Press, 2007), 102.

38. See I. Bennett Capers, "Against Prosecutors," *Cornell Law Review* 105, no. 6 (2020): 1561–1610.

39. See Angélica Cházaro, "Challenging the 'Criminal Alien' Paradigm," *UCLA Law Review* 63, no. 3 (2016): 594–664.

40. See Hiroshi Motomura, *Immigration Outside the Law* (Oxford: Oxford University Press, 2014); Adam B. Cox and Cristina M. Rodríguez, "The President and Immigration Law Redux," *Yale Law Journal* 125, no. 1 (October 2015): 197–205.

41. See Rachel E. Barkow, "The Ascent of the Administrative State and the Demise of Mercy," *Harvard Law Review* 121, no. 5 (March 2008): 1332, 1339, https://

harvardlawreview.org/2008/03/the-ascent-of-the-administrative-state-and-the
-demise-of-mercy/.

42. See Shalini Bhargava Ray, "Immigration Law's Arbitrariness Problem," *Columbia Law Review* 121, no. 7 (2021): 2049-2118.

43. Napolitano, "Anatomy of a Legal Decision."

44. Napolitano, "Anatomy of a Legal Decision."

45. *Dep't of Homeland Sec. v. Regents of the Univ. of Calif.*, 591 U.S. ___ (2020). The Court rejected the argument that the DHS had violated the Administrative Procedures Act when it implemented DACA without notice and comment rulemaking.

46. See Marc L. Miller and Ronald F. Wright, "The Black Box," *Iowa Law Review* 94, no. 1 (2008): 125, 129 (describing prosecutorial decision-making as a "black box" due to a lack of regulation compelling transparency).

47. See Careen Shannon, *"Regulating Immigration Legal Service Providers: Inadequate Representation and Notario Fraud,"* *Fordham Law Review* 78, no. 2 (2009): 577–622.

48. Napolitano, "Anatomy of a Legal Decision."

49. See Nanette Asimov, "UC Regents Appoint Napolitano Amid Protest," *SF Gate*, July 18, 2013, https://www.sfgate.com/education/article/UC-regents-appoint-Napolitano-amid-protest-4673527.php.

Chapter 3

1. In 1999, spouses of H-1 visa holders (also known as H-4 visa holders) were not granted authorization to work, an indication of the barriers faced even by those who hold valid visas. This policy changed in 2015. See Employment Authorization for Certain H-4 Dependent Spouses, 80 Fed. Reg. 10283 (Feb. 25, 2015). See also 8 C.F.R. § 214.2(h)(9)(iv). See also Pallavi Banerjee, *The Opportunity Trap: High-Skilled Workers, Indian Families, and the Failures of the Dependent Visa Program* (New York: NYU Press, 2022).

2. Marrying a US citizen does not automatically grant the right to obtain permanent residency. Individuals who entered the United States without authorization and who marry US citizens must leave the country in order to obtain permanent residency. When they do so, those who have lived in the US without lawful status for at least a year trigger a ten-year bar on lawful reentry. It is possible to apply for a provisional waiver of unlawful presence, so that before leaving the country, visa beneficiaries will know whether or not this bar on lawful reentry has been waived in their case. "Provisional Unlawful Presence Waivers," US Citizenship and Immigration Services, last modified January 5, 2018, https://www.uscis.gov/family/family-us-citizens/provisional-unlawful-presence-waivers. The visa process is therefore complex and drawn-out. For an analysis of the uncertainty, emotional

anguish, and material costs of the spousal visa process, see Ruth Gomberg-Muñoz, *Becoming Legal: Immigration Law and Mixed Status Families* (Oxford: Oxford University Press, 2016).

3. For a discussion of this law, A.B. 540, see Leisy Abrego, "Legitimacy, Social Identity, and the Mobilization of Law: The Effects of Assembly Bill 540 on Undocumented Students in California," *Law & Social Inquiry* 33, no. 3 (Summer 2008): 709–734.

4. The US economy has long depended on the very immigrant labor that the country prohibits, the category of "citizen" is defined in relation to and therefore dependent on that of "alienage," and the United States has played a key role in uprooting the very immigrants whose presence the government ostensibly seeks to bar. See Nicholas P. De Genova, "Migrant 'Illegality' and Deportability in Everyday Life," *Annual Review of Anthropology* 31, no. 1 (2002): 419–447; Robert L. Bach, "Mexican Immigration and the American State," *International Migration Review* 12, no. 4 (Winter 1978): 536–558; J. Craig Jenkins, "The Demand for Immigrant Workers: Labor Scarcity or Social Control?," *International Migration Review* 12, no. 4 (Winter 1978): 514–535; Mae M. Ngai, *Impossible Subjects: Illegal Aliens and the Making of Modern America* (Princeton, NJ: Princeton University Press, 2014).

5. See, e.g., *Texas v. United States*, 809 F.3d 134, 150 (5th Cir. 2015), aff'd ___ U.S. ___ (2016) (reasoning that the deferred action described in the DAPA Memorandum was "much more than nonenforcement: It would affirmatively confer 'lawful presence' and associated benefits on a class of unlawfully present aliens."); Dep't of Homeland Sec. v. Regents of the Univ. of California, 207 L. Ed. 2d 353, 140 S. Ct. 1891, 1896 (2020) (Finding the DHS's attempted rescission of DACA likely violated the APA because "removing benefits eligibility while continuing forbearance remained squarely within the discretion of Acting Secretary Duke, who was responsible for "[e]stablishing national immigration enforcement policies and priorities." 116 Stat. 2178, 6 U.S.C. § 202(5). But Duke's memo offers no reason for terminating forbearance. She instead treated the Attorney General's conclusion regarding the illegality of benefits as sufficient to rescind both benefits and forbearance, without explanation."); United States v. Texas, 599 U.S. ___ (U.S. June 23, 2023) ("a challenge to an Executive Branch policy that involves both the Executive Branch's arrest or prosecution priorities *and* the Executive Branch's provision of legal benefits or legal status could lead to a different standing analysis. That is because the challenged policy might implicate more than simply the Executive's traditional enforcement discretion.").

6. The state of Georgia, for example, bars all three. In 2019, a federal appeals court upheld the state's ban on undocumented students in the state's three most prestigious public universities. Bill Rankin & Eric Stirgis, Atlanta court upholds

University System ban on unauthorized immigrants, Atlanta Journal Constitution, March 6, 2019 (https://www.ajc.com/news/local/atlanta-court-upholds-university-system-ban-unauthorized-immigrants/IxwkDzIV8VAwjRHY76fPiK/). Rankin and Stirgis also notes that some DACA students can enroll in some of the state's institutions, but only if the schools are not fully enrolled. And those students, though residents of the state, must pay out-of-state tuition.

7. See Ines Hasselberg, *Enduring Uncertainty: Deportation, Punishment and Everyday Life* (New York: Berghahn Books, 2016); Cecilia Menjívar, "Liminal Legality: Salvadoran and Guatemalan Immigrants' Lives in the United States," *American Journal of Sociology* 111, no. 4 (2006): 999–1037; Luin Goldring and Patricia Landolt, "The Conditionality of Legal Status and Rights: Conceptualizing Precarious Non-Citizenship in Canada," in *Producing and Negotiating Non-Citizenship: Precarious Legal Status in Canada*, ed. Luin Goldring and Patricia Landolt (Toronto: University of Toronto Press, 2013), 3–27.

8. Paloma E. Villegas, "Fishing for Precarious Status Migrants: Surveillant Assemblages of Migrant Illegalization in Toronto, Canada," *Journal of Law and Society* 42, no. 2 (June 2015): 232.

9. Bridget Anderson, "Migration, Immigration Controls and the Fashioning of Precarious Workers," *Work, Employment and Society* 24, no. 2 (2010): 300–317; Nicholas De Genova, "The Legal Production of Mexican/Migrant 'Illegality,'" *Latino Studies* 2, no. 2 (2004): 160–185.

10. Villegas, "Fishing for Precarious Status Migrants," 230.

11. Luis F. B. Plascencia, "The 'Undocumented' Mexican Migrant Question: Re-Examining the Framing of Law and Illegalization in the United States," *Urban Anthropology and Studies of Cultural Systems and World Economic Development* 38, no. 2/3/4 (2009): 375–434; Catherine Dauvergne, "Making People Illegal," in *Migrants and Rights*, ed. Mary Crock (Oxfordshire: Routledge, 2015), 77–94.

12. Sébastien Chauvin and Blanca Garcés-Mascareñas, "Becoming Less Illegal: Deservingness Frames and Undocumented Migrant Incorporation," *Sociology Compass* 8, no. 4 (April 2014): 422–432.

13. Marcel Paret and Shannon Gleeson, "Precarity and Agency through a Migration Lens," *Citizenship Studies* 20, no. 3/4 (2016): 281.

14. Paret and Gleeson, "Precarity and Agency."

15. Guy Standing, *The Precariat: The New Dangerous Class* (London: Bloomsbury Academic, 2011).

16. Hannah Lewis and Louise Waite, "Asylum, Immigration Restrictions and Exploitation: Hyper-precarity as a Lens for Understanding and Tackling Forced Labour," *Anti-Trafficking Review*, no. 5 (2015): 49–67, https://www.antitraffickingreview.org/index.php/atrjournal/article/view/83/138.

17. Goldring and Landolt, "The Conditionality of Legal Status and Rights," 3.

18. Chloe Ahmann, "'It's Exhausting to Create an Event out of Nothing': Slow Violence and the Manipulation of Time," *Cultural Anthropology* 33, no. 1 (2018): 144.

19. Stephen Lee, "Family Separation as Slow Death," *Columbia Law Review* 119, no. 8 (2019): 2319–2384.

20. Ruben Andersson, "Time and the Migrant Other: European Border Controls and the Temporal Economics of Illegality," *American Anthropologist* 116, no. 4 (December 2014): 795–809; Melanie B. E. Griffiths, "Out of Time: The Temporal Uncertainties of Refused Asylum Seekers and Immigration Detainees," *Journal of Ethnic and Migration Studies* 40, no. 12 (2014): 1991–2009; Bridget Anderson, "Battles in Time: The Relation between Global and Labour Mobilities," Working Paper No. 55, Centre on Migration, Policy and Society, University of Oxford, 2007, https://www.compas.ox.ac.uk/wp-content/uploads/WP-2007-055-Anderson _Global_Labour_Mobilities.pdf; Hasselberg, *Enduring Uncertainty*.

21. Andersson, "Time and the Migrant Other," 796.

22. See Elizabeth F. Cohen, *The Political Value of Time: Citizenship, Duration, and Democratic Justice* (Cambridge: Cambridge University Press, 2018); Ahmann, "'Exhausting to Create an Event'" (discussing deferral as a resistance tactic that mimics but subverts the form of slow violence).

23. Temporary Protected Status is a parallel case. See Alison Mountz et al., "Lives in Limbo: Temporary Protected Status and Immigrant Identities," *Global Networks* 2, no. 4 (2002): 335–356. Note also that such broken promises are the opposite of entitlement.

24. In some cases, even US citizens have been deported. See Jacqueline Stevens, "U.S. Government Unlawfully Detaining and Deporting U.S. Citizens as Aliens," *University of Virginia Journal of Social Policy and the Law* 18, no. 3 (Fall 2011): 606–720.

25. See Paret and Gleeson, "Precarity and Agency."

26. See Dauvergne, "Making People Illegal"; Ngai, *Impossible Subjects*; Nicholas De Genova and Nathalie Mae Peutz, eds., *The Deportation Regime: Sovereignty, Space, and the Freedom of Movement* (Durham, NC: Duke University Press, 2010).

27. Laura E. Enriquez, "Gendering Illegality: Undocumented Young Adults' Negotiation of the Family Formation Process," *American Behavioral Scientist* 61, no. 10 (September 2017): 1153–1171; Joanna Dreby, *Everyday Illegal: When Policies Undermine Immigrant Families* (Oakland: University of California Press, 2015); Heide Castañeda, *Borders of Belonging: Struggle and Solidarity in Mixed-Status Immigrant Families* (Redwood City: Stanford University Press, 2019).

28. For a discussion of gender dynamics within immigration and deportation, see Pierrette Hondagneu-Sotelo, *Gendered Transitions: Mexican Experiences of*

Immigration (Oakland: University of California Press, 1994); Beth Caldwell, "Deported by Marriage: Americans Forced to Choose Between Love and Country," *Brooklyn Law Review* 82, no. 1 (2016): 1–48.

29. See Beth Caldwell, *Deported Americans: Life after Deportation to Mexico* (Durham, NC: Duke University Press, 2019); Gomberg-Muñoz, *Becoming Legal.*

30. Aristide R. Zolberg, "The Roots of American Refugee Policy," *Social Research* 55, no. 4 (Winter 1988): 649–678.

31. US citizens can petition for their spouses, parents, and children, while lawful permanent residents can petition for their spouses and unmarried children. For further details, see "Green Card Eligibility Categories," US Citizenship and Immigration Services, last modified July 11, 2022, https://www.uscis.gov/green card/eligibility-categories.

32. "Ayer escuche el mensaje del presidente Obama. Finalmente se siente un alivio, es como tener un respiro despues de haber estado ahogandose. Creo que las cosas van a ser diferentes de ahora en adelante, hay muchos proyectos en nuestras mentes y un optimismo increible. Todavia tenemos un poco de miedo y es normal, pero el deseo de luchar por una residencia es grande."

33. See also Gray Albert Abarca and Susan Bibler Coutin, "Sovereign Intimacies: The Lives of Documents within US State-Noncitizen Relationships," *American Ethnologist* 45, no. 1 (February 2018): 7–19.

34. Aurora Chang, "Undocumented to Hyperdocumented: A Jornada of Protection, Papers, and PhD Status," *Harvard Educational Review* 81, no. 3 (2011): 508–520; Juan Thomas Ordóñez, "Documents and Shifting Labor Environments among Undocumented Migrant Workers in Northern California," *Anthropology of Work Review* 37, no. 1 (July 2016): 24–33.

35. Examples of such litigation include Biden's attempted rescission of the Migrant Protection Protocols, the September 2021 Mayorkas prosecutorial discretion memo, and DACA. See Jennifer Lee Koh, "Executive Discretion and First Amendment Constraints on the Deportation State," *Georgia Law Review* 56, no. 4 (2022): 1473–1510.

36. At a 2016 "Community Navigator" training conducted by one of the organizations participating in our study, the presenter characterized deferred action recipients neither as "immigrants" nor as "nonimmigrants."

37. "Estamos en el aire."

38. Advocates who worked with the Asian and Pacific Islander communities stressed that this message was especially important, as the deeper stigma associated with being undocumented was an additional barrier to seeking relief.

39. Fieldnotes that Susan Coutin wrote regarding one such workshop read: "During this portion of the event those around the table got out their piles of paper,

folders, or portfolios and leafed through the documents that they were hoping would help them qualify for DAPA."

40. See generally Chapter 1 and Jennifer M. Chacón, "Overcriminalizing Immigration," *Journal of Criminal Law and Criminology* 102, no. 3 (2012): 613–652.

41. Susan Bibler Coutin et al., "Deferred Action and the Discretionary State: Migration, Precarity and Resistance," *Citizenship Studies* 21, no. 8 (2017): 951–968.

Chapter 4

1. See Amna A. Akbar, Sameer M. Ashar, and Jocelyn Simonson, "Movement Law," *Stanford Law Review* 73, no. 4 (April 2021): 854.

2. See Amna A. Akbar, Sameer M. Ashar, and Jocelyn Simonson, "Movement Law," *Stanford Law Review* 73, no. 4 (April 2021): 854.

3. Aimee Meredith Cox, *Shapeshifters: Black Girls and the Choreography of Citizenship* (Durham, NC: Duke University Press, 2015), 7.

4. Cox, *Shapeshifters*, 9.

5. See Amna A. Akbar, Sameer M. Ashar, and Jocelyn Simonson, "Movement Law," *Stanford Law Review* 73, no. 4 (April 2021): 854.

6. Leti Volpp, "Migrant Justice Now," *University of Colorado Law Review* 92, no. 4 (2021): 1163–1188.

7. See Devon Carbado, "From Stop and Frisk to Shoot and Kill: *Terry v. Ohio*'s Pathway to Police Violence," *UCLA Law Review* 64, no. 6 (2017): 1508–1553.

8. Elise C. Boddie, "Racial Territoriality," *UCLA Law Review* 58, no. 2 (December 2010): 401–464.

9. Careen Shannon, "Regulating Immigration Legal Service Providers: Inadequate Representation and Notario Fraud," *Fordham Law Review* 78, no. 2 (2009): 577–622.

10. See "Welcome," Los Angeles County Office of Immigrant Affairs, accessed February 26, 2023, https://oia.lacounty.gov/.

11. In 2023, Orange County developed an Office of Immigrant and Refugee Affairs. See Gillian Morán Pérez, 2023, "Orange County is Creating a Hub to Help Immigrants and Refugees," *LAist,* April 26. Available at https://laist.com/news/oc-supervisors-vote-to-establish-office-to-help-immigrants-refugees. Accessed July 9, 2023.

12. See Seema Mehta, "Orange County, Longtime GOP Stronghold, Now Has More Registered Democrats than Republicans," *Los Angeles Times,* August 7, 2019, https://www.latimes.com/politics/story/2019-08-07/orange-county-turns-blue-with-more-registered-democrats-than-republicans. In this way, the old image of conservative Orange County (OC) is changing. At the same time, there are still quite a few registered voters with no party preference, which means that the old OC is fading but the new OC has yet to be negotiated or settled upon. This

is one of the reasons why it is hard for elected officials to take strong positions on immigration in OC. In LA, a clear majority of voters would support pro-immigrant measures but in OC there is so much divergence on this issue that it would be riskier for elected officials to take such a position.

13. We reviewed several sources to attempt to verify this claim. Transactional Records Access Clearinghouse (TRAC) data on city and state of deportation through 2020 reveal that in California, cities near the US-Mexico border were three of the top four, with LA being the third. "Immigration and Customs Enforcement Removals: ICE Data Through June 2020," TRAC Immigration, accessed February 26, 2023, https://trac.syr.edu/phptools/immigration/remove/. TRAC data on detainers by county and jail through 2021 identify LA County and Orange County as the top two. "Immigration and Customs Enforcement Detainers," TRAC Immigration, accessed February 26, 2023, https://trac.syr.edu/phptools/immigration/detain/. Likewise, LA and Orange County are the two counties in California with the largest undocumented population. Joseph Hayes and Laura Hill, *Undocumented Immigrants in California* (Public Policy Institute of California, 2017), https://www.ppic.org/publication/undocumented-immigrants-in-california/.

14. Cesar Alesi Perez, Marisol Cuellar Mejia, and Hans Johnson, *Immigrants in California* (Public Policy Institute of California, 2023), https://www.ppic.org/publication/immigrants-in-california/.

15. See Alejandro Sanchez-Lopez, Manuel Pastor, and Victor Sanchez, *The State of Black Immigrants in California* (Black Alliance for Just Immigration, USC Center for the Study of Immigrant Integration, 2018), 20–21 (discussing the erasure of Black immigrants from conventional contemporary immigrant narratives).

16. Abrams, Kathryn. *Open Hand, Closed Fist: Practices of Undocumented Organizing in a Hostile State*. Univ of California Press, 2022.

17. Second Chances report (https://www.law.uci.edu/academics/real-life-learning/clinics/UCILaw_SecondChances_dec2013.pdf); news article on how Orange County Probation Department referred juveniles to ICE especially from 2008-2012 (https://voiceofoc.org/2015/08/lost-boys-undocumented-juveniles-face-perilous-journey-through-justice-system/).

18. One study found that in 2007, the number of migrants from El Salvador, Guatemala, and Honduras totaled an estimated 1,990,000 migrants. In 2015, migrants from those countries rose to an estimated 3,030,000. Importantly, however, by 2014 the overall unauthorized migrant population had dropped to 11 million from its peak of 12.2 million in 2007—during the Republican administration of President Bush. See Jeffrey S. Passel and D'Vera Cohn, *Overall Number of U.S. Unauthorized Immigrants Holds Steady Since 2009* (Pew Research Center, 2016), https://www.pewresearch.org/hispanic/2016/09/20/overall-number-of-u-s-unauthorized-immigrants-holds-steady-since-2009.

19. In challenging DAPA, the plaintiffs sought a preliminary injunction, asking the court to stop the federal government from implementing the program before holding a trial on the program's legality. Ordinarily, when a lawsuit is filed, the parties assert and refine claims, gather evidence, and proceed to trial (or settlement). If a plaintiff prevails in a lawsuit seeking to prevent an official policy from going into effect, then they are entitled to relief in the form of an injunction. The *preliminary* injunction is a departure from the ordinary litigation process because it is imposed before the evidence gathering state of the litigation. A court should only grant a preliminary injunction if it concludes that there is a "substantial likelihood of success on the merits," among other things. Once the Supreme Court declined to lift the preliminary injunction of DAPA and DACA+ imposed by the district court, the case was sent back to the same district court judge who had imposed the injunction in the first place. Since the Fifth Circuit decision, affirmed by the Supreme Court, had reasoned that the challenge to DAPA/DACA+ was likely to succeed on the merits, the district court was almost inevitably poised to strike it down. See *Texas v. United States*, 809 F.3d 134, 150 (5th Cir. 2015).

20. Jamie's reflections tap into a broader set of questions over the fight for universal immigrant representation. See Angélica Cházaro, Due Process Deportation, N.Y.U. Law Review 98, no. 2 (2023): 407-484.

21. See "ICE Detained Parents Directive," US Immigration and Customs Enforcement, last modified January 24, 2023, https://www.ice.gov/detain/parental-interest.

22. Under federal immigration law, certain convictions can qualify as "aggravated felonies" provided they result in at least one-year of imprisonment. See 8 U.S.C. § 1101(a)(43)(F) (defining aggravated felony to include "a crime of violence . . . for which the term of imprisonment at least one years") and (G) (defining aggravated felony to include a "theft offense . . . for which the term of imprisonment at least one year").

23. See Amna A. Akbar, Sameer M. Ashar, and Jocelyn Simonson, "Movement Law," *Stanford Law Review* 73, no. 4 (April 2021): 854.

24. See Cházaro, Due Process Deportations.

25. See Akbar, Ashar, and Simonson, "Movement Law," 851–852.

Chapter 5

1. Byrhonda Lyons, "California's bill for fighting Trump in court? $41 million so far," Cal Matters, January 22, 2021, last visited June 28, 2023, https://calmatters.org/justice/2021/01/california-cost-trump-lawsuits/.

2. See Cal. Gov't Code §§ 7282, 7282.5 (West 2019); see also Cal. Health and Safety Code § 11369 (West 2007).

3. TRUST Act, A.B. 4, 2013 State Assemb., 2013–2014 Reg. Sess. (Cal. 2013).

4. A.B. 60, 2013 State Assemb., 2013–2014 Reg. Sess. (Cal. 2013).

5. California prohibited unauthorized immigrants from obtaining driver's licenses in 1993, at the same time that it mandated state employment agencies to perform checks of federal immigration status and required state prisons to cooperate with federal immigration authorities. Allan Colbern and S. Karthick Ramakrishnan, "Citizens of California: How the Golden State Went from Worst to First on Immigrant Rights," *New Political Science* 40, no. 2 (2018): 360, https://doi.org/10.1 080/07393148.2018.1449065.

6. See, e.g., Amada Armenta and Rocío Rosales, "Beyond the Fear of Deportation: Understanding Unauthorized Immigrants' Ambivalence Toward the Police," *American Behavioral Scientist* 63, no. 9 (2019): 1350–1369; Laura E. Enriquez and Daniel Millán, "Situational Triggers and Protective Locations: Conceptualising the Salience of Deportability in Everyday Life," *Journal of Ethnic and Migration Studies* 47, no. 9 (2021): 2089–2108; Laura E. Enriquez, "A 'Master Status' or the 'Final Straw'? Assessing the Role of Immigration Status in Latino Undocumented Youths' Pathways out of School, *Journal of Ethnic and Migration Studies* 43, no. 9 (2017): 1526–1543.

7. See, e.g., Ingrid V. Eagly, "Local Immigration Prosecution: A Study of Arizona before SB 1070," *UCLA Law Review* 58, no. 6 (August 2011): 1749–1818 (documenting the use of state smuggling laws to prosecute immigrants for "self-smuggling"); Leticia M. Saucedo, "Immigration Enforcement Versus Employment Law Enforcement: The Case for Integrated Protections in the Immigrant Workplace," *Fordham Urban Law Journal* 38, no. 1 (2010): 303, 308–10, https://ir.lawnet.ford ham.edu/ulj/vol38/iss1/9/ (discussing the use of identity theft prosecutions to target immigrant workers caught in workplace immigration raids).

8. See, e.g., *Kansas v. Garcia*, 140 S. Ct. 791 (2020) (upholding as against a federal preemption challenge Kansas identity theft prosecutions against immigrants who used false Social Security numbers to obtain work); see also *Arizona v. United States*, 567 U.S. 387 (2012) (striking down several Arizona laws as preempted by federal immigration law, but leaving in place a requirement that state law enforcement agents ascertain immigration status of individuals they stopped upon reasonable suspicion that they were present in violation of federal immigration law).

9. See, for example, People v. Vivar, 43 Cal. App. 5th 2016 (2021) applying California Penal Code section 1473.7 to vacate the conviction of a long-time California resident as procedurally deficient where that individual had pled guilty to an offense without understanding the severe immigration consequences of the plea.

10. While the number of misdemeanor entry and illegal reentry charges peaked in 2013 (at 65,597 and 20,159 respectively) and then began to decline, they never receded to the numbers that had been the norm prior to the Obama administration.

American Immigration Council, *Prosecuting People for Coming to the United States* (Washington, DC: August 23, 2021), https://www.americanimmigrationcouncil .org/research/immigration-prosecutions/.

11. Muzzafar Chishti and Sarah Pierce, "Trump's Promise of Millions of Deportations Is Yet to Be Fulfilled," *Migration Information Source*, October 29, 2020, https://www.migrationpolicy.org/article/trump-deportations-unfinished -mission.

12. The discussion from here through note 76 is a revised, updated, and edited version of work previously published in Jennifer M. Chacón, "Immigration Federalism in the Weeds," *UCLA Law Review* 66, no. 6 (December 2019): 1330–1393.

13. TRUST Act, A.B. 4, 2013 State Assemb., 2013–2014 Reg. Sess. (Cal. 2013).

14. 8 U.S.C. § 1373.

15. See Cal. Gov't Code §§ 7285.1–3 (West 2019); Cal. Labor Code §§ 90.2, 1019.2 (West 2019).

16. See Cal. Gov't Code §§ 7310–11 (West 2019); see also Cal. Gov't Code § 12532 (West 2018).

17. See Cal. Gov't Code §§ 7282, 7282.5 (West 2019); see also Cal. Health and Safety Code § 11369 (West 2007).

18. Amy Howe, "Court Turns Down Government's 'Sanctuary State' Petition," *SCOTUSblog*, June 15, 2020, https://www.scotusblog.com/2020/06/court-turns -down-governments-sanctuary-state-petition/.

19. Patrick McGreevy, "Gov. Brown Signs Bill to Reduce Deportations for Minor Crimes," *Los Angeles Times*, July 21, 2014, https://www.latimes.com/local/ crime/la-me-pol-brown-364-days-20140722-story.html [https://perma.cc/CLS9 -CVXE]; see Cal. Penal Code § 18.5 (West 2014).

20. Some common criminal convictions will only qualify as aggravated felonies if they carry a possible sentence of a year or more. See, e.g., 8 U.S.C. § 1101(a)(43) (F) (crimes of violence) and (G) (theft offenses). For a discussion of the full immigration consequences of committing an "aggravated felony," see Daniel Kanstroom, *Deportation Nation: Outsiders in American History* (Cambridge, MA: Harvard University Press, 2007), 227–28; Teresa A. Miller, "Blurring the Boundaries between Immigration and Crime Control after September 11th," *Boston College Third World Law Journal* 25, no. 1 (2005): 81, 83–85; Nancy Morawetz, "Rethinking Retroactive Deportation Laws and the Due Process Clause," *New York University Law Review* 73, no. 1 (April 1998): 97, 108 n48.

21. For a discussion of this and other previously mentioned reforms, see generally Ingrid V. Eagly, "Local Immigration Prosecution," supra note 223.

22. "AB 60 Driver's Licenses," State of California Department of Motor Vehicles, accessed February 27, 2023, https://www.dmv.ca.gov/portal/dmv/detail/ ab60 [https://perma.cc/A9RL-XS47].

23. "QuickFacts: Los Angeles City, California; Los Angeles County, California" [hereinafter "QuickFacts LA"], US Census Bureau, accessed February 27, 2023, https://www.census.gov/quickfacts/fact/table/losangelescitycalifornia,losangelescountycalifornia/PST045221.

24. "Children Living with Foreign-Born Parents," KidsData, accessed February 27, 2023, https://www.kidsdata.org/topic/573/foreign-born-parents/table#fmt=786&loc=2,127,1657,331,1761,171,2168,345,357,324,369,362,360,2076,364,356,217,354,1663,339,2169,365,343,367,344,366,368,265,349,361,4,273,59,370,326,341,338,350,2145,359,363,340&tf=108.

25. "QuickFacts Los Angeles County" https://www.census.gov/quickfacts/losangelescountycalifornia

26. Norma Stoltz Chinchilla, Nora Hamilton, and James Loucky, "The Sanctuary Movement and Central American Activism in Los Angeles," *Latin American Perspectives* 36, no. 6 (2009): 101–126, https://www.jstor.org/stable/20684688.

27. Daryl F. Gates, Chief of Los Angeles Police Department, "Special Order No. 40: Undocumented Aliens," November 27, 1979, https://perma.cc/6VVU-2NMV.

28. Gates, "Special Order No. 40." On the short-lived city sanctuary declaration, see Victor Merina, "L.A. Council Backs Down on Sanctuary Plan," *Los Angeles Times*, February 8, 1986, https://www.latimes.com/archives/la-xpm-1986-02-08-mn-5516-story.html.

29. Elana Zilberg, "A Troubled Corner: The Ruined and Rebuilt Environment of a Central American Barrio in Post-Rodney-King-Riot Los Angeles," *City and Society* 14, no. 2 (2002): 34–35.

30. Rick Su, "Police Discretion and Local Immigration Policymaking," *UMKC Law Review* 79, no. 4 (2011): 907.

31. Su, "Police Discretion," 914–915.

32. This is not to discount the long and deep history of anti-Asian police violence in Los Angeles. See, e.g., Kelly Lytle Hernández, *City of Inmates: Conquest, Rebellion, and the Rise of Human Caging in Los Angeles, 1771–1965* (Chapel Hill, NC: University of North Carolina Press, 2017), 64–91 (recounting the anti-Chinese animus of local law enforcement in Los Angeles in the late nineteenth century).

33. Elaine H. Kim, "Home Is Where the Han Is: A Korean American Perspective on the Los Angeles Upheavals," *Social Justice* 20, no. 1/2 (Spring-Summer 1993): 1–21; see also Lisa C. Ikemoto, "Traces of the Master Narrative in the Story of African American/ Korean American Conflict: How We Constructed 'Los Angeles,'" *Southern California Law Review* 66, no. 4 (May 1993): 1581, 1582.

34. Los Angeles, Cal., Exec. Directive No. 20, March 21, 2017, 1, [https://perma.cc/TDD4-VH9M].

35. Los Angeles, Cal., Exec. Directive No. 20, March 21, 2017, 2, [https://perma.cc/TDD4-VH9M].

36. Los Angeles, Cal., Exec. Directive No. 20, March 21, 2017, 3, [https://perma .cc/TDD4-VH9M].

37. Los Angeles, Cal., Exec. Directive No. 20, March 21, 2017, 3, [https://perma .cc/TDD4-VH9M].

38. Los Angeles, Cal., Exec. Directive No. 20, March 21, 2017, 3, [https://perma .cc/TDD4-VH9M].

39. Los Angeles, Cal., Exec. Directive No. 20, March 21, 2017, 4, [https://perma .cc/TDD4-VH9M].

40. Memorandum from Michael R. Moore, Assistant Chief, Director, Office of Operations, L.A. Police Department, to Geographic Bureau Commanding Officers, "Joint Operations with Federal Immigration Authorities – Notification Requirement," June 24, 2016, http://libguides.law.ucla.edu/ld.php?content _id=25214160 [https://perma.cc/DAV4-62XY].

41. See generally Memorandum from Charlie Beck, Chief of Police, L.A. Police Department, to All Department Personnel, "Immigration Enforcement Procedures," December 29, 2017, https://scng-dash.digitalfirstmedia.com/wp-content/ uploads/2018/02/immigrationocop.pdf [https://perma.cc/3AR4-Y5AR].

42. Chacón, "Immigration Federalism," 1366.

43. Kate Linthicum and Joseph Tanfani, "L.A. County Ends Contract with ICE, Then Oks Future Collaboration," *Los Angeles Times*, May 12, 2015, 9:00 PM, http://www.latimes.com/local/lanow/la-me-ln-ice-los-angeles-287g-20150512 -story.html [https://perma.cc/W8XX-ZN42].

44. See Los Angeles County Sheriff's Department, *Manual of Policies and Procedures* § 05-09/271.00 (2015) http://libguides.law.ucla.edu/ld.php?content _id=19104938 [https://perma.cc/QH57-QRA5].

45. Letter from Jim McDonnell, Sheriff of Los Angeles County, to the Los Angeles County Board of Supervisors, "The Los Angeles County Sheriff's Department Report Back Regarding the Priority Enforcement Program," September 22, 2015, http://file.lacounty.gov/SDSInter/bos/bc/233871_PEPICEReportBack09-22-15OrigLtr..pdf.

46. See Max Huntsman, *Immigration: Public Safety and Public Trust* (Los Angeles County Office of Inspector General, 2017), 13–14, [https://perma.cc/S2HP -VP3S].

47. "Security," Metrolink, accessed February 26, 2023, https://metrolinktrains .com/rider-info/safety--security/security/.

48. The vote on the motion is at Los Angeles County Board of Supervisors, "Meeting Transcript of the Los Angeles County Board of Supervisors," December 6, 2016, 310–311, https://docs.google.com/gview?url=https%3A%2F%2Flacounty .granicus.com%2FDocumentViewer.php%3Ffile%3Dlacounty_7d1a8011bad 9b60796dbc5f15c471b41.PDF%26view%3D1&embedded=true. Los Angeles

County Board of Supervisors, "Revised Motion by Supervisors Hilda L. Solis and Sheila Kuehl: Protecting Los Angeles County Residents Regardless of Immigration Status," December 6, 2016, http://file.lacounty.gov/SDSInter/bos/sup docs/109929.pdf.On October 17, 2017, the Los Angeles County Board of Supervisors also adopted a "Sensitive Locations Policy" that prohibited county officials from voluntarily allowing federal civil immigration enforcement agents access to "non-public areas of County properties" in the absence of a judicial warrant. This effort was directly responsive to increased ICE presence in county courthouses—purportedly in response to their decreased access to county jails.

49. Huntsman, *Public Safety and Public Trust*, 10–13, [https://perma.cc/S2HP-VP3S].

50. Huntsman, *Public Safety and Public Trust*, 12, [https://perma.cc/S2HP-VP3S].

51. Huntsman, *Public Safety and Public Trust*, 17–19, [https://perma.cc/S2HP-VP3S].

52. See Statement by Sheriff Jim McDonnell, "Regarding the Passage of Senate Bill 54: Final Bill Reflects Law Enforcement Mission Already Underway," September 16, 2017, http://libguides.law.ucla.edu/ld.php?content_id=41925223 [https://perma.cc/V6R8-X8SR] [hereinafter McDonnell Statement].

53. See Los Angeles County Sheriff's Department, "Immigration Policies, Protocols, and Procedures," March 8, 2018, https://www.lasd.org/pdf/18-06 .pdf. The Los Angeles sheriff opposed earlier versions of S.B. 54, but when the law was enacted, his department issued a statement in support of the measure as enacted. See McDonnell Statement. The Los Angeles County police chiefs also played an active role in reshaping and narrowing the protections of the bill prior to passage. See, e.g., Letter from Bob Guthrie, President, Los Angeles County Police Chiefs' Association and Kevin L. McClure, Chairman, Los Angeles County Police Chiefs' Association, to Assemblyman Anthony Rendon, Speaker of the Assembly, California State Assembly, April 20, 2017, https://lac hiefs.com/wp-content/uploads/2017/05/Oppose-Proposed-SB54.pdf [https://perma.cc/5YDY-D5KH].

54. See, e.g., ICE Out of LA Coalition and International Human Rights Clinic of UCLA School of Law, *The Human Rights Consequences of LASD-ICE Collaboration: A Toxic Entanglement* (2017), 4, http://iceoutofla.org/wp-content/up loads/2017/01/ICEoutofLA-UCLA-HR-Clinic-1-12-2017.pdf.

55. Maya Lau, "In Historic Upset, Alex Villanueva Beats Incumbent Jim McDonnell in Race for Los Angeles County Sheriff," *Los Angeles Times*, November 26, 2018, 9:25 PM, https://www.latimes.com/local/lanow/la-me-sheriff-election -20181126-story.html [https://perma.cc/R56Q-DT89] ("'The immigrant community was not happy about the way the department was dealing with its relationship

with ICE,' said former Los Angeles County Supervisor Zev Yaroslavsky, who supported McDonnell in both his campaigns.").

56. See, e.g., Corina Knoll and Jill Cowan, "Democrats Ushered In the Los Angeles Sheriff. Now Many Want Him Gone," *New York Times*, November 5, 2022 (Villanueva "frequently says that he made good on a promise to prevent U.S. Immigration and Customs Enforcement officials from accessing the jails, though critics say he did so only under pressure from county supervisors and watchdog organizations.").

57. See "Sheriff Robert Luna Says Things Going 'Extremely Well' after His First Month in Office," *KCAL News*, January 6, 2023, https://www.cbsnews.com/losangeles/news/sheriff-robert-luna-says-things-going-extremely-well-after-his-first-month-in-office/.

58. "QuickFacts: Orange County, California," US Census Bureau, https://www.census.gov/quickfacts/fact/table/orangecountycalifornia/PST045218 [https://perma.cc/K8FG-WNPA].

59. "QuickFacts: Orange County, California." For a discussion of settler attempts to eliminate the Native American presence in Southern California, see, e.g., Hernández, *City of Inmates*.

60. "QuickFacts: Orange County, California, " https://www.census.gov/quickfacts/orangecountycalifornia. For a history of the anti-Black racism in Orange County, see, e.g., Elyse Joseph, "Sundown Towns in Orange County," *Los Angeles Review of Books*, May 3, 2018, https://blog.lareviewofbooks.org/essays/sundown-towns-orange-county/.

61. Krsna Avila, Belinda Escobosa Helzer, and Annie Lai, *The State of Orange County: An Analysis of Orange County's Policies on Immigration and a Blueprint for an Immigrant Inclusive Future* (Immigrant Legal Resource Center, Resilience Orange County, and UC Irvine School of Law Immigrant Rights Clinic, 2019), 8, https://resilienceoc.org/wp-content/uploads/2019/01/State-of-OC-Report.pdf [https://perma.cc/72RL-8NV4].

62. Avila, Helzer, and Lai, *The State of Orange County*, 8.

63. Cindy Carcamo, "Orange County Quits Program That Exemplified Its Tough Stance on Illegal Immigration," *Los Angeles Times*, January 6, 2018, https://www.latimes.com/local/california/la-me-orangecounty-halts-immigration-program-20180103-story.html [https://perma.cc/2VKU-GQJH].

64. Avila, Helzer, and Lai, *The State of Orange County*, 9.

65. Spencer Custodio, "OC to Join Federal Lawsuit against California Sanctuary Laws," *Voice of OC*, March 28, 2018, https://voiceofoc.org/2018/03/oc-to-join-federal-lawsuit-against-california-sanctuary-laws [https://perma.cc/MKC6-3V7U].

66. See "Orange County, California—Patrol Areas," Orange County Sheriff's Department, http://www.ocsd.org/patrol [https://perma.cc/4ETS-5KWK].

67. In late March 2019, OCSD announced its plans to terminate these agreements to comply with state law. Theresa Sears, "Orange County Sheriff's Department Ends Its Immigrant Detention Contract with ICE," *Voice of OC*, March 29, 2019, https://voiceofoc.org/2019/03/orange-county-sheriffs-department-ends-its -immigrant-detention-contract-with-ice/.

68. "City News: Mayor's SB54 Message—Sanctuary State Law," City of Huntington Beach, California, March 23, 2018, https://www.huntingtonbeachca .gov/announcements/announcement.cfm?id=1203 [https://perma.cc/D2LW -A8TK].

69. Letter from Allan Bernstein, Mayor, Tustin, California, to Kevin de Leon, Senate President Pro Tempore, California State Senate, "Senate Bill 54 (Oppose as Amended 3/6/17)," March 22, 2017, http://www.tustinca.org/documents/SB%20 54%20Oppose.pdf [https://perma.cc/A28G-QJRZ].

70. Petition for Writ of Mandamus and Complaint for Declaratory Relief and Injunctive Relief at 3, *City of Huntington Beach v. California*, No. 2018–80002876-CV, April 5, 2018, https://www.huntingtonbeachca.gov/government/elected_off icials/city_attorney/city-of-huntington-beach-vs-state-of-california-ref-sb54.pdf [https://perma.cc/HX2E-GDF5].

71. City of Santa Ana, California, Resolution No. NS-2016-086, December 6, 2016, https://santaana.granicus.com/MediaPlayer.php?view_id=2&clip _id=937&meta_id=40722. The resolution was amended on January 17, 2017. City of Santa Ana, California, "Request for Council Action," January 17, 2017, https:// santaana.granicus.com/MetaViewer.php?view_id=2&clip_id=971&meta_id =42408.

72. City of Santa Ana, California, Resolution No. NS-2016-086, December 6, 2016, as amended January 17, 2017, https://santaana.granicus.com/MetaViewer .php?view_id=2&clip_id=971&meta_id=42408.

73. Cindy Carcamo, "Immigration Officials Abruptly Announce End to Controversial Contract at Santa Ana Jail," *Los Angeles Times*, February 24, 2017, https:// www.latimes.com/local/california/la-me-immigration-contract-santa-ana-jail -20170224-story.html.

74. Thy Vo, "Anaheim Leaders Criticized for Muddled Approach to Sanctuary City Issue, *Voice of OC*, January 9, 2017, https://voiceofoc.org/2017/01/anaheim -leaders-criticized-for-muddled-approach-to-sanctuary-city-issue [https://perma .cc/G35U-EZL6].

75. City of Anaheim, California, Resolution No. 2017–158, October 24, 2017, http://www.anaheim.net/DocumentCenter/View/20613/Welcoming-Ana

heim-Resolution?bidId [https://perma.cc/CB8K-5EAZ]; City of Orange, California, Resolution No. 11074, April 10, 2018, http://cityoforange.granicus.com/MetaViewer.php?view_id=2&clip_id=329&meta_id=28035 [https://perma.cc/4XRW-NE5F].

76. Gabriel San Ramón, "Orange County Board of Supervisors Seats First Democratic Majority in Decades," *Los Angeles Times,* November 18, 2022, https://www.latimes.com/california/story/2022-11-18/orange-county-board-of-supervisors-poised-to-seat-first-democratic-majority-in-decades.

77. See, e.g. Armenta and Rosales, "Beyond the Fear of Deportation."

78. "OCTA Transit Police Services Overview," Mass Transit Bureau, Orange County Sheriff's Department, http://www.ocsd.org/divisions/fieldops/security/mtb [https://perma.cc/3XWD-YN8Y].

79. Doris Marie Provine et al., *Policing Immigrants: Local Law Enforcement on the Front Lines* (Chicago: University of Chicago Press, 2016).

80. See also Jennifer M. Chacón and Susan Bibler Coutin, "Racialization through Enforcement," in *Race, Criminal Justice, and Migration Control: Enforcing the Boundaries of Belonging,* ed. Mary Bosworth, Alpa Parmar, and Yolanda Vázquez (Oxford: Oxford University Press, 2018), 169–70; Jennifer M. Chacón, "Citizenship Matters: Conceptualizing Belonging in an Era of Fragile Inclusions," *U.C. Davis Law Review* 52, no. 1 (2018): 1, 63–65.

81. Racial and Identity Profiling Advisory Board, *2022 Annual Report,* 66, https://oag.ca.gov/system/files/media/ripa-board-report-2022.pdf.

82. See also Chacón, "Citizenship Matters," 30–31n99 (citing examples from respondents' transcripts expressing the sense that A.B. 60 helped protect them from this practice). At least one study also has demonstrated the positive social spill-over effects of A.B. 60: the number of hit-and-run accidents have decreased since the implementation of the act. See generally Hans Lueders, Jens Hainmueller, and Duncan Lawrence, "Providing Driver's Licenses to Unauthorized Immigrants in California Improves Traffic Safety," *Proceedings of the National Academy of Science* 114, no. 16 (2017): 4111–4116.

83. James Queally, "Ku Klux Klan Rally in Anaheim Erupts in Violence; 3 Are Stabbed and 13 Arrested," *Los Angeles Times,* February 27, 2016, https://www.latimes.com/local/lanow/la-me-ln-klan-rally-in-anaheim-erupts-in-violence-one-man-stabbed-20160227-story.html.

84. Angela S. García, *Legal Passing: Navigating Undocumented Life and Local Immigration Law* (Oakland, CA: University of California Press, 2019), 128.

85. Alene Tchekmedyian, Ben Poston, and Julia Barajas, "L.A. Sheriff's Deputies Use Minor Stops to Search Bicyclists, with Latinos Hit Hardest," *Los Angeles Times,* November 4, 2021, https://www.latimes.com/projects/la-county-sheriff-bike-stops-analysis/.

86. Bill Ong Hing, *Deporting Our Souls: Values, Morality, and Immigration Policy* (Cambridge: Cambridge University Press, 2006).

87. See also Jennifer A. Zelnick, "Suspicious Citizenship, Bureaucratic Coordination, and the Deportation of Cambodian American Refugees," *Political and Legal Anthropology Review* 44, no. 2 (November 2021): 271–286.

Chapter 6

1. See also Laura E. Enriquez, Daisy Vazquez Vera, and S. Karthick Ramakrishnan, "Driver's Licenses for All? Racialized Illegality and the Implementation of Progressive Immigration Policy in California," *Law & Policy* 41, no. 1 (January 2019): 34–58.

2. As we discussed in Chapter 1, within our interview sample, police stops were often moments when interviewees were asked for driver's licenses. If they did not have them for any reason, including being undocumented, interviewees' cars were impounded, resulting in considerable expense and financial loss. In 2015, California Assembly Bill A.B. 60 permitted California residents to qualify for driver's licenses regardless of their immigration status.

3. Angela S. García, *Legal Passing: Navigating Undocumented Life and Local Immigration Law* (Oakland, CA: University of California Press, 2019), 6.

4. See Rebecca Sharpless, "'Immigrants Are Not Criminals': Respectability, Immigration Reform, and Hyperincarceration," *Houston Law Review* 53, no. 3 (2016): 691–765, https://houstonlawreview.org/article/3949-immigrants-are-not-criminals-respectability-immigration-reform-and-hyperincarceration.

5. See also Genevieve Negrón-Gonzales, Leisy Abrego, and Kathleen Coll, "Introduction: Immigrant Latina/o Youth and Illegality: Challenging the Politics of Deservingness," *Association of Mexican American Educators Journal* 9, no. 3 (2015): 7–10, https://amaejournal.utsa.edu/index.php/AMAE/article/view/178/169.

6. We thank Carrie Rosenbaum for this point.

7. Shoba Sivaprasad Wadhia, "The Rise of Speed Deportation and the Role of Discretion," *Columbia Journal of Race and Law* 5, no. 1 (2014): 1–27, https://journals.library.columbia.edu/index.php/cjrl/article/view/2304/1199.

8. Aimee Meredith Cox, *Shapeshifters: Black Girls and the Choreography of Citizenship* (Durham, NC: Duke University Press, 2015). For additional discussion of Cox's work, see Chapter 3.

9. Cox, *Shapeshifters.*

10. Angélica Cházaro, "Beyond Respectability: Dismantling the Harms of 'Illegality,'" *Harvard Journal on Legislation* 52, no. 2 (Summer 2015): 355–422.

11. See Cházaro, "Beyond Respectability."

12. Bonnie Honig writes that the "supercitizen immigrant [is] neither needy nor threatening, as such, but always mirrored by and partnered with those others. . . .

The supercitizen immigrant is the object of neither American hostility nor charity but of outright adoration. . . . He is the screen onto which we project our idealized selves." Bonnie Honig, *Democracy and the Foreigner* (Princeton, NJ: Princeton University Press, 2001), 67.

13. Ana Muñiz, "Bordering Circuitry: Crossjurisdictional Immigration Surveillance," *UCLA Law Review* 66, no. 6 (2019): 1636–1680, https://www.uclalawreview.org/bordering-circuitry-crossjurisdictional-immigration-surveillance/.

14. See also Jennifer M. Chacón, "Whose Community Shield? Examining the Removal of the 'Criminal Street Gang Member,'" *University of Chicago Legal Forum* 2007 (2007): 317–358.

15. Sarah Horton, "Identity Loan: The Moral Economy of Migrant Document Exchange in California's Central Valley," *American Ethnologist* 42, no. 1 (2015): 55–67, https://doi.org/10.1111/amet.12115. Not only federal charges, but also state identity theft prosecutions can flow from these violations. *Kansas v. Garcia*, 140 S. Ct. 791 (2020).

16. Interviewees' reports of being racially profiled are borne out by the 2021 Annual Report of the Racial Identity Profiling Advisory Board, available at https://oag.ca.gov/sites/all/files/agweb/pdfs/ripa/ripa-board-report-2021.pdf.

17. See Sharpless, "'Immigrants Are Not Criminals'"; Cházaro, "Beyond Respectability"; Paisley Jane Harris, "Gatekeeping and Remaking: The Politics of Respectability in African American Women's History and Black Feminism," *Journal of Women's History* 15, no. 1 (Spring 2003): 212–220; Grace J. Yoo, "Immigrants and Welfare: Policy Constructions of Deservingness," *Journal of Immigrant & Refugee Studies* 6, no. 4 (2008): 490–507; Rosemary Sales, "The Deserving and the Undeserving? Refugees, Asylum Seekers and Welfare in Britain," *Critical Social Policy* 22, no. 3 (August 2002): 456–478.

18. For a discussion of de facto citizenship, see Christian Joppke, "Transformation of Citizenship: Status, Rights, Identity," *Citizenship Studies* 11, no. 1 (2007): 37–48.

19. Sarah J. Mahler, *American Dreaming: Immigrant Life on the Margins* (Princeton, NJ: Princeton University Press, 1995).

20. Hiroshi Motomura, "Who Belongs? Immigration outside the Law and the Idea of Americans in Waiting," *UC Irvine Law Review* 2, no. 1 (2012): 359–379.

21. Ruth Gomberg-Muñoz, "The Punishment/El Castigo: Undocumented Latinos and US Immigration Processing," *Journal of Ethnic and Migration Studies* 41, no. 14 (2015): 2235–2252.

22. Sharpless, "'Immigrants Are Not Criminals.'"

23. Cházaro, "Beyond Respectability"; Grace Yukich, "Constructing the Model Immigrant: Movement Strategy and Immigrant Deservingness in the New Sanctuary Movement," *Social Problems* 60, no. 3 (2013): 302–320.

24. Seth M. Holmes, *Fresh Fruit, Broken Bodies: Migrant Farmworkers in the United States* (Oakland, CA: University of California Press, 2013).

25. See also Yukich, "Constructing the Model Immigrant."

26. See Kimmy Yam, "Anti-Asian Hate Crimes Increased 399 Percent Nationwide Last Year, Report Says," *NBC News*, February 14, 2022, https://www.nbc news.com/news/asian-america/anti-asian-hate-crimes-increased-339-percent -nationwide-last-year-repo-rcna14282.

27. Tanya Katerí Hernández, *Racial Innocence: Unmasking Latino Anti-Black Bias and the Struggle for Equality* (Boston, MA: Beacon Press, 2022).

28. Jennifer M. Chacón et al., "Citizenship Matters: Conceptualizing Belonging in an Era of Fragile Inclusions," *UC Davis Law Review* 52, no. 1 (2018): 1–80.

29. Michelle Alexander, *The New Jim Crow: Mass Incarceration in the Age of Colorblindness* (New York: The New Press, 2020).

30. Kitty Calavita and Valerie Jenness, "Inside the Pyramid of Disputes: Naming Problems and Filing Grievances in California Prisons," *Social Problems* 60, no. 1 (February 2013): 50–80.

31. Chloe Ahmann, "'It's Exhausting to Create an Event out of Nothing': Slow Violence and the Manipulation of Time," *Cultural Anthropology* 33, no. 1 (2018): 142–171; Heide Castañeda et al., "Immigration as a Social Determinant of Health," *Annual Review of Public Health* 36 (2015): 375–392, https://doi.org/10.1146/ annurev-publhealth-032013-182419.

32. Cecilia Menjívar and Leisy J. Abrego, "Legal Violence: Immigration Law and the Lives of Central American Immigrants," *American Journal of Sociology* 117, no. 5 (March 2012): 1380–1421.

33. "Ya" has multiple meanings in Spanish, including, "now" and "already." It seems presumptuous of us to translate this term, uttered at a highly emotional moment, so we have also left "ya" in the original Spanish.

34. See Genevieve Negrón-Gonzales, "Undocumented, Unafraid and Unapologetic: Re-Articulatory Practices and Migrant Youth 'Illegality.'" *Latino Studies* 12, no. 2 (2014): 259–278; Kathryn Abrams, Open Hand, Closed Fist: Practices of Undocumented Organizing in a Hostile State (Berkeley: University of California Press, 2022).

35. Kevin R. Johnson, "Bringing Racial Justice to Immigration Law," *Northwestern University Law Review Online* 116 (2021): 1–22.

36. For a discussion of voting and citizenship, see Rainer Bauböck, "Expansive Citizenship: Voting Beyond Territory and Membership," *PS: Political Science and Politics* 38, no. 4 (2005): 683–687.

37. Carole McGranahan, "Theorizing Refusal: An Introduction," *Cultural Anthropology* 31, no. 3 (2016): 319–325.

Conclusion

1. Citizenship has its limits in protecting against expulsion, particularly for individuals whose racial identity triggers assumptions of "illegality" for enforcement agents. See, e.g., Jacqueline Stephens. "US government unlawfully detaining and deporting US citizens as aliens." *Virginia Journal of Social Policy & the Law* 18 (2010): 606.

2. Chae Chan Ping v. U.S. (Chinese Exclusion Case), 130 U.S. 581 (1889).

3. See "Profile of the Unauthorized Population: United States," Data Hub, Migration Policy Institute, accessed October 13, 2021, https://www.migrationpolicy .org/data/unauthorized-immigrant-population/state/US.

4. Racial and Identity Profiling Advisory Board, *2022 Annual Report*, https:// oag.ca.gov/system/files/media/ripa-board-report-2022.pdf; Charles R. Epp, Steven Maynard-Moody, and Donald P. Haider-Markel, *Pulled Over: How Police Stops Define Race and Citizenship* (Chicago: University of Chicago Press, 2014).

5. See Seth M. Holmes, *Fresh Fruit, Broken Bodies: Migrant Farmworkers in the United States* (Oakland, CA: University of California Press, 2013). Commentators have noted that organizing migrants on the basis of nationality to the exclusion of other identifying data like tribal affiliation compounds the effects of family separation and denial of asylum. See Tristan Ahtone, "Indigenous Immigrants Face Unique Challenges at the Border," *High Country News*, June 21, 2018.

6. See, e.g., Paul Butler, *Let's Get Free: A Hip-Hop Theory of Justice* (New York: The New Press, 2010); Devon Carbado, *Unreasonable: Black Lives, Police Power, and the Fourth Amendment* (New York: The New Press, 2022); Aya Gruber, *The Feminist War on Crime: The Unexpected Role of Women's Liberation in Mass Incarceration* (Oakland, CA: University of California Press, 2021); Cynthia Lee, "Reasonableness with Teeth: The Future of Fourth Amendment Reasonableness Analysis," *Mississippi Law Journal* 81, no. 5 (2012): 1152; Angela J. Davis, "Race, Cops, and Traffic Stops," *University of Miami Law Review* 51, no. 2 (January 1997): 425–444.

7. See Devon W. Carbado, "Racial Naturalization," *American Quarterly* 57, no. 3 (2005): 633, 649.

8. See Carbado, "Racial Naturalization."

9. See Kevin R. Johnson, "Racial Profiling in the War on Drugs Meets the Immigration Removal Process: The Case of *Moncrieffe v. Holder*," *University of Michigan Journal of Law Reform* 48, no. 4 (2015): 967–970.

10. See, e.g., Kelly Lytle Hernández, *City of Inmates: Conquest, Rebellion, and the Rise of Human Caging in Los Angeles, 1771–1965* (Chapel Hill, NC: University of North Carolina Press, 2017) (documenting the role of local police in enacting violence against Chinese immigrants in Southern California).

11. See, e.g., Monica Muñoz Martínez, *The Injustice Never Leaves You: Anti-Mexican Violence in Texas* (Cambridge, MA: Harvard University Press, 2018)

(documenting the anti-Mexican and anti-Mexican American violence of the Texas Rangers and other Texas law enforcement in the early twentieth century).

12. See Aimee Meredith Cox, *Shapeshifters: Black Girls and the Choreography of Citizenship* (Durham, NC: Duke University Press, 2015), 234.

13. California did not require proof of lawful status to obtain a driver's license until 1993 and some undocumented residents who had received driver's licenses before the change in the law were able to keep their driver's licenses through the renewal process. See *AB 60 Driver's License Frequently Asked Questions: April 2015* (Immigrant Legal Resource Center, 2015), https://www.ilrc.org/sites/default/files/resources/ab_60_4_27_15.pdf.

14. These acts of protest often demonstrated the mutually constitutive relationship between play and protest that Cox described in her own work: "the joy in working collectively to confront the most subtle and difficult to define aspects of institutionalized injustice and everyday instances in which Black girls find themselves dismissed and/or violated." See Cox, *Shapeshifters*, 141. We witnessed the same kind of creativity in the advocates and organizers who staged events such as the viewing of Obama's announcement of DAPA and DACA+ on a large, inflated screen outside of a detention facility in downtown Los Angeles.

15. See US Department of Homeland Security, "*DHS Announces Process Enhancements for Supporting Labor Enforcement Investigations,*" January 13, 2023, https://www.dhs.gov/news/2023/01/13/dhs-announces-process-enhancements-supporting-labor-enforcement-investigations.

INDEX

Administrative Procedures Act, 3, 44, 281n45

advocacy: abolitionist and protoabolitionist approaches, 128, 130–131, 161, 164, 170–171, 224, 229–230, 234–236; bottom-up approach, 134, 168–169; community-based resistance, 160–172; deservingness and, 131, 143, 161, 171–172; spatialized organizational networks, 132–146; temporality and uncertainty, 146–160

Ahmann, Chloe, 95

Akbar, Amna, 128

alienation, 44, 250

American Dream, 225

Andersson, Ruben, 95

anti-Black racism, 21, 24, 143, 145–146. 189, 225–230, 235, 250, 256

"API," use of the term, 23. *See also* Asian and Pacific Islander (API) immigrants

Ashar, Sameer, 22

Asian and Pacific Islander (API) immigrants, 23, 31; access to driver's licenses, 39, 208, 271n41; Latinx/

API comparisons, 48–50, 141–146, 191, 208–209, 232–233, 249, 251–252; law enforcement and, 48–50; in Los Angeles County, 183, 185; in Orange County, 189; racial profiling and, 49; stereotypes of, 253–254

asylum seekers, 11, 99–100, 123, 133, 155, 181, 220, 259

Baca, Lee, 198

Becerra, Xavier, 174, 182

belonging, 25, 104, 129, 194, 213–215, 222–223, 225, 242–244

bicycle stops, 203–204

Biden, Joseph R.: attempted rescission of Migrant Protection Protocols, 285n35; campaign platform, 11, 100, 110, 129, 180; Criminal Apprehension Program and, 33; DACA and, 3, 5, 10, 11, 57, 110; DACA litigation and, 11, 57, 110; DACA Rule 2022, 275–276n2; deferred action benefits expansion, 259; immigration policies and executive actions, 10, 11; notice-and-comment rulemaking,

and DACA+, 3, 10, 121, 155; Secure
Communities program under, 149,
181, 187
TRUST Act (California), 148, 167, 175,
181–182, 185–189, 192, 242
287(g) program, 31, 34–35, 147, 164, 185,
187, 189

"unauthorized," use of the term, 22
"undocumented," use of the term, 22
United States v. Texas (2016), 20, 44,
109, 112, 114–121, 152, 171, 218
United States v. Texas (2023), 4, 51, 57,
84, 258
University of California, Irvine, 196,
206
US Citizenship and Immigration
Services (USCIS): DACA and, 44,
51, 78–81, 84–87; DHS organization
and, 63–64; interviews and removal
orders, 55–56; Morton memos and,

64–65, 69; Obama administration, 69, 78–81, 84–87, 253; reentry
waivers, 98

Villanueva, Alex, 188, 198, 294n56
Violence Against Women Act
(VAWA), 133, 217
visa program, 51–52, 55–56, 64, 90–93,
98–100, 281–282n2; application
process, 84; family-based visas,
55–56, 274n59; family visa petition,
102, 120, 221; H-1 visas, 90, 93,
281n1; H-4 visas, 281n1; overstays,
52, 72, 74, 93; tourist visas, 51, 91,
100, 233; U visas, 51–52, 121, 133, 175,
217, 238–239
Volpp, Leti, 129

whiteness, 225, 231–232, 235, 249, 256
white supremacism, 155, 160, 202
workplace injuries, 95, 240

Printed in the USA
CPSIA information can be obtained
at www.ICGtesting.com
JSHW081937171123
52217JS00002B/3